Fundamental Differences

Fundamental Differences

Feminists Talk Back to Social Conservatives

Edited by Cynthia Burack
and Jyl J. Josephson

ROWMAN & LITTLEFIELD PUBLISHERS, INC.
Lanham • *Boulder* • *New York* • *Oxford*

ROWMAN & LITTLEFIELD PUBLISHERS, INC.

Published in the United States of America
by Rowman & Littlefield Publishers, Inc.
A Member of the Rowman & Littlefield Publishing Group
4501 Forbes Boulevard, Suite 200, Lanham, Maryland 20706
www.rowmanlittlefield.com

P.O. Box 317, Oxford OX2 9RU, United Kingdom

British Library Cataloguing in Publication Information Available

Library of Congress Cataloging-in-Publication Data

Fundamental differences : feminists talk back to social conservatives /
edited by Cynthia Burack and Jyl J. Josephson.
    p. cm.
Includes bibliographical references and index.
    ISBN 0-7425-1929-5 (cloth : alk. paper) — ISBN 0-7425-1930-9 (pbk. : alk. paper)
    1. Feminism—United States. 2. Conservatism—United States. 3. Right and left
(Political science) I. Burack, Cynthia, 1958– II. Josephson, Jyl J., 1960–
    HQ1426 .F883 2003
    305.42—dc21
                                                                    2002155386

♾™ The paper used in this publication meets the minimum requirements of
American National Standard for Information Sciences—Permanence of Paper for
Printed Library Materials, ANSI/NISO Z39.48-1992.

This volume is dedicated to the memory of Rhonda M. Williams, whose life bent toward justice.

Contents

Tables

Acknowledgments

We would like to thank our family members, Laree Martin, James Nelson, and David Foster, for their enthusiasm and encouragement throughout the process of writing and assembling this book. Thanks to Jennifer Knerr at Rowman & Littlefield for recognizing the value of this project. In addition, we recognize the research and editorial assistance of Lu Zhang in the department of women's studies at The Ohio State University. An additional thank you to David Foster for his help with formatting the tables.

In November 2001, Jyl Josephson organized a "Fundamental Differences" panel at the annual meeting of the Southern Political Science Association in Atlanta, Georgia, at which some of the authors presented their work. Thanks to Suzanne Franks, Valerie Lehr, and Claire Snyder for joining us at that panel and to Kathy Dolan and the Women's Caucus of the SPSA for including it on the program.

Permission to reprint the following materials is gratefully acknowledged: Chapter 2, Judith Stacey and Timothy Biblarz, "(How) Does the Sexual Orientation of Parents Matter?" was first published in *American Sociological Review* 66, no. 2 (April 2001): 159–83. Reprinted with permission of the American Sociological Association. Chapter 3, "The Politics of Child Sexual Abuse Research" by Janice Haaken and Sharon Lamb was first published in *Society* 37, no. 4 (May/June 2000): 7–14. Reprinted with permission of Transaction Publishers. Chapter 12, Gwendolyn Mink, "From Welfare to Wedlock: Marriage Promotion and Poor Mothers' Inequality" was first published in *The Good Society: A PEGS Journal* 11, no. 3 (2002). Reprinted with permission of Penn State University Press.

Introduction

Cynthia Burack and Jyl J. Josephson

GETTING TO FUNDAMENTALS

During the 2000 presidential election campaign, George W. Bush represented himself as a new kind of conservative against his more strident and exclusionary colleagues on the American Right. Although Bush used the slogan "compassionate conservatism" to position himself as a centrist politician, it turns out that compassionate conservatives differ from their colleagues on the Right in presentation but not in substance. Today, the president supports—and sometimes openly espouses—the agenda of the New Right, but he is only one of many exponents of an ideology that combines social and economic conservatism in ways that pose a threat to many Americans. Indeed, he is more a potent symbol of conservative ideology than an informed and challenging intellectual leader of the contemporary Right. For intellectual leaders of the Right, we may look to academia, think tanks and political organizations, and the media and popular press.

In this volume, we are pleased to bring together feminist critiques of New Right thinkers and their political ideas, policies, and practices. "Feminists" serve as an all-purpose mobilizing and demonizing symbol for many on both the secular and Christian Right. To New Right ideologists, this category is often uninformed by the nuances of political differences among feminists or by respect for the values that feminists bring to debates about social and political issues. Here, feminists talk back to particular leaders, thinkers, and activist organizations on the Right, confronting their values and ideals and exposing their intellectual and political strategies. Talking back to those who formulate and promulgate the ideas of the Right is an important project for feminists. There are differences in the concerns,

1

arguments, and justifications expressed by those on the U.S. Right, just as there are among feminists and other critics. Attending closely to these differences facilitates more careful and fine-grained analyses of what can otherwise appear as a homogeneous and ahistorical political enterprise.

The chapters that follow offer cogent and accessible scholarly critiques of selected aspects of social conservative ideology and agendas in the contemporary United States. Although the topics are various, readers may find productive links between the chapters as authors grapple with social conservative convictions and recommendations regarding sexuality, family formation, gendered roles and characteristics, socialization and education, the norms and politics of scholarship, and public policies and institutions. Besides collecting feminist critiques of social conservative politics, *Fundamental Differences* offers two important features. First, the volume is interdisciplinary, with perspectives from political science and policy, history, sociology, psychology, philosophy, women's studies, and biological science. This interdisciplinary approach highlights the complexities of social and political debates as familiar subjects are conceptualized and engaged anew through multiple intellectual lenses.

The second unique feature of the volume is the attention in one set of chapters to critiques of methods employed by contemporary social conservatives. Political debates are often incommensurable and irreducible debates about values. In political contests, those who represent different values and ideals—those who stand on different "sides"—work to fashion a compelling narrative through which to express their arguments and persuade their fellow citizens. One way of authorizing such political narratives is to write with an eye to scholarly legitimacy, and many social conservatives who disseminate their ideas to popular audiences do so with an eye to cultivating this legitimacy. The quest for legitimacy takes many forms, from citing scholarly authorities and invoking respected historical figures to linking discursive conclusions and political programs to respected research methods. In responding to politics fundamentally different than our own, we can examine the ways in which research methods can distort texts and data, disclaim ambiguity, and dismiss alternative forms of explanation.

New Right social conservatism is not only central to U.S. domestic politics at the turn of the millennium but is also "centered" as conservatives represent themselves and their commitments as expressions of common sense and popular will that balance political "extremes" of left and right.[1] In fact, as these chapters show, the rightward movement of official U.S. ideology and policy is driven by concerted campaigns that deny the existence of an ideological agenda, target resources to conservative goals, mischaracterize adversaries' goals and values, and exploit the conservative moves of more centrist politicians and policy advocates. We do not suggest that there is a single grand consensus among social conservatives, coordinated by political leadership and executed by the foot soldiers of a 1990s-style conservative "revolution." Rather, what we find are common general themes, tropes, aspirations, and enemies whose historical appearance is traceable to social events and formations of the latter half of the twentieth century.

FOCUS ON FAMILIES AND SOCIAL INSTITUTIONS

When feminists turn to the social conservative Right at the turn of the twenty-first century, we confront a web of discourses, policies, practices, and institutions whose domains include gender, race, sexuality, and family structure. In the "family values" of current U.S. political discourse, these domains intersect in complex ways. Although different New Right ideologists take up these domains in different ways and degrees, the domains intersect with one another in patterns linked to individual morality as well as to collective—and "natural"—forms of belief and practice. "Family values" rhetoric is usually blunt and unequivocal in prescribing appropriate norms and behavior in the areas of gender, sexuality, and family structure. Gendered characteristics and roles are "natural" and essential to social order and child well-being.

Often social conservative claims for "natural" gender differences and their effects are embedded in legitimizing scientific or social scientific discourse. Suzanne E. Franks discovers that behind the scientific claims of Randy Thornhill and Craig Palmer's *A Natural History of Rape* stands a ready antifeminist rhetoric that attempts to construct a strict and mutually exclusive binary between "science" and "feminist politics" to the detriment of the latter. In fact, as Franks shows, the putatively scientific account of rape as an evolutionary adaptation fails as science, and its defense by scholar Daphne Patai confirms that reactionary and antifeminist politics can exist in a mutually reinforcing relationship with spurious "science." In "Not Really a 'New Attitude': Dr. Laura on Gender and Morality," Victoria Davion confronts this discourse of nature in the words and work of popular conservative talk-radio host and author Dr. Laura Schlessinger. Davion is particularly concerned with examining Schlessinger's case for natural gender complementarity and the way that it is built upon a basis of nearly irresistible male biological drives. Davion argues that Schlessinger's exhortations to women to domesticate, indeed, to humanize, men display Schlessinger's own antimale bias. This bias is evident, argues Davion, in the way that, while men's responsibility for destructive behaviors is slighted, women are figured as forces of humanity and moral responsibility.

It is not surprising that social conservative anxieties about gender, sexuality, and families frequently play out as concerns about protecting children.[2] Indeed, because children are increasingly at the center of debates over a wide variety of social goals and political initiatives, this volume includes several chapters that speak directly to social conservative ideology with regard to children. Examining a popular conservative text on "fatherlessness," Cynthia Burack finds that what is identified as a careful and objective study of family structure and its impact on children is premised, in part, on dubious interpretations of psychological discourse. In "Defense Mechanisms: Using Psychoanalysis Conservatively," Burack traces author David Blankenhorn's deployment of selective and mendacious readings of orthodox psychoanalytic literature to support his a priori conservative conclusions on fatherhood, masculine authority, and "natural" gender complementarity. She suggests that Blankenhorn's strategy of avoiding contemporary psychological, and particularly feminist, research casts undeserved merit on the assumptions that undergird his theory of fatherhood and child well-being.

In their already widely recognized article "(How) Does the Sexual Orientation of Parents Matter?" Judith Stacey and Timothy J. Biblarz analyze scholarly research and debates on child development in lesbian and gay families. Stacey and Biblarz focus on the heteronormative nature of most dialogues and research designs on the subject of lesbigay families and parenting. They confirm that research on children of lesbians and gay men finds no negative effects on child outcomes that would validate the fears and predictions of antigay authors and political activists such as Paul Cameron and Maggie Gallagher. However, the authors challenge researchers who are sympathetic to lesbian and gay parents and families to undertake research that is less defensive, more attentive to positive effects of lesbigay parenting, and more open to the multiple ways in which parents' sexual identities may influence children's gender and sexual repertoires.

Janice Haaken and Sharon Lamb also examine conservative reactions to scholarly research on child well-being, this time with regard to the phenomenon of child sexual abuse, or adult–child sex. In "The Politics of Child Sexual Abuse Research," Haaken and Lamb survey the debate between social conservatives (such as activists in the Christian Coalition and Family Research Council) and advocates of scientific independence that erupted in 1998 over the publication of a meta-analysis of studies on the long-term impact of child sexual abuse on college students. Refusing merely to take the side of the researchers in a case of scientific objectivity versus moral panic, the authors seek to complicate the domain of sexuality research itself. They urge researchers and others to consider the ways in which gender inequalities, the cultural equation of sexuality with morality and shame, and the denial of children's sexuality and agency work to undermine the pursuit of knowledge about the vexed subject of intergenerational sex.

In "The Missing Children: Safe Schools for Some," Jyl J. Josephson addresses another aspect of concerns about schools and sexuality: the conservative attack on programs that seek to make schools safer places for youth who are subjected to homophobic harassment. Despite consistent evidence that many youth—and not only self-identified gay, lesbian, bisexual, or transgender youth—are subject to and harmed by homophobic harassment in U.S. public schools, social conservatives have developed comprehensive strategies to counter programs that seek to reduce antigay harassment in schools. They depict efforts to reduce harassment as the promotion of sex, homosexuality, disease, and perversion to young children and as discrimination against social conservative rights of free speech. Thus, social conservatives deny protections to real children who are harmed by antigay harassment in favor of abstract fears of disease and perversion.

From school prayer to the teaching of U.S. history, public schools have functioned as an important site for what some social conservatives have termed the "culture wars." Both Josephson and Valerie C. Johnson examine the ways in which public schools function as political arenas in which the subject of controversy is both the maintenance of order and the subject matter to which students are exposed. A frequent subtext of the social conservative moral agenda in public schools, however, is anxiety over increased diversity within schools and in U.S. society. Concerns over maintaining order and discipline in public schools have led to the adoption of increasingly punitive discipline policies, including zero-tolerance policies. In "Leaving Children Behind: Criminalizing Youth in American Schools," Johnson outlines the development of such policies and notes the implicit and explicit linkage between two types of policies addressed to youth: juvenile justice and public school discipline policies. Discussing the well-publicized 1999 incident in the Decatur, Illinois, schools, Johnson shows both the inequity in that particular incident and the ways in which applications of zero-tolerance policies exacerbate racial inequalities.

A number of feminists argue that, far from being the threats to culture and to children that social conservatives claim, diverse families are a valuable feature of a desirable pluralist society. A number of feminist studies criticize New Right depictions and popular understandings of the history of families as deeply flawed either because they are based more on myth than on empirical reality or because they rely upon a putatively "natural" gender order and complementarity.[3] Because they do not exemplify this natural order, lesbians and gay men remain groups against which normality and heteronormativity are defined. In spite of the fact that recent scholarship shows growing tolerance for lesbians and gay men in American society, lesbians and gay men continue to find themselves harassed by fellow citizens and denied basic civil rights by states and by the federal government.[4] Critics who focus on New Right campaigns in the area of same-sex sexuality focus on the organizations, discourse, political activities, and policies through which the Right seeks to circumvent democratic pluralism and threaten sexual minorities. It is often a difficult enterprise to trace New Right activity against lesbians and gay men because "the right undermines the gay and lesbian civil rights quest in two conflicting ways: by denying discrimination against gay people and by defending it."[5]

In "Neopatriarchy and the Antihomosexual Agenda," R. Claire Snyder analyzes a variety of conservative ideologies, including the Christian antifeminism of Concerned Women for America and the democratic conservatism of philosopher William Galston, to consider the variety of forms that opposition to same-sex marriage takes in political discourse. Snyder demonstrates that in spite of rhetoric to the contrary, the varied forms of conservative opposition to same-sex marriage share implicit heterosexist and antifeminist values that also conflict with liberal principles of personal liberty and liberal equality. She concludes that respect for political liberalism requires support for same-sex civil marriage and that civil unions should be legally disentangled from religious forms of marriage recognition.

In "'Family Values': Social Conservative Power in Diverse Rhetorics," Valerie Lehr indicts social conservatives' accounts of "family values" as discourses that deflect the attention of U.S. citizens from global economic change and declining standards of living. Lehr argues that family values rhetoric inscribes and masks a range of ideas regarding dependence, responsibility, social control, authority, citizenship, and resource distribution. However, it is not only in the work of conservatives such as gay journalist and author Andrew Sullivan that such rhetoric performs its obfuscating work. Lehr shows how it is that putative liberals, such as Hillary Rodham Clinton and scholar Elinor Burkett, reinforce conservative family values and, thus, inhibit the feminist task of social and political critique.

Feminist scholarship reveals the conservative assumptions and the multiple effects, especially with respect to race and gender, at the root of social policy and reform. Policies such as those in the welfare arena frequently are constructed to reconcile laissez-faire economic principles with social conservative ideals such as complementary gender roles and social reliance on women's care work. At the core of both economic and social strands of the New Right is an ideology of individual responsibility and commitment to the "basic values of work, faith, and family."[6] Naturally, New Right ideologists are insensible to feminist interrogations of these values as well as to the cynical uses to which they may be put in establishing the rights and status of members of disfavored groups.

A timely intervention into the welfare policy arena is Gwendolyn Mink's "From Welfare to Wedlock: Marriage Promotion and Poor Mothers' Inequality." Mink shows that the federal government violates personal and associational rights associated with marital and reproductive freedom established in the 1967 Supreme Court decision in *Loving v. Virginia* when it tries to coerce poor women into marriage or to withhold benefits of citizenship from them if they do not marry. Mink assesses the Temporary Assistance for Needy Families (TANF) program and the 1996 Personal Responsibility and Work Opportunity Reconciliation Act (PRWORA) and concludes that both constitute assaults on core aspects of democratic personhood for poor women, and particularly for poor women of color. However, she is even more critical of recent attempts by the Bush administration to strengthen these initiatives, reinforce patriarchy, use the levers of government to "promote" marriage, and deny citizenship to poor women.

For Jenrose Fitzgerald, the merger of recent welfare discourse and social conservative rhetoric substitutes a behavioral paradigm of individual and familial dysfunction for any discussion of structural economic changes or inequalities. In "A Liberal Dose of Conservatism: The 'New Consensus' on Welfare and Other Strange Synergies," Fitzgerald uses government debates to document and analyze the contributions to the conservative rhetoric on welfare of conservatives such as Charles Murray and of liberals such as Daniel Patrick Moynihan. Along with Lehr and Mink, Fitzgerald suggests that the rhetoric and political practices of New Right social conservatives have been strengthened by the—sometimes witting, often unwitting—support of liberal thinkers and political actors.

As these chapters suggest, "compassionate conservatism" is more of a mystifying rhetoric than it is a serious attempt to modify the ideology and activism for which the New Right is known. Nancy D. Campbell takes up this theme in "Reading the Rhetoric of 'Compassionate Conservatism,'" tracing the genealogy of the idea and the functions of its current deployment. She finds that compassionate conservative theorists such as Marvin Olasky and William J. Bennett wield a flawed historical narrative of U.S. social policy and a set of contemporary initiatives that hinge upon such tropes as "addiction" and "dependency." Campbell argues that behind the rhetoric of compassionate conservatism lies a set of responses to the current crisis of social reproduction that operates by directing, indeed by coercing, the behavior of citizens, especially the labor of women.

CONCLUSION

In her historical account of the "clash of ideas" and policies between feminism and New Right conservatism from the late 1970s to the 1990s, Sylvia Bashevkin notes that "right wing leaders shaped organized feminism and vice versa."[7] Bashevkin's insight is trenchant. From the mobilization of African American women in the wake of the first President Bush's nomination of Clarence Thomas to the Supreme Court to battles over welfare and same-sex families, feminisms are as much in dialectical relation with existing political realities as they are a reflection of many women's social, economic, and political aspirations. As feminists, it is our task not only to enunciate our own aspirations and to propose our own political arrangements, but also to explain our fundamental differences with other social and political ideals. The authors in this volume take up the challenge.

NOTES

1. Anna Marie Smith, "The Centering of Right-Wing Extremism through the Construction of an 'Inclusionary' Racism and Homophobia," in *Playing with Fire: Queer Politics, Queer Theories*, ed. Shane Phelan (New York: Routledge, 1997), 113–38; Anna Marie Smith, *New Right Discourse on Race and Sexuality: Britain, 1968–1990* (Cambridge: Cambridge University Press, 1994).

2. Jyl J. Josephson and Cynthia Burack, "The Political Ideology of the Neo-Traditional Family," *Political Ideologies* 3, no. 2 (1998): 213–31.

3. Stephanie Coontz, *The Way We Never Were: American Families and the Nostalgia Trap* (New York: Basic, 1992); Judith Stacey, *In the Name of the Family: Rethinking Family Values in the Postmodern Age* (Boston: Beacon, 1992).

4. See Jeni Loftus, "America's Liberalization in Attitudes toward Homosexuality, 1973–1998," *American Sociological Review* 66, no. 5 (2001): 762–82.

5. Urvashi Vaid, *Virtual Equality: The Mainstreaming of Gay and Lesbian Liberation* (New York: Doubleday, 1997), 330.

6. Ann Withorn, "Fulfilling Fears and Fantasies: The Role of Welfare in Right-Wing Social Thought and Strategy," in *Unraveling the Right: The New Conservatism in American Thought and Politics*, ed. Amy E. Ansell (Boulder, Colo.: Westview, 1998), 140.

7. Sylvia Bashevkin, *Women on the Defensive: Living through Conservative Times* (Chicago: Chicago University Press, 1998), 234.

I

TAKING ISSUE: INQUIRIES ON METHODS

The search for fundamental causes

1

They Blinded Me with Science: Misuse and Misunderstanding of Biological Theory

Suzanne E. Franks

In 2000, MIT Press published a book by Randy Thornhill and Craig T. Palmer entitled *A Natural History of Rape: Biological Bases of Sexual Coercion.*[1] One consequence of this is that I spent $35 to purchase the book and several months reading and thinking about it to produce this chapter. The experience has not been unlike what Samuel Johnson must have felt in responding to Bishop Berkeley's theory of the nonexistence of matter. Exposing Thornhill and Palmer's theoretical holes and lapses of logic is no more difficult than giving a swift kick to a large stone. But it's just about as painful, too—painful to read for anyone accustomed to thinking logically, painful to see work like this embraced and promoted by the media as scientific fact, and painful to contemplate the low level of scientific literacy that must therefore obtain.

Thornhill is described on the book jacket as a Regents' professor and professor of biology at the University of New Mexico; Palmer, as instructor of anthropology at the University of Colorado. Thornhill and Palmer declare that rape is about sex and sexual reproduction, not violence. Their theory is based on evolutionary psychology (formerly known as sociobiology) and asserts that rape is an adaptive behavior that promotes reproductive success for males. Further, Thornhill and Palmer claim that proposals for eliminating rape that do not take evolution into account are doomed to failure.

In evolutionary theory, an *adaptation* is a trait directly selected for, because the trait's function tends to promote the differential survival of those who possess it over those who do not. *Differential survival* means that an individual with the trait survives and produces more offspring with the trait, who in turn survive and produce more offspring, and so

11

forth. Adaptations arose as solutions to past environmental problems. Thornhill and Palmer tell us that rape is an adaptive solution to a particular problem males face—"the difficulty of gaining sexual access to choosy females."[2]

Combining a selective attention to evidence with a misunderstanding of the limits of scientific certainty and explanatory power, the authors remake biological theory to promote a limited, scientifically untenable, and socially conservative view of human nature and sexual behavior. "Scientific" arguments are presented as irrefutable and final and may easily be interpreted as such by a naïve audience and/or used to lend the aura of scientific truth to political claims of all sorts. An example of this is Daphne Patai's essay on *Natural History,* in which she uses Thornhill and Palmer's arguments to attack feminism in general.[3] Despite her self-proclaimed lack of scientific credentials, and her acknowledgment of scientific critiques of *Natural History,* she finds Thornhill and Palmer compelling—or useful—enough to help advance her antifeminist political aims.

For both in the writing and in the marketing of *Natural History,* the authors are explicitly critical of feminists and feminism. According to Thornhill and Palmer, feminists insist on a monolithic account of rape as a violent act that has nothing to do with sex. This, along with feminists' inability to embrace evolutionary theory, prevents feminists from producing accurate accounts of why men rape and so from arriving at useful solutions. This claim itself misrepresents feminist perspectives on rape. As Natalie Angier notes, "Most of us have long known that rape is about sex and power and a thousand other things as well, and that rape is not a monolithic constant but varies in incidence and meaning from culture to culture and epoch to epoch." Angier also rightly notes that it is feminists who "sought to have the word 'rape' replaced in the legal lexicon by the terms 'sex crime' and 'sexual battery,' the better to include offenses that don't involve intercourse but are clearly sexual in nature, such as . . . forced fellatio, anal penetration, the shoving of a gun barrel up the vagina, and the like."[4] Rape clearly is not limited to a single type of behavior or pattern of behavior that is found in every case. Feminists have always been attentive to this reality and to the fact that in the real world of sexual offenses it is difficult to ignore the ways in which sex *and* violence are often fused.

Thornhill himself asserts that the conclusions in *A Natural History of Rape* "are not debatable issues" and has accused his critics of being antiscience and of presenting misleading views about the nature of science.[5] And, in their preface, Thornhill and Palmer invoke Karl Popper's theory of scientific progression through the falsification of ideas mainly to outline the ways in which they may not be critiqued.[6] Any critique that relies on any theory other than evolutionary psychology is deemed by Thornhill and Palmer to be a priori invalid. Declaring issues nondebatable and placing one's theory beyond critique does not match with any definition of science I ever learned in the classroom or the laboratory. Other critics have pointed out that Thornhill and Palmer make assertions that cannot be tested, and that by presenting a totalizing theory that purports to explain everything, they rule out nothing, undermining their own claims of scientific authority and betraying their ideological bias.[7]

Nevertheless, I shall take Thornhill and Palmer at their word that what they present is a scientific study, and I offer in this essay a scientist's critique of their theory and methods. I explicitly position myself in this endeavor as a scientist who self-identifies as a feminist. This is important because Thornhill and Palmer, as well as their supporters, portray feminists as antiscience and as unwilling or incapable of embracing science and its methods.

Rather than revisit scientific critiques made so well elsewhere, I shall focus, as Thornhill and Palmer insist would-be critics must, on "the very heart of the perceived difficulty with [their] idea"; that is, with their foundational assumptions.[8] I shall also discuss the significance of their rhetorical move to align feminism and all social science with ignorance, emotion, and antiscientific beliefs, while aligning themselves and evolutionary psychology with logic, reason, and scientific truth. I begin with a brief summary of the propositions that underlie their theory.

SEEKING THE CAUSE OF THINGS THAT WEIGH TEN POUNDS

A variety of scientists (both biological and social), who may or may not identify as feminists, have offered reasoned critiques of *Natural History*.[9] These critics have pointed out flaws such as lack of empirical evidence, overreliance on pop literature surveys versus scientific literature, inattention to cross-cultural patterns of rape and an assumption that U.S. patterns are universal, and misinterpretation of data, including misrepresenting data that appeared in a paper authored by Thornhill and his wife.[10] Furthermore, Matt Cartmill persuasively contends:

> It's a mistake to argue about the causes of rape. . . .We define [rape, murder, and war] by their properties and their effects, not their causes, and there's no reason to think that acts that share an effect also share a cause. . . . [A]ll homicides share the same effect . . . but they don't all have the same cause. . . . Seeking the cause of murder, war, or rape may be a fundamental mistake, like asking for the cause of things that weigh 10 pounds.[11]

Thornhill and Palmer make critical errors in their assumptions that what has happened (evolution) is the key to knowing what will happen (development), that a single unified theory of causation for rape exists, and that such a theory will explain how to prevent rape.

Thornhill and Palmer's evolutionary psychological explanation of the cause of rape, and their claim of its superiority as an explanatory tool, rests on two propositions. First, while research and theory in the social sciences is ideologically shaped and driven, evolutionary psychology is a true science, free of ideology and based on facts. Second, all human behavior has two levels of causation: proximate and ultimate. Proximate causes of behavior operate over the short term, and most social scientists are exclusively concerned with proximate causes. Ultimate causes underlie all proximate causes. Proximate causes explain how developmental or physiological mechanisms cause something to happen, but ultimate causes explain why particular proximate mechanisms exist. For example, Thornhill and Palmer note that the proximate cause of vision is the structure of rods and cones in the eye, but the ultimate cause of the rods and cones is evolutionary adaptation that favored development of rods and cones. It is important to know ultimate causes because some possible proximate explanations may be incompatible with ultimate causes. Evolutionary psychologists are concerned with the ultimate causes of human behavior, and evolutionary theory, with its explanation of how natural selection leads to adaptations, is the only source of information about them. In order to develop effective solutions to problems like rape, we must have knowledge of ultimate causes. Otherwise, the solutions we propose may not only be ineffective, but may actually exacerbate the situation.

Two additional concepts are important for Thornhill and Palmer's theory—the notion of "evolved differences between male and female sexuality"[12] and the idea that the "cultural behavior of individuals is *never* independent of the human evolutionary history of selection for individual reproductive success."[13] So, in their view, the behaviors around sex, including rape, are the result of evolutionary adaptations that promoted the differential survival of offspring.

The cornerstone of Thornhill and Palmer's theoretical edifice is this truism: "No aspect of life can be completely understood until both its proximate and its ultimate causes are fully known."[14] Proximate causes exist and are complements, not alternatives, to the ultimate cause of millions of years of natural selection. So far, so good—there's nothing here that even a feminist social scientist could argue with. Thornhill and Palmer go on to argue that the best and most useful solutions to social and biological problems can only arise from awareness of ultimate (evolutionary) causes of behavior. Ultimate explanations will "lead to the best insights about proximate causes, and identifying proximate causes is the key to changing human behavior."[15] Without knowing ultimate causes, one can be misled about proximate causes, and therefore workable solutions will be unattainable. Thornhill and Palmer believe that science explains why things are and that this knowledge is what allows us to develop useful solutions and innovations. But solutions and innovations are, for the most part, developed by engineers, and often an innovation predates our scientific understanding of why it works. Science can give us an explanation of why something works but that is not the same thing as giving us a solution or a practical application, as I shall now show.

ULTIMATE CAUSES AND EFFECTIVE SOLUTIONS

Let us examine the proposition that knowledge of ultimate causes is necessary for development of effective solutions. As a first test of this proposition, consider Thornhill and Palmer's own example of vision. The science of optics, and the development of spectacles for the improvement of vision, did not require an understanding of the evolutionary adaptations that promoted the development of the system of rods and cones found in the human eye. Both spectacles and the science of optics predated Darwin and the development of evolutionary theory. Furthermore, it is not just the rods and cones, or the evolutionary history which produced them, that are responsible for vision. The nature and properties of light are also necessary for vision to exist. In the absence of light, there is no vision, no matter how evolved your rods and cones may be. Knowing the evolutionary origins of a behavior, or even of a physical trait, is in many cases not sufficient or even necessary to arriving at a solution for a problem or an improvement for an existing situation. Humans *always* exist and operate within a context that is shaped by their current physical and intellectual environment. Human evolutionary history sets parameters for what is possible, but those parameters are wide and far-reaching. I saw this every day in my research on human cancer cell lines. All the cells in a particular line shared a common genetic makeup, yet minimal changes in environmental conditions (the amount of glucose or other common nutrients they were fed) were sufficient to evoke widely different outcomes of cell function, morphology (shape), and growth patterns.[16]

A corollary proposition is that effective solutions indeed follow from perfect knowledge of ultimate causes. But perfect knowledge of the evolutionary causes of human behavior does not necessarily guarantee that the knowledge will be useful for crafting any kind of practical solution to issues of concern. One could also argue that evolution itself has an ultimate cause, that is, the Big Bang, which could be given as the ultimate cause of everything. Yet, it is hard to see how knowledge of Big Bang theory would be either useful or necessary to crafting an effective solution to rape, or even how Big Bang theory as an ultimate cause would be useful for developing and understanding evolutionary theory. Certainly, one hesitates to suggest that no theory of evolution can be considered valid unless it takes the Big Bang into account.

Ultimate causality could, in fact, be interesting without being useful (as in the case of vision and eyeglasses). For example, some scientists say that the laws of quantum mechanics ultimately govern the behavior of all material. Suppose I want to design a plastic bottle cap that can withstand temperature extremes from −50 degrees to 120 degrees Fahrenheit. I also want the bottle cap to be recyclable. I do not need to understand the quantum mechanical underpinnings of the behavior and characteristics of plastics to be able to design and produce my cap, which is a good thing, since no one has that knowledge. Yet, such bottle caps are designed and produced. If I did have perfect knowledge of the quantum mechanical behavior of plastics, it would not change the fact that I had already designed an effective bottle cap that met my design criteria.

The universal claim that evolution, not culture, is the ultimate cause of all human behavior, and that culture itself is behavior ultimately caused by evolution, leads Thornhill and Palmer into the trap of a theory that explains everything, and therefore nothing.[17] Taken to its extreme, their theory makes it impossible to determine what, if anything, is true. For example, they state repeatedly that social science has proposed solutions to rape that are doomed to failure because they are political and not based in evolutionary theory. But if all human behavior is ultimately caused by evolution, then we may say that the proposing of solutions, a human behavior, is caused by evolution. A priori, what is the difference between the solutions proposed by feminists and the solutions proposed by Thornhill and Palmer, if both are the result of evolution? Thornhill and Palmer will insist that a difference does exist (so would I) but how one chooses between the two cannot be explained by evoking the evolution-as-ultimate-cause theory, since that could be applied to any theory proposed and is therefore not a criterion that can be used to choose between competing theories.

WHAT'S WRONG WITH THIS SOLUTION?

If Thornhill and Palmer are correct that evolutionary theory is necessary to understand and eliminate rape, and that their particular theory provides the correct evolutionary perspective, we might expect some startling new recommendations. The antirape program they outline is as follows: educate young men about how their evolved sexual desires may lead them to want to commit rape, but tell them they should resist doing so. Tell them about the penalties for rape. Educate young women about the Darwinist history that leads men to be rapists. Make them aware "of the costs associated with attractiveness."[18] Dressing sexy may help attract desirable males, but it will also attract undesirable ones. Women should not be encouraged "to place themselves in dangerous situations" just because men don't have the right to rape.[19] In the absence of official structural barriers restricting the access of men to women, women should interact with men only in public places in the early stages of relationships, and carefully consider in what conditions they will consent to be alone with men. In other words, men should try to be good, and women should restrict their mobility, dress modestly, and endeavor to be chaperoned. Rape's ultimate explanation identifies rape's proximate causes as women and their behavior.

If this sounds familiar, you may be thinking of white upper-class norms of Victorian culture, or the Taliban, or the rules for student behavior at Liberty College. Social conservatives in the United States and religious fundamentalists of many descriptions arrive at strikingly similar conclusions about the necessity for women to limit their activities, dress, movements, and sexual practices without recourse to indisputable "scientific" explanations. It is hard to see why an evolutionary approach was necessary to arrive at these solutions, since all of them have been proposed before and even carried out in other times and places. These so-called solutions place a burden on women to prevent the misbehavior of men, stopping just short of blaming the victim.

The unspoken assumption within Thornhill and Palmer's theory and proposals is that, given the opportunity, all men would choose to commit rape, unless they have been educated to struggle against their Darwinian inheritance. If this theory is correct, does it follow that their proposals are inevitably and uniquely correct? In a word, no. There are many possible behavioral and policy suggestions for eliminating rape that are consistent with their theory. For example, one could propose that all men should be locked up twenty-four hours a day and be let out only under the guard of heavily armed women who would escort them to places where they would perform useful work. Men would never be allowed to have intercourse with women, but would be periodically harvested for sperm as needed to continue propagating the species. This would effectively eliminate rape.

Whether Thornhill and Palmer are right or wrong about evolution's explanatory value for rape, it is certainly possible that their recommendations could contribute to reducing the incidence of male–female rape, just as my modest proposal for locking up all men would reduce the incidence of male–female rape (though perhaps it would have the opposite effect on the incidence of male–male rape). Whether or not either course of action is found to be a socially acceptable solution—and who might find it acceptable or not—is another question, and one that cannot be answered by science.

MEN WANT SEX, WOMEN WANT MATES—NATURALLY!

A central tenet of the evolutionary view of human sexuality espoused by Thornhill and Palmer is the assumption that only women care about mate choice. Women are evolutionarily designed to resist rape and to suffer psychological pain after rape, because rape thwarts their mate choice. Men are evolutionarily designed for rape, because it lets them spread their seed far and wide. But why is it rational to assume that men would have no care about where their seed gets spread? If women want to mate with the best males, why don't men want to mate with the best females? Why will any old—or young—female do? Why aren't men choosy about their mates? This gender-unbalanced theory disregards male mate preference as a possible evolutionary influence and limits mate choice/preference solely to women—which implies one of two preexisting biases.

Bias 1: Men contribute everything to the child; the woman is only an incubator. Therefore, any woman will do and men need not be choosy. Women must be choosy, in order to get the best male possible. Aristotle and many others thought this was basically the truth, but developmental biology established that women are more than incubators.

Bias 2: Women invest a great deal in each egg; therefore, it pays them to be choosy, whereas men have very little invested in each sperm, since they make so many all the time, and so don't have to be choosy. This is the bias that Thornhill and Palmer hold. As they clearly state, "We . . . discuss these psychological adaptations in terms of male *sexual preferences* and female *mate choice*. The reason we use two different terms is that hu-

[handwritten margin notes: mostly illegible — "people don't know about C chromosomes T can't be motivated by them"]

man females have a tremendous minimum necessary investment in each of their offspring" while men have a very small minimal investment.[20]

But there's a problem with this yin and yang theory of reproduction. Each egg can accommodate only one sperm. Males contribute just as much genetic material to the offspring as females do and have just as much of a genetic interest in the offspring—perhaps even more, since females provide only an X chromosome while males can give an X or a Y, and therefore determine the sex of the offspring.

Isn't it interesting how, whether men contribute everything, as in the pre-Darwin scenario 1, or so little it's hardly worth their bother to care where it goes, as in the post-Darwin scenario 2, the end conclusion is that men have a vested interest in spreading their seed around as far as possible while women have a vested interest in being choosy? Is this why choosy mothers choose Jif? Or could it be that the starting assumption is that it's natural for men to spread seed widely and natural for women to be choosy, and, lo and behold, a theory (pre- or post-Darwin) is found to provide a support for that belief? Maybe this is why choosy mothers choose Jif! Or maybe choosy mothers choose Jif because they fear that otherwise they will be perceived as bad moms. And maybe rapists rape in part because they think other men will admire them for it or that it's their prerogative as a male to have access to any woman they want at any time.[21]

"DO THEY HAVE TO BE WRONG?"

Thornhill and Palmer would argue that it doesn't matter what any individual man gives as his reason for committing rape, since this is just the proximate cause. Ultimately, evolution is behind it all. As they state, "Rape behavior arises from elements of men's sexual nature—their sexual psychology . . . [which] is characteristic of men in general."[22] They deny that their theory is one of genetic determinism, but their proposed solution assumes that all boys are potential rapists unless they are educated to be men who can resist their "evolved sexual desires."[23] As Margaret Wertheim has noted, this view of human male nature is strikingly similar to that of "feminist extremists like Andrea Dworkin . . . [who] is routinely portrayed in the media as a half-crazed man-hating harpy."[24] Yet, Thornhill and Palmer's call for a *Minority Report*-like societal solution to rape has been presented by the media as a respectable and scientifically grounded approach that undermines feminist analyses of rape.[25]

Thornhill and Palmer devote an entire chapter of their book to the question, "Why have social scientists failed to Darwinize?" and another to denouncing the social scientific explanation of rape.[26] By *social scientists,* they mean feminists, as they explain: "Because the phrase 'feminist psychosocial analysis' is a bit awkward, we will refer to it as 'the social science explanation.'"[27] Feminists are depicted as suffering from biophobia, the sources of which are several: the naturalistic fallacy, or the belief that to admit something is natural is to admit it is good; the myth of genetic determinism, or the assumption that evolutionary explanations are based on the notion of genetically determined behavior; the failure to distinguish proximate from ultimate explanations; the perceived threat of biology to cherished ideology; and the perceived threat of biology to the status of those whose success is based on nonevolutionary theories.

The bulk of their argument against feminist theories of rape is devoted to (1) the red herring claim that feminists deny that rape is about sex, and (2) the claim that a combination of ideology and ignorance prevents feminists from accepting biological truth. Thornhill and Palmer disavow that culturally specific learning is relevant to the cause of rape, yet they propose a solution to rape that features a cultural-learning activity—teaching men not to rape. They accuse feminist, culturally based explanations of rape of being deterministic and inconsistent with free will. The evolutionary approach, however, offers the power of predicting "the developmental events of interest [that] occur in response to specific cues" that are likely to increase the proclivity of males to rape. This would allow humans to alter "environmental factors" that would help men consciously choose not to rape.[28]

It would appear that both evolutionary psychologists and feminists agree that changes in environment/culture and in educational programs/learning are key to eliminating rape. So, what is really at stake here in setting up the feminism versus evolutionary psychology battle? In their chapter "Social Influences on Male Sexuality," the real issue is at last identified. It is the fear that acceptance of feminist theories of rape will degrade the status of males and destroy "male traditions" and traditional families. "The feminist view predicts that rape can be prevented only by a wholesale abandonment of male traditions."[29] Evolutionary psychology promises to eliminate rape while leaving male privilege intact. "In reality, though many aspects of patriarchal traditions may be undesirable for a variety of reasons, the abandonment of all male traditions that might be deemed patriarchal would be likely to *increase* the frequency of rape."[30] Feminists are cast in an ideologically motivated, antiscience role while science is claimed by evolutionary psychology in the service of patriarchy.

In her essay on *A Natural History of Rape*, Daphne Patai builds on Thornhill and Palmer's case against feminism.[31] She argues that the problem with feminism is that it is nonscientific—that feminists are neither inspired nor limited in their conceptualizations of the problem of rape by scientific data or theory. In Patai's view, feminists are antagonistic to biological approaches to gender and sexuality. Indeed, feminism appears to require antagonism to scientific accounts of gender and sexuality to accomplish what Patai sees as its broader purpose of problematizing and attacking heterosexual sexual orientation and desire. Social constructivist accounts of gender, by contrast, give feminists the ability to create a world of their own liking and to keep the less desirable dimensions of scientific explanation at bay. In fact, Patai argues, it is because feminists misunderstand the scientific account of such phenomena as rape as utterly deterministic that they reject all uncomfortable scientific accounts.

There are several problems with this account of the repudiation of Thornhill and Palmer, but the most obvious one to those who examine the plethora of critical responses to *Natural History* is the overwhelmingly negative reception of the theory from scientists who make no claim to feminist political identification.[32] In spite of the critiques of scientists who contend, for example, that the theory is "more of an ideological rant than an empirical, well-reasoned analysis,"[33] media accounts of the book and interviews with the authors focused attention on the divergence between science and politics. The implication is clear: only biophobic ideologists could disagree with Thornhill and Palmer's scientific narrative of rape as an adaptive sexual behavior.

For Thornhill and Palmer, as well as for their enthusiastic apologist Patai, culture is a product of biology so that cultural accounts—and condemnations—of rape attack the symptom of the issue, the proximate cause, rather than the ultimate cause. The ultimate cause of such social and cultural forms of behavior as rape is evolutionary development. Therefore, rape is not amenable to the kinds of feminist and social science critiques leveled at the problem by virtually all previous scholars.

"Do they have to be wrong?" is the plaintive question asked by Daphne Patai. They don't "have" to be wrong; that is, their conclusions should not be rejected merely because they are inconvenient to proponents of women's civil and political rights. However, as many critics have now pointed out, there is little to recommend their theory as science. And as I have shown, even if accepted as scientifically based, their theory contains numerous flaws and contradictions, and their proposed solutions are neither unique nor inevitable.

Why do the media + others accept this acct.
+ not scientific or feminist ones?

CONCLUSION

Patai defends Thornhill and Palmer against feminist critique of their theory while affirming its scientific basis and implications. She acknowledges the existence of scientific critiques but denies that these are the basis for any feminist rejections of Thornhill and Palmer's theory. Both Thornhill and Palmer and Patai draw a false dichotomy between feminists (who are not only not scientists but are, in addition, ideologically predisposed to reject scientific explanations) and scientists (who are unaffected by ideology and insulated against it by scientific method itself). Furthermore, ignorance and antiscience bias among feminists—and feminists only—are claimed to fuel the hostility against Thornhill and Palmer and the rejection of their theory.

Far from being impaired by a feminist lack of scientific knowledge and sophistication, as Patai suggests in her review, Thornhill and Palmer benefit from this lack in the general public. More, they appear to cultivate the look and feel of science for naïve readers and busy news consumers, which may explain why Patai is so easily convinced of the theory's validity and scientific nature. Journalists, political commentators, humanistic scholars, and ordinary citizens who lack the scientific sophistication to evaluate Thornhill and Palmer's theory, evidence, and conclusions are likely to be too impressed by the researchers' scientific claims and credentials and more credulous about the social implications they derive.

But who is to blame for the theory's reception as science: naïve readers or the authors who deliberately and deceptively claim the indisputable mantle of science with frequent assertions of the incontestability of their approach and findings? As an alumna of MIT, I find it particularly embarrassing to see the imprimatur of science given to this work through its publication by MIT Press. The extensive and uncritical media coverage that hailed the appearance of Thornhill and Palmer's book prompted MIT Press to push up the publication date by two months in an effort to capitalize on the "logical scientists versus angry feminists" controversy created by Thornhill and Palmer in their text and cultivated by and through the media.[34]

In 2003, MIT Press will publish a book entitled *Gender, Evolution, and Rape*. Designed as a rebuttal to *Natural History,* Cheryl Travis's edited volume will offer "alternative models of rape, which incorporate psychology and cultural systems, as well as a broader interpretation of evolutionary theory."[35] This is reminiscent of another pairing of volumes that appeared at the end of the nineteenth century. In 1873, Edward H. Clarke published *Sex in Education, or, A Fair Chance for the Girls.*[36] Clarke's main thesis was that education would cause a woman's uterus to wither and decay, and he, too, claimed the mantle of science to support his selective use of biological theory and data. In 1874, Julia Ward Howe spearheaded publication of a volume dedicated to a rebuttal of Clarke, based on actual data and experiences of women who had received higher education.[37]

When I reflect on the time spent on this essay, the time spent by Howe and her colleagues over a hundred years ago on their book, or that spent by Travis and her colleagues today, I am frustrated by the loss to critique of time that could have been given to creative activity. However, it is every scientist's responsibility to engage in critique as well as creation; critique is an integral part of the scientific process. Furthermore, scientists have a responsibility to the public to share both creation and critique, to aid nonscientists in making reasoned choices about the influence and application of science in society. It will not do to lament in the laboratory that ideology draped in science is so easily accepted by the public, for if it is, it means we as scientists have not been engaged in sufficient dialogue with that public.

Social conservatives today can effectively wield "science" to support the conservative agenda in part because practicing scientists have in the past cared little for the scientific education of the general public. Far from being antiscience, feminism in the academy is one of the few places where large numbers of nonscientists are encouraged to grapple with what science has had to say about biology and destiny. Feminism, for me, has always been about asking more and better questions and continually questioning received wisdom, a description that can also be applied to science at its best. Feminists have been talking science for over a hundred years, and we'll keep doing so, wherever we find science misunderstood and misused.

NOTES

The title of this chapter refers to the song "She Blinded Me with Science" by Thomas Dolby from the 1982 album *Golden Age of Wireless* on EMD/Capitol Records.

1. Randy Thornhill and Craig T. Palmer, *A Natural History of Rape: Biological Basis of Sexual Coercion* (Cambridge, Mass.: MIT Press, 2000).
2. Thornhill and Palmer, *Natural History,* 53.
3. Daphne Patai, "Do They Have to Be Wrong?" *Gender Issues* (Fall 2000): 74–82.
4. Natalie Angier, "Biological Bull," *Ms.,* June/July 2000, 80–82.
5. Jennifer L. Pozner, "In Rape Debate, Controversy Trumps Credibility," *Fairness and Accuracy in Reporting,* 2000, at www.fair.org/extra/0005/thornhill.html

(accessed February 7, 2002); APB News.com, "Scientists Assail Controversial Rape Book," *APB News.com,* 2000, at www.apbonline.com/safetycenter/family/2000/03/08/rapebook0308_01.html (accessed February 7, 2002).

6. Thornhill and Palmer, *Natural History,* xii–xiii.

7. Margaret Wertheim, "Born to Rape?" *Salon.com,* 2000, at www.salon.com/books/feature/2000/02/29/rape/print.html (accessed February 7, 2002); Matt Cartmill, "Understanding the Evil that Men Do," *Chronicle of Higher Education* 46, no. 39 (2000), at www.chronicle.com/weekly/v46/i39/39b00401.htm (accessed February 7, 2002); Craig B. Stanford, "Darwinians Look at Rape, Sex, and War," *American Scientist,* July/August 2000, at www.sigmaxi.org/amsci/bookshelf/leads00/Stanford.html (accessed February 7, 2002).

8. Thornhill and Palmer, *Natural History,* xii.

9. Cartmill, "Understanding the Evil"; Stanford, "Darwinians Look at Rape"; Jerry A. Coyne and Andrew Berry, "Rape as an Adaptation," *Nature* 404 (March 9, 2000): 121–22; Wertheim, "Born to Rape?"; Dan Vergano, *USA Today,* 2000, at www.usatoday.com/life/health/sexualit/lhsex021.htm (accessed February 7, 2002).

10. Randy Thornhill and Nancy W. Thornhill, "Evolutionary Analysis of Psychological Pain of Rape Victims I: The Effects of Victim's Age and Marital Status," *Ethnology and Sociobiology* 11 (1990): 155–76. The criticism that the data in this paper are misinterpreted is made in Coyne and Berry, "Rape as an Adaptation."

11. Cartmill, "Understanding the Evil."

12. Thornhill and Palmer, *Natural History,* 14.

13. Thornhill and Palmer, *Natural History,* 29, emphasis in original.

14. Thornhill and Palmer, *Natural History,* 5.

15. Thornhill and Palmer, *Natural History,* 12–13.

16. Suzanne E. Franks, Annette C. Kuesel, Norbert W. Lutz, and William E. Hull, "^{31}P-MRS of Human Tumor Cells: Effects of Culture Media and Conditions on Phospholipid Metabolite Levels," *Anticancer Research* 16 (1996): 1365–74; Suzanne F. Shedd, Norbert W. Lutz, and William E. Hull, "The Influence of Medium Formulation on Phosphomonoester and UDP-hexose Levels in Cultured Human Colon Tumor Cells as Observed by ^{31}P-NMR Spectroscopy," *NMR in Biomedicine* 6 (1993): 254–63.

17. This philosophical quandary was humorously depicted in Douglas Adams's book *The Hitchhiker's Guide to the Galaxy* (Ballantine Books, 1995), wherein the ultimate answer to the ultimate question of life, the universe, and everything is found to be 42.

18. Thornhill and Palmer, *Natural History,* 181.

19. Thornhill and Palmer, *Natural History,* 182.

20. Thornhill and Palmer, *Natural History,* 39–40; emphasis in original.

21. Diana Scully and Joseph Marolla, "'Riding the Bull at Gilley's: Convicted Rapists Describe the Rewards of Rape," *Social Problems* 32, no. 3 (February 1985): 251–63.

22. Thornhill and Palmer, *Natural History,* 194.

23. Thornhill and Palmer, *Natural History,* 180.

24. Wertheim, "Born to Rape?"

25. In the 2002 movie *Minority Report,* individuals are punished for murders they have not yet committed but which the authorities believe will occur if they are left alone.

26. Thornhill and Palmer, *Natural History,* ch. 5 and 6.

27. Thornhill and Palmer, *Natural History,* 123.

28. Thornhill and Palmer, *Natural History,* 153–54.

29. Thornhill and Palmer, *Natural History,* 176.

30. Thornhill and Palmer, *Natural History,* 177.

31. Daphne Patai, "Do They Have to Be Wrong?"

32. Cartmill, "Understanding the Evil"; Stanford, "Darwinians Look at Rape"; Coyne and Berry, "Rape as an Adaptation."

33. Stanford, "Darwinians Look at Rape."

34. Pozner, "In Rape Debate"; FAIR, "In Rape Debate, NBC Prioritizes Controversy over Scientific Credibility," *Fairness and Accuracy in Reporting,* 2000, at www.fair.org/activism/nbc-thornhill.html (accessed February 7, 2002).

35. Cheryl Brown Travis, *Evolution, Gender, and Rape* (Cambridge, Mass.: MIT Press, forthcoming 2003), at mitpress.mit.edu/catalog/item/default.asp?sid=DA6AE115-4FA5-43E6-B268-965C34EDFB57&ttype=2&tid=9228 (accessed July 6, 2002).

36. Edward Hammond Clarke, *Sex in Education; Or, A Fair Chance for the Girls* (New York: Arno Press, [1873] 1972).

37. Julia Ward Howe, *Sex and Education; a Reply to Dr. E. H. Clarke's "Sex in Education"* (New York: Arno Press, [1874] 1972).

2

(How) Does the Sexual Orientation of Parents Matter?

Judith Stacey and Timothy J. Biblarz

Today, gay marriage is taking on an air of inevitability." So observed a U.S. newspaper from the heartland in September 1999, reporting that one-third of those surveyed in an *NBC News/Wall Street Journal* poll endorsed the legalization of same-sex marriage, while 65 percent predicted such legislation would take place in the new century.[1] During the waning months of the last millennium, France enacted national registered partnerships, Denmark extended child custody rights to same-sex couples, and the state supreme courts in Vermont and in Ontario, Canada, ruled that same-sex couples were entitled to full and equal family rights. Most dramatically, in September 2000 the Netherlands became the first nation to realize the inevitable when the Dutch parliament voted overwhelmingly to grant same-sex couples full and equal rights to marriage. As the new millennium begins, struggles by nonheterosexuals to secure equal recognition and rights for the new family relationships they are now creating represent some of the most dramatic and fiercely contested developments in Western family patterns.

It is not surprising, therefore, that social science research on lesbigay family issues has become a rapid growth industry that incites passionate divisions. For the consequences of such research are by no means "academic," but bear on marriage and family policies that encode Western culture's most profoundly held convictions about gender, sexuality, and parenthood. As advocates and opponents square off in state and federal courts and legislatures, in the electoral arena, and in culture wars over efforts to extend to nonheterosexuals equal rights to marriage, child custody, adoption, foster care, and fertility services, they heatedly debate the implications of a youthful body of research, conducted primarily by psychologists, that investigates if and how the sexual orientation of parents affects children.

This body of research, almost uniformly, reports findings of no notable differences between children reared by heterosexual parents and those reared by lesbian and gay parents, and it finds lesbigay parents to be as competent and effective as heterosexual parents. Lawyers and activists struggling to defend child custody and adoption petitions by lesbians and gay men, or to attain same-gender marriage rights and to defeat preemptive referenda against such rights (e.g., the victorious Knight Initiative on the 2000 ballot in California) have drawn on this research with considerable success.[2] Although progress is uneven, this strategy has promoted a gradual liberalizing trend in judicial and policy decisions. However, backlash campaigns against gay family rights have begun to challenge the validity of the research.

In 1997, the *University of Illinois Law Review Journal* published an article by Lynn D. Wardle, a Brigham Young University law professor, that impugned the motives, methods, and merits of social science research on lesbian and gay parenting.[3] Wardle charged the legal profession and social scientists with an ideological bias favoring gay rights that has compromised most research in this field and the liberal judicial and policy decisions it has informed. He presented a harshly critical assessment of the research and argued for a presumptive judicial standard in favor of awarding child custody to heterosexual married couples. The following year, Wardle drafted new state regulations in Utah that restrict adoption and foster care placements to households in which all adults are related by blood or marriage. Florida, Arkansas, and Mississippi also have imposed restrictions on adoption and/or foster care, and such bills have been introduced in the legislatures of ten additional states.[4] In March 2000, a paper presented at a "Revitalizing Marriage" conference at Brigham Young University assailed the quality of studies that had been cited to support the efficacy of lesbigay parenting.[5] Characterizing the research methods as "dismal," Robert Lerner and Althea K. Nagai claimed, "The methods used in these studies were sufficiently flawed so that these studies could not and should not be used in legislative forums or legal cases to buttress any arguments on the nature of homosexual vs. heterosexual parenting."[6] Shortly afterward, Maggie Gallagher, of the Institute for American Values, broadcast Lerner and Nagai's argument in her nationally syndicated *New York Post* column in order to undermine the use of "the science card" by advocates of gay marriage and gay "normalization."[7]

We depart sharply from the views of Wardle and Gallagher on the merits and morals of lesbigay parenthood as well as on their analysis of the

focus on PR + policy

child development research. We agree, however, that ideological pressures constrain intellectual development in this field. In our view, it is the pervasiveness of social prejudice and institutionalized discrimination against lesbians and gay men that exerts a powerful policing effect on the basic terms of psychological research and public discourse on the significance of parental sexual orientation. The field suffers less from the overt ideological convictions of scholars than from the unfortunate intellectual consequences that follow from the implicit heteronormative presumption governing the terms of the discourse—that healthy child development depends upon parenting by a married heterosexual couple. While few contributors to this literature personally subscribe to this view, most of the research asks whether lesbigay parents subject their children to greater risks or harm than are confronted by children reared by heterosexual parents. Because antigay scholars seek evidence of harm, sympathetic researchers defensively stress its absence.

We take stock of this body of psychological research from a sociological perspective. We analyze the impact that this heteronormative presumption exacts on predominant research strategies, analyses, and representations of findings. After assessing the basic premises and arguments in the debate, we discuss how the social fact of heterosexism has operated to constrain the research populations, concepts, and designs employed in the studies to date.

We wish to acknowledge that the political stakes of this body of research are so high that the ideological "family values" of scholars play a greater part than usual in how they design, conduct, and interpret their studies. Of course, we recognize that this is equally true for those who criticize such studies.[8] The inescapably ideological and emotional nature of this subject makes it incumbent on scholars to acknowledge the personal convictions they bring to the discussion. Because we personally oppose discrimination on the basis of sexual orientation or gender, we subject research claims by those sympathetic to our stance to a heightened degree of critical scrutiny and afford the fullest possible consideration to work by scholars opposed to parenting by lesbians and gay men.

THE CASE AGAINST LESBIAN AND GAY PARENTHOOD

Wardle is correct that contemporary scholarship on the effects of parental sexual orientation on children's development is rarely critical of lesbigay parenthood.[9] Few respectable scholars today oppose such parenting. However, a few psychologists subscribe to the view that homosexuality represents either a sin or a mental illness and continue to publish alarmist works on the putative ill effects of gay parenting.[10] Even though the American Psychological Association expelled Paul Cameron, and the American Sociological Association denounced him for willfully misrepresenting research, his publications continue to be cited in amicus briefs, court decisions, and policy hearings.[11] For example, the chair of the Arkansas Child Welfare Agency Review Board repeatedly cited publications by Cameron's group in her testimony at policy hearings, which, incidentally, led to restricting foster child placements to heterosexual parents.[12]

Likewise, Wardle draws explicitly on Cameron's work to build his case against gay parent rights.[13] Research demonstrates, Wardle maintains, that gay parents subject children to disproportionate risks; that children of gay parents are more apt to suffer confusion over their gender and sexual identities and are more likely to become homosexuals themselves; that homosexual parents are more sexually promiscuous than are heterosexual parents and are more likely to molest their own children; that children are at greater risk of losing a homosexual parent to AIDS, substance abuse, or suicide, and to suffer greater risks of depression and other emotional difficulties; that homosexual couples are more unstable and likely to separate; and that the social stigma and embarrassment of having a homosexual parent unfairly ostracizes children and hinders their relationships with peers. Judges have cited Wardle's article to justify transferring child custody from lesbian to heterosexual parents.[14]

Wardle, like other opponents of homosexual parenthood, also relies on a controversial literature that decries the putative risks of "fatherlessness" in general.[15] Thus, Wardle cites books by David Popenoe,[16] David Blankenhorn,[17] and Barbara Dafoe Whitehead[18] when he argues:

> Children generally develop best, and develop most completely, when raised by both a mother and a father and experience regular family interaction with both genders' parenting skills during their years of childhood. It is now undeniable that, just as a mother's influence is crucial to the secure, healthy, and full development of a child, [a] paternal presence in the life of a child is essential to the child emotionally and physically.[19]

Wardle, like Blankenhorn, extrapolates (inappropriately) from research on single-mother families to portray children of lesbians as more vulnerable to everything from delinquency, substance abuse, violence, and crime, to teen pregnancy, school dropout, suicide, and even poverty.[20] In short, the few scholars who are opposed to parenting by lesbians and gay men provide academic support for the convictions of many judges, journalists, politicians, and citizens that the sexual orientation of parents matters greatly to children, and that lesbigay parents represent a danger to their children and to society. Generally, these scholars offer only limited, and often implicit, theoretical explanations for the disadvantages of same-sex parenting—typically combining elements of bioevolutionary theory with social and cognitive learning theories.[21] Cameron et al. crudely propose that homosexuality is a "learned pathology" that parents pass on to children through processes of modeling, seduction, and "contagion."[22] The deeply rooted heteronormative convictions about what constitutes healthy and moral gender identity, sexual orientation, and family composition held by contributors to this literature hinder their ability to conduct or interpret research with reason, nuance, or care.

THE CASE FOR LESBIAN AND GAY PARENTHOOD

Perhaps the most consequential impact that heterosexism exerts on the research on lesbigay parenting lies where it is least apparent—in the far more responsible literature that is largely sympathetic to its subject. It is easy to expose the ways in which the prejudicial views of those directly hostile to lesbigay parenting distort their research.[23] Moreover, because antigay scholars regard homosexuality itself as a form of pathology, they tautologically interpret any evidence that children may be more likely to engage in homoerotic behavior as evidence of harm. Less obvious, however, are the ways in which heterosexism also hampers research and analysis among those who explicitly support lesbigay parenthood. With rare exceptions, even the most sympathetic proceed from a highly defensive posture that accepts heterosexual parenting as the gold standard and investigates whether lesbigay parents and their children are inferior.

This sort of hierarchical model implies that differences indicate deficits.[24] Instead of investigating whether (and how) differences in adult sexual orientation might lead to meaningful differences in how individuals parent and how their children develop, the predominant research designs place the burden of proof on lesbigay parents to demonstrate that they are not less successful or less worthy than heterosexual parents. Too often scholars seem to presume that this approach precludes acknowledging almost any differences in parenting or in child outcomes. A characteristic review of research on lesbian-mother families concludes: "a rapidly growing and highly consistent body of empirical work has failed to identify significant differences between lesbian mothers and their heterosexual counterparts or the children raised by these groups. Researchers have been unable to establish empirically that detriment results to children from being raised by lesbian mothers."[25]

Given the weighty political implications of this body of research, it is easy to understand the social sources of such a defensive stance. As long as sexual orientation can deprive a gay parent of child custody, fertility services, and adoption rights, sensitive scholars are apt to tread gingerly around the terrain of differences. Unfortunately, however, this reticence compromises the development of knowledge not only in child development and psychology, but also within the sociology of sexuality, gender, and family more broadly. For if homophobic theories seem crude, too many psychologists who are sympathetic to lesbigay parenting seem hesitant to theorize at all. When researchers downplay the significance of any findings of differences, they forfeit a unique opportunity to take full advantage of the "natural laboratory" that the advent of lesbigay-parent families provides for exploring the effects and acquisition of gender and sexual identity, ideology, and behavior.

This reticence is most evident in analyses of sexual behavior and identity—the most politically sensitive issue in the debate. Virtually all of the published research claims to find no differences in the sexuality of children reared by lesbigay parents and those raised by nongay parents but none of the studies that report this finding attempts to theorize about such an implausible outcome. Yet it is difficult to conceive of a credible theory of sexual development that would not expect the adult children of lesbigay parents to display a somewhat higher incidence of homoerotic desire, behavior, and identity than children of heterosexual parents. For example, biological determinist theory should predict at least some difference in an inherited predisposition to same-sex desire; a social constructionist theory would expect lesbigay parents to provide an environment in which children would feel freer to explore and affirm such desires; psychoanalytic theory might hypothesize that the absence of a male parent would weaken a daughter's need to relinquish her preoedipal desire for her mother or that the absence of a female parent would foster a son's preoedipal love for his father that no fear of castration or oedipal crisis would interrupt. Moreover, because parents determine where their children reside, even one who subscribed to Judith Rich Harris's maverick theory—that parents are virtually powerless when compared with peers to influence their children's development—should anticipate that lesbigay parents would probably rear their children among less homophobic peers.[26]

Bern's "exotic becomes erotic" theory of sexual orientation argues that in a gender-polarized society, children eroticize the gender of peers whose interests and temperaments differ most from their own.[27] Most children thereby become heterosexual, but boys attracted to "feminine" activities and girls who are "tomboys" are apt to develop homoerotic desires. The impact of parental genes and child-rearing practices remains implicit because parents contribute genetically to the temperamental factors Bern identifies as precursors to a child's native activity preferences, and parental attitudes toward gender polarization should affect the way those innate preferences translate into children's cognition and play. In fact, the only "theory" of child development we can imagine in which a child's sexual development would bear no relationship to parental genes, practices, environment, or beliefs would be an arbitrary one.[28] Yet this is precisely the outcome that most scholars report, although the limited empirical record does not justify it.

Over the past decade, prominent psychologists in the field began to call for less defensive research on lesbian and gay family issues.[29] Rethinking the "no differences" doctrine, some scholars urge social scientists to look for potentially beneficial effects children might derive from such distinctive aspects of lesbigay parenting as the more egalitarian relationships these parents appear to practice.[30] More radically, a few scholars[31] propose abandoning comparative research on lesbian and heterosexual parenting altogether and supplanting it with research that asks "why and how are lesbian parents oppressed and how can we change that?"[32] While we perceive potential advantages from these agendas, we advocate an alternative strategy that moves beyond heteronormativity without forfeiting the fruitful potential of comparative research. Although we agree with Celia Kitzinger and Adrian Coyle[33] and Victoria Clarke[34] that the social obstacles to lesbian (and gay) parenthood deserve rigorous attention, we believe that this should supplement, not supplant, the rich opportunity planned lesbigay parenthood provides for the exploration of the interactions of gender, sexual orientation, and biosocial family structures on parenting and child development. Moreover, while we welcome research attuned to potential strengths as well as vulnerabilities of lesbigay parenting, we believe that knowledge and policy will be best served when scholars feel free to replace a hierarchical model, which assigns "grades" to parents and children according to their sexual identities, with a more genuinely pluralist approach to family diversity. Sometimes, to bowdlerize Freud's famous dictum, a difference *really* is just a difference!

PROBLEMS WITH CONCEPTS, CATEGORIES, AND SAMPLES

The social effects of heterosexism constrain the character of research conducted on lesbigay parenting in ways more profound than those deriving from the ideological stakes of researchers. First, as most researchers recognize, because so many individuals legitimately fear the social consequences of adopting a gay identity, and because few national surveys have included questions about sexual orientation, it is impossible to gather reliable data on such basic demographic questions as how many lesbians and gay men there are in the general population, how many have children, or how many children reside (or have substantial contact) with lesbian or gay parents. Curiously, those who are hostile to gay parenting tend to minimize the incidence of same-sex orientation, while sympathetic scholars typically report improbably high numerical estimates. Both camps thus implicitly presume that the rarer the incidence, the less legitimate would be lesbigay claims to rights. One could imagine an alternative political logic, however, in which a low figure might undermine grounds for viewing lesbigay parenting as a meaningful social threat. Nonetheless, political anxieties have complicated the difficulty of answering basic demographic questions.

Since 1984, most researchers have statically reproduced numbers, of uncertain origin, depicting a range of from 1 to 5 million lesbian mothers, from 1 to 3 million gay fathers, and from 6 to 14 million children of gay or lesbian parents in the United States.[35] More recent estimates by Charlotte J. Patterson and Lisa V. Freil[36] extrapolate from distributions observed in the National Health and Social Life Survey.[37] Depending upon the definition of parental sexual orientation employed, Patterson and Freil suggest a current lower limit of 800,000 lesbigay parents ages 18 to 59 with 1.6 million children and an upper limit of 7 million lesbigay parents with 14 million children. However, these estimates include many "children" who are actually adults. To estimate the number who are dependent children (age 18 or younger), we multiplied the child counts by .66, which is the proportion of dependent children among all offspring of 18- to 59-year-old parents in the representative National Survey of Families and Households.[38] This adjustment reduces the estimates of current dependent children with lesbigay parents to a range of 1 to 9 million, which implies that somewhere between 1 percent and 12 percent of all (78 million) children ages 19 and under in the United States have a lesbigay parent.[39] The 12 percent figure depends upon classifying as a lesbigay parent anyone who reports that even the idea of homoerotic sex is appealing, while the low (1 percent) figure derives from the narrower, and in our view more politically salient, definition of a lesbigay parent as one who self-identifies as such.[40]

Across the ideological spectrum, scholars, journalists, and activists appear to presume that the normalization of lesbigay sexuality should steadily increase the ranks of children with lesbian and gay parents. In contrast, we believe that normalization is more likely to reduce the proportion of such children. Most contemporary lesbian and gay parents procreated within heterosexual marriages that many had entered hoping to escape the social and emotional consequences of homophobia. As homosexuality becomes more legitimate, far fewer people with homoerotic desires should feel compelled to enter heterosexual marriages, and thus fewer should become parents in this manner.

On the other hand, with normalization, intentional parenting by self-identified lesbians and gay men should continue to increase, but it is unlikely to do so sufficiently to compensate for the decline in the current ranks of formerly married lesbian and gay parents. Thus, the proportion of lesbian parents may not change much. Many women with homoerotic desires who once might have married men and succumbed to social pressures to parent will no longer do so; others who remained single and childless because of their homoerotic desires will feel freer to choose lesbian maternity. It is difficult to predict the net effect of these contradictory trends. However, as fewer closeted gay men participate in heterosexual marriages, the ranks of gay fathers should thin. Even if gay men were as eager as lesbians are to become parents, biology alone sharply constrains their ability to do so. Moreover, there is evidence that fewer men of any sexual orientation actually desire children as strongly as do comparable women,[41] and most demographic studies of sexual orientation find a higher incidence of homosexuality among men than women.[42] Thus, although the ranks of intentional paternity among gay men should increase, we do not believe this will compensate for the declining numbers of closeted gay men who will become fathers through heterosexual marriages. Hence, the estimate of 1 to 12 percent of children with a lesbigay parent may represent a peak interval that may decline somewhat with normalization.

A second fundamental problem in sampling involves the ambiguity, fluidity, and complexity of definitions of sexual orientation. "The traditional type of surveys on the prevalence of 'homosexuality,'" remarks a prominent Danish sociologist, "are already in danger of becoming antiquated even before they are carried out; the questions asked are partially irrelevant; sexuality is not what it used to be."[43] What defines a parent (or adult child) as lesbian, gay, bisexual, or heterosexual? Are these behavioral, social, emotional, or political categories? Historical scholarship has established that sexual identities are modern categories whose definitions vary greatly not only across cultures, spaces, and time, but even among and within individuals.[44] Some gay men, for example, practice celibacy; some heterosexual men engage in "situational" homosexual activity. Some lesbians relinquish lesbian identities to marry; some relinquish marriage for a lesbian identity. What about bisexual, transsexual, or transgendered parents, not to mention those who repartner with individuals of the same or different genders? Sexual desires, acts, meanings, and identities are not expressed in fixed or predictable packages.

Third, visible lesbigay parenthood is such a recent phenomenon that most studies are necessarily of the children of a transitional generation of self-identified lesbians and gay men who became parents in the context of heterosexual marriages or relationships that dissolved before or after they assumed a gay identity. These unique historical conditions make it impossible to fully distinguish the impact of a parent's sexual orientation on a child from the impact of such factors as divorce, remating, the secrecy of the closet, the process of coming out, or the social consequences of stigma. Only a few studies have attempted to control for the number and gender of a child's parents before and after a parent decided to identify as lesbian or gay. Because many more formerly married lesbian mothers than gay fathers retain custody of their children, most research is actually on postdivorce lesbian motherhood. A few studies compare heterosexual and gay fathers after divorce.[45] If fewer self-identified lesbians and gay men will become parents through heterosexual marriages, the published research on this form of gay parenthood will become less relevant to issues in scholarly and public debates.

Fourth, because researchers lack reliable data on the number and location of lesbigay parents with children in the general population, there are no studies of child development based on random, representative samples of such families. Most studies rely on small-scale, snowball, and convenience samples drawn primarily from personal and community networks or agencies. Most research to date has been conducted on white lesbian mothers who are comparatively educated, mature, and reside in relatively progressive urban centers, most often in California or the northeastern states.[46]

Although scholars often acknowledge some of these difficulties, few studies explicitly grapple with these definitional questions.[47] Most studies simply rely on a parent's sexual self-identity at the time of the study, which contributes unwittingly to the racial, ethnic, and class imbalance of the populations studied. Ethnographic studies suggest that "lesbian," "gay," and "bisexual" identity among socially subordinate and nonurban populations is generally less visible or less affirmed than it is among more privileged white, educated, and urban populations.[48]

Increasingly, uncloseted lesbians and gay men actively choose to become parents through diverse and innovative means.[49] In addition to adoption and foster care, lesbians are choosing motherhood using known and unknown sperm donors (as single mothers, in intentional co-mother couples, and in complex variations of biosocial parenting). Both members of a lesbian couple may choose to become pregnant sequentially or simultaneously. Pioneering lesbian couples have exchanged ova to enable both women to claim biological, and thereby legal, maternal status to the same infant.[50] It is much more difficult (and costly) for gay men to choose to become fathers, particularly fathers of infants. Some (who reside in states that permit this) become adoptive or foster parents; others serve as sperm donors in joint parenting arrangements with lesbian or other mothers. An affluent minority hire women as "surrogates" to bear children for them.

The means and contexts for planned parenthood are so diverse and complex that they compound the difficulties of isolating the significance of parental sexual orientation. To even approximate this goal, researchers would need to control not only for the gender, number, and sexual orientation of parents, but for their diverse biosocial and legal statuses. The handful of studies that has attempted to do this focuses on lesbian motherhood. The most rigorous research designs compare donor-insemination (DI) parenthood among lesbian and heterosexual couples or single mothers.[51] To our knowledge, no studies have been conducted exclusively on lesbian or gay adoptive parents or compare the children of intentional gay fathers with children in other family forms. Researchers do not know the extent to which the comparatively high socioeconomic status of the DI parents studied accurately reflects the demographics of lesbian and gay parenthood generally, but given the degree of effort, cultural and legal support, and, frequently, the expense involved, members of relatively privileged social groups would be the ones most able to make use of reproductive technology and/or independent adoption.

In short, the indirect effects of heterosexism have placed inordinate constraints on most research on the effects of gay parenthood. We believe, however, that the time may now be propitious to begin to reformulate the basic terms of the enterprise.

RECONSIDERING THE PSYCHOLOGICAL FINDINGS

Toward this end, we examined the findings of twenty-one psychological studies[52] published between 1981 and 1998 that we considered best equipped to address sociological questions about how parental sexual orientation matters to children. One meta-analysis of eighteen such studies (eleven of which are included among our twenty-one)

Table 2.1. Findings on the Associations between Parents' Sexual Orientations and Selected Child Outcomes: Twenty-One Studies, 1981 to 1998

Variable Measured	Direction of Effect
Gender Behavior/Preferences	
Girls' departure from traditional gender role expectations and behaviors—in dress, play, physicality, school activities, occupational aspirations (Hoeffer 1981; Golombok et al. 1983; R. Green et al. 1986; Steckel 1987; Hotvedt and Mandel 1982)	0/+
Boys' departure from traditional gender role expectations and behaviors—in dress, play, physicality, school activities, occupational aspirations (Hoeffer 1981; Golombok et al. 1983; R. Green et al. 1986; Steckel 1987; Hotvedt and Mandel 1982)	0/+
Boys' level of aggressiveness and domineering disposition (Steckel 1987)	−
Child wishes she/he were the other sex (Green et al. 1986)	0
Sexual Behavior/Sexual Preferences	
Young adult child has considered same-sex sexual relationship(s); has had same-sex sexual relationship(s) (Tasker and Golombok 1997)	+
Young adult child firmly self-identifies as bisexual, gay, or lesbian (Tasker and Golombok 1997)	0
Boys' likelihood of having a gay sexual orientation in adulthood, by sexual orientation of father (Bailey et al. 1995)	(+)
Girls' number of sexual partners from puberty to young adulthood (Tasker and Golombok 1997)	+
Boys' number of sexual partners from puberty to young adulthood (Tasker and Golombok 1997)	(−)
Quality of intimate relationships in young adulthood (Tasker and Golombok 1997)	0
Have friend(s) who are gay or lesbian (Tasker and Golombok 1997)	+
Self-Esteem and Psychological Well-Being	
Children's self-esteem, anxiety, depression, internalizing behavioral problems, externalizing behavioral problems, total behavioral problems, performance in social arenas (sports, friendships, school), use of psychological counseling, mothers' and teachers' reports of children's hyperactivity, unsociability, emotional difficulty, conduct difficulty, other behavioral problems (Golombok, Spencer, and Rutter 1983; Huggins 1989; Patterson 1994; Flaks et al. 1995; Tasker and Golombok 1997; Chan, Raboy, and Patterson 1998; Chan, Brooks, et al. 1998)	0
Daughters' self-reported level of popularity at school and in the neighborhood (Hotvedt and Mandel 1982)	+
Mothers' and teachers' reports of child's level of affection, responsiveness, and concern for younger children (Steckel 1987)	+

Table 2.1. *continued*

Variable Measured	Direction of Effect
Self-Esteem and Psychological Well-Being *(continued)*	
Experience of peer stigma concerning own sexuality (Tasker and Golombok 1997)	+
Cognitive functioning (IQ, verbal, performance, and so on) (Flaks et al. 1995; R. Green et al. 1986)	0
Experienced problems gaining employment in young adulthood (Tasker and Golombok 1997)	0

+ = significantly higher in lesbigay than in heterosexual parent context.
0 = no significant difference between lesbigay and heterosexual parent context.
− = significantly lower in lesbigay than in heterosexual parent context.
( ) = borders on statistical significance.
0/+ = evidence is mixed.
Sources: See note 52.

characteristically concludes that "the results demonstrate no differences on any measures between the heterosexual and homosexual parents regarding parenting styles, emotional adjustment, and sexual orientation of the child(ren)."[53] To evaluate this claim, we selected for examination only studies that (1) include a sample of gay or lesbian parents and children and a comparison group of heterosexual parents and children; (2) assess differences between groups in terms of statistical significance; and (3) include findings directly relevant to children's development. The studies we discuss compare relatively advantaged lesbian parents (eighteen studies) and gay male parents (three studies) with a roughly matched sample of heterosexual parents. Echoing the conclusion of metanalysts Mike Allen and Nancy Burrell, the authors of all twenty-one studies almost uniformly claim to find no differences in measures of parenting or child outcomes.[54] In contrast, our careful scrutiny of the findings they report suggests that on some dimensions—particularly those related to gender and sexuality—the sexual orientations of these parents matter somewhat more for their children than the researchers claimed.[55]

The empirical findings from these studies are presented in tables 2.1 and 2.2. Table 2.1 summarizes findings on the relationship between parental sexual orientation and three sets of child "outcome" variables: (1) gender behavior/gender preferences, (2) sexual behavior/sexual preferences, and (3) psychological well-being. Table 2.2 summarizes findings on the relationship between parental sexual orientation and other attributes of parents, including (1) behavior toward children's gender and sexual development, (2) parenting skills, (3) relationships with children, and (4) psychological well-being. Positive signs (+) indicate a statistically significant higher level of the variable for lesbigay parents or their children, while negative signs (–) indicate a higher level for heterosexual parents or their children. Zero (0) indicates no significant difference.

While table 2.1 reports the results of all twenty-one studies, our discussion here emphasizes findings from six studies we consider to be best designed to isolate whatever unique effects parents' sexual orientations might have on children. Four of these—David K. Flaks et al.,[56] A. Brewaeys et al.;[57] Raymond W. Chan, Barbara Raboy, and Patterson;[58] and Chan, Risa C. Brooks, et al.[59]—focus on planned parenting and compare children of lesbian mothers and heterosexual mothers who conceived through DI. This focus reduces the potential for variables like parental divorce, repartnering, coming out, and so on to confound whatever effects of maternal sexual orientation may be observed. The other two studies—Richard Green et al.[60] and Fiona L. Tasker and Susan Golombok[61]—focus on children born within heterosexual marriages who experienced the divorce of their biological parents before being raised by a lesbian mother with or without a new partner or spouse. Although this research design heightens the risk that in statistical analyses the effect of maternal sexual orientation may include the effects of other factors, distinctive strengths of each study counterbalance this limitation.

Table 2.2. Findings on the Associations between Parents' Sexual Orientations, Other Attributes of Parents, and Parent–Child Relationships: Twenty-One Studies, 1981 to 1998

Variable Measured	Direction of Effect
Parental Behavior toward Children's Gender and Sexual Development	
Mother prefers child engages in gender-appropriate play activities (Hoeffer 1981; R.Green et al. 1986; M. Harris and Turner 1986).	0/−
Mother classifies the ideal child as masculine (if boy) and feminine (if girl) (Kweskin and Cook 1982).	0
Mother prefers that child be gay or lesbian when grown up (Golombok et al. 1983; Tasker and Golombok 1997).	0
Child believes that mother would prefer that she/he has lesbigay sexual orientation (Tasker and Golombok 1997).	+
Parenting Practices: Developmental Orientations and Parenting Skills	
Mother's developmental orientation in child rearing and parenting skill (Miller et al.1982; McNeill et al. 1998; Flaks et al. 1995).	0/+
Spouse/partner's developmental orientation in child rearing and parenting skill (Flaks et al. 1995; Brewaeys et al. 1997).	+
Spouse/partner's desire for equal/shared distribution of child care (Chan, Brooks, et al. 1998).	+
Degree to which mother and spouse/partner share child care work (Brewaeys et al. 1997; Chan, Brooks, et al. 1998).	+
Similarity between mother's and spouse/partner's parenting skills (Flaks et al. 1995).	+

Table 2.2. continued

Variable Measured	Direction of Effect
Parenting Practices: Developmental Orientations and Parenting Skills (continued)	
Similarity between mother's and spouse/partner's assessment of child's behavior and well-being (Chan, Raboy, and Patterson 1998; Chan, Brooks, et al. 1998).	+
Mother allowed adolescent child's boyfriend/girlfriend to spend the night (Tasker and Golombok 1997).	0
Residential Parent/Child Relationships	
Mother's rating of quality of relationship with child (Golombok et al. 1983; M. Harris and Turner 1986; Brewaeys et al. 1997; McNeill et al. 1998).	0
Mother's likelihood of having a live-in partner postdivorce (Kweskin and Cook 1982; R. Green et al. 1986).	+
Spouse/partner's rating of quality of relationship with child (Brewaeys et al. 1997).	+
Child's report of closeness with biological mother growing up (Tasker and Golombok 1997; Brewaeys et al. 1997).	0
Child's report of closeness with biological mother's partner/spouse growing up (Tasker and Golombok 1997; Brewaeys et al. 1997).	0/+
Child felt able to discuss own sexual development with parent(s) while growing up (Tasker and Golombok 1997).	+
Nonresidential Parent/Child Relationships	
(Noncustodial) father's level of involvement with children, limit setting, and developmental orientation in child rearing (Bigner and Jacobsen 1989, 1992).	0/+
Mother's encouragement of child's contact with nonresidential father (Hotvedt and Mandel 1982).	0
Divorced mother's contact with children's father in the past year (Golombok et al. 1983).	+
Child's frequency of contact with nonresidential father (Golombok et al. 1983).	+
Child's positive feelings toward nonresidential father (Hotvedt and Mandel 1982; Tasker and Golombok 1997).	0/+
Parent's Self-Esteem and Psychological Well-Being	
Mother's level of depression, self-esteem (Rand et al. 1982; R. Green et al. 1986; Chan, Raboy and Patterson 1998; Golombok et al. 1983).	0/+
Mother's level of leadership, independence, achievement orientation (R. Green et al. 1986; Rand et al. 1982).	0/+
Mother's use of sedatives, stimulants, in- or outpatient psychiatric care in past year (Golombok et al. 1983).	0
Mother ever received psychiatric care in adult life (Golombok et al. 1983).	+
Mother's level of self-reported stress associated with single parenthood (R. Green et al. 1986).	0

+ = significantly higher in lesbigay than in heterosexual parent context.
0 = no significant difference between lesbigay and heterosexual parent context.
− = significantly lower in lesbigay than heterosexual parent context.
( ) = borders on statistical significance.
0/+ = evidence is mixed.
Sources: See note 52.

R. Green et al.[62] rigorously attempt to match lesbian mothers and heterosexual mothers on a variety of characteristics, and they compare the two groups of mothers as well as both groups of children on a wide variety of dimensions.[63] Tasker and Golombok offer a unique long-term, longitudinal design.[64] Their data collection began in 1976 on 27 heterosexual single mothers and 39 of their children (average age 10) and 27 lesbian mothers and 39 of their children (also average age 10) in England. Follow-up interviews with 46 of the original children were conducted 14 years later, allowing for a rare glimpse at how children with lesbian mothers and those with heterosexual mothers fared over their early life courses into young adulthood.

CHILDREN'S GENDER PREFERENCES AND BEHAVIOR

The first panel of table 2.1 displays findings about the relationship between the sexual orientation of parents and the gender preferences and behaviors of their children. The findings demonstrate that, as we would expect, on some measures meaningful differences have been observed in predictable directions. For example, lesbian mothers in R. Green et al. reported that their children, especially daughters, more frequently dress, play, and behave in ways that do not conform to sex-typed cultural norms.[65] Likewise, daughters of lesbian mothers reported greater interest in activities associated with both "masculine" and "feminine" qualities and that involve the participation of both sexes, whereas daughters of heterosexual mothers report significantly greater interest in traditionally feminine, same-sex activities.[66] Similarly, daughters with lesbian mothers reported higher aspirations to nontraditional gender occupations.[67] For example, in R. Green et al., 53 percent (16 out of 30) of the daughters of lesbians aspired to careers such as doctor, lawyer, engineer, and astronaut, compared with only 21 percent (6 of 28) of the daughters of heterosexual mothers.[68]

Sons appear to respond in more complex ways to parental sexual orientations. On some measures, such as aggressiveness and play preferences, the sons of lesbian mothers behave in less traditionally masculine ways than those raised by heterosexual single mothers. However, on other measures, such as occupational goals and sartorial styles, they also exhibit greater gender conformity than do daughters with lesbian mothers (but they are not more conforming than sons with heterosexual mothers).[69] Such evidence, albeit limited, implies that lesbian parenting may free daughters and sons from a broad but uneven range of traditional gender prescriptions. It also suggests that the sexual orientation of mothers interacts with the gender of children in complex ways to influence gender preferences and behavior. Such findings raise provocative questions about how children assimilate gender culture and interests—questions that the propensity to downplay differences deters scholars from exploring.[70]

Consider, for example, the study by R. Green et al. that, by our count, finds at least fifteen intriguing, statistically significant differences in gender behavior and preferences among children (4 among boys and 11 among girls) in lesbian and heterosexual single-mother homes.[71] Yet the study's abstract summarizes: "Two types of single-parent households [lesbian and heterosexual mothers] and their effects on children ages 3–11 years were compared. . . . No significant differences were found between the two types of households for boys and few significant differences for girls."[72]

Similarly, we note an arresting continuum of data reported, but ignored, by A. Brewaeys et al.[73] Young boys (ages 4 to 8) conceived through DI in lesbian co-mother families scored the lowest on a measure of sex-typed masculine behaviors (the PSAI-preschool activities inventory, rated by parents), DI boys in heterosexual two-parent families were somewhat more sex-typed, while "naturally" conceived boys in heterosexual two-parent families received the highest sex-typed masculine scores. By our calculation, the difference in the magnitude of scores between DI boys with lesbian co-mothers and conventionally conceived sons with heterosexual parents is sufficient to reach statistical significance, even though the matched groups contained only 15 and 11 boys, respectively. Rather than exploring the implications of these provocative data, the authors conclude: "No significant difference was found between groups for the mean PSAI scores for either boys or girls."[74]

CHILDREN'S SEXUAL PREFERENCES AND BEHAVIOR

The second panel of table 2.1 shifts the focus from children's gender behavior and preferences to their sexual behavior and preferences, with particular attention to thought-provoking findings from the Tasker and Golombok study, the only comparative study we know of that follows children raised in lesbian-headed families into young adulthood and hence that can explore the children's sexuality in meaningful ways.[75] A significantly greater proportion of young adult children raised by lesbian mothers than those raised by heterosexual mothers in the Tasker and

Golombok sample reported having had a homoerotic relationship (6 of the 25 young adults raised by lesbian mothers—24 percent—compared with 0 of the 20 raised by heterosexual mothers). The young adults reared by lesbian mothers were also significantly more likely to report having thought they might experience homoerotic attraction or relationships. The difference in their openness to this possibility is striking: 64 percent (14 of 22) of the young adults raised by lesbian mothers report having considered same-sex relationships (in the past, now, or in the future), compared with only 17 percent (3 of 18) of those raised by heterosexual mothers. Of course, the fact that 17 percent of those raised by heterosexual mothers also report some openness to same-sex relationships, while 36 percent of those raised by lesbians do not, underscores the important reality that parental influence on children's sexual desires is neither direct nor easily predictable.

If these young adults raised by lesbian mothers were more open to a broad range of sexual possibilities, they were not statistically more likely to self-identify as bisexual, lesbian, or gay. To be coded as such, the respondent not only had to currently self-identify as bisexual/lesbian/gay, but also to express a commitment to that identity in the future. Tasker and Golombok employ a measure of sexual identity with no "in-between" categories for those whose identity may not yet be fully fixed or embraced.[76] Thus, although a more nuanced measure or a longer period of observation could yield different results, Golombok and Tasker[77] choose to situate their findings within the "overall no difference" interpretation:

> The commonly held assumption that children brought up by lesbian mothers will themselves grow up to be lesbian or gay is not supported by the findings of the study: the majority of children who grew up in lesbian families identified as heterosexual in adulthood, and there was no statistically significant difference between young adults from lesbian and heterosexual family backgrounds with respect to sexual orientation.[78]

This reading, while technically accurate, deflects analytic attention from the rather sizeable differences in sexual attitudes and behaviors that the study actually reports. The only other comparative study we found that explores intergenerational resemblance in sexual orientation is J. Michael Bailey et al. on gay fathers and their adult sons.[79] This study also provides evidence of a moderate degree of parent-to-child transmission of sexual orientation.

Tasker and Golombok also report some fascinating findings on the number of sexual partners children report having had between puberty and young adulthood.[80] Relative to their counterparts with heterosexual parents, the adolescent and young adult girls raised by lesbian mothers appear to have been more sexually adventurous and less chaste, whereas the sons of lesbians evince the opposite pattern—somewhat less sexually adventurous and more chaste (the finding was statistically significant for the twenty-five-girl sample but not for the eighteen-boy sample). In other words, once again, children (especially girls) raised by lesbians appear to depart from traditional gender-based norms, while children raised by heterosexual mothers appear to conform to them. Yet, this provocative finding of differences in sexual behavior and agency has not been analyzed or investigated further.

Both the findings and nonfindings discussed previously may be influenced by the measures of sexual orientation employed. All of the studies measure sexual orientations as a dichotomy rather than as a continuum. We have no data on children whose parents do not identify their sexuality neatly as one of two dichotomous choices, and we can only speculate about how a more nuanced conceptualization might alter the findings reported. Having parents less committed to a specific sexual identity may free children to construct sexualities altogether different from those of their parents, or it may give whatever biological predispositions exist freer reign to determine eventual sexual orientations, or parents with greater ambiguity or fluidity of sexual orientation might transmit some of this to their children, leading to greater odds of sexual flexibility.

CHILDREN'S MENTAL HEALTH

Given historic social prejudices against homosexuality, the major issue deliberated by judges and policymakers has been whether children of lesbian and gay parents suffer higher levels of emotional and psychological harm. Unsurprisingly, therefore, children's "self-esteem and psychological well-being" is a heavily researched domain. The third panel of table 2.1 shows that these studies find no significant differences between children of lesbian mothers and children of heterosexual mothers in anxiety, depression, self-esteem, and numerous other measures of social and psychological adjustment. The roughly equivalent level of psychological well-being between the two groups holds true in studies that test children directly, rely on parents' reports, and solicit evaluations from teachers. The few significant differences found actually tend to favor children with lesbian mothers (see table 2.1).[81] Given some credible evidence that children with gay and lesbian parents, especially adolescent children, face homophobic teasing and ridicule that many find difficult to manage, the children in these studies seem to exhibit impressive psychological strength.[82]

Similarly, across studies, no relationship has been found between parental sexual orientation and measures of children's cognitive ability. Moreover, to our knowledge no theories predict such a link. Thus far, no work has compared children's long-term achievements in education, occupation, income, and other domains of life.[83]

Links between parental sexual orientation, parenting practices, and parent–child relationships may indicate processes underlying some of the links between parents' sexual orientation and the child outcomes in table 2.1. Table 2.2 presents empirical findings about the parents themselves and the quality of parent–child relationships.

PARENTAL BEHAVIOR TOWARD
CHILDREN'S GENDER AND SEXUAL DEVELOPMENT

The scattered pieces of evidence cited previously imply that lesbigay parenting may be associated with a broadening of children's gender and sexual repertoires. Is this because lesbigay parents actively attempt to achieve these outcomes in their children? Data in the first panel of table 2.2 provide little evidence that parents' own sexual orientations correlate strongly with their preferences concerning their children's gender or sexual orientations. For example, the lesbian mothers in Sally L. Kweskin and Alicia S. Cook's study were no more likely than heterosexual mothers to assign masculine and feminine qualities to an "ideal" boy or girl, respectively, on the well-known Bern Sex Role Inventory.[84] However, mothers did tend to desire gender traits in children that resembled those they saw in themselves, and the lesbians saw themselves as less feminine-typed than did the heterosexual mothers. This suggests that a mother's own gender identity may mediate the connection between maternal sexual orientation and maternal gender preferences for her children.

Also, in some studies lesbian mothers were less concerned than heterosexual mothers that their children engage in gender "appropriate" activities and play, a plausible difference most researchers curiously downplay. For example, Beverly Hoeffer's summary reads:

> Children's play and activity interests as indices of sex-role behavior were compared for a sample of lesbian and heterosexual single mothers and their children. More striking than any differences were the similarities between the two groups of children on acquisition of sex-role behavior and between the two groups of mothers on the encouragement of sex-role behavior.[85]

Yet, from our perspective, the most interesting (and statistically significant) finding in Hoeffer is one of difference.[86] While the heterosexual single mothers in the sample were significantly more likely to prefer that their boys engage in masculine activities and their girls in feminine ones, lesbian mothers had no such interests. Their preferences for their children's play were gender neutral.

Differences in parental concern with children's acquisition of gender and in parenting practices that do or do not emphasize conformity to sex-typed gender norms are understudied and underanalyzed. The sparse evidence to date based on self-reports does not suggest strong differences between lesbigay and heterosexual parents in this domain.

PARENTING PRACTICES: DEVELOPMENTAL ORIENTATIONS AND PARENTING SKILLS

The second panel of table 2.2 displays findings about parenting skills and child-rearing practices—developmental orientations, parental control and support, parent–child communication, parental affection, time spent with children—that have been shown to be central for many aspects of children's development (introversion/extroversion, success in school, and so on).[87] The many findings of differences here coalesce around two patterns. First, studies find the nonbiological lesbian co-mothers (referred to as lesbian "social mothers" in Brewaeys et al.)[88] to be more skilled at parenting and more involved with the children than are stepfathers. Second, lesbian partners in the two-parent families studied enjoy a greater level of synchronicity in parenting than do heterosexual partners.

For example, the lesbian birth mothers and heterosexual birth mothers who conceived through DI studied by Flaks et al.[89] and Brewaeys et al.[90] scored about the same on all measures of parenting. However, the DI lesbian social mothers scored significantly higher than the DI heterosexual fathers on measures of parenting skills, practices, and quality of interactions with children. DI lesbian social mothers also spent significantly more time than did DI heterosexual fathers in child-care activities including disciplinary, control, and limit-setting activities. In fact, in the Brewaeys et al. study, lesbian social mothers even scored significantly higher on these measures than did biological fathers in heterosexual couples who conceived conventionally.[91] Similarly, in Chan, Raboy, and Patterson, whereas the lesbian birth mothers and co-mother partners evaluated their children's emotional states and social behaviors in almost exactly the same way, heterosexual mothers and fathers evaluated their children differently: fathers identified fewer problems in the children than did mothers (a similar pattern is observed in Chan, Brooks et al.,[92] table 4).[93]

These findings imply that lesbian co-parents may enjoy greater parental compatibility and achieve particularly high quality parenting skills, which may help explain the striking findings on parent–child relationships in the third panel of table 2.2 DI lesbian social mothers report feeling closer to the children than do their heterosexual male counterparts. The children studied report feeling closer to DI lesbian social mothers as well as to lesbian stepmothers than to either DI fathers or stepfathers (measures of emotional closeness between birth mothers and children did not vary by mother's sexual orientation). Children of lesbian mothers also report feeling more able than children of heterosexual parents to discuss their sexual development with their mothers and their mothers' partners.[94] If lesbian social mothers and stepmothers have more parenting awareness and skill, on average, than heterosexual DI fathers or stepfathers, and if they spend more time taking care of children, they may be more likely to earn the children's affection and trust.

We believe that the comparative strengths these lesbian co-parents seem to exhibit have more to do with gender than with sexual orientation.[95] Female gender is probably the source of the positive signs for parenting skill, participation in child rearing, and synchronicity in child evaluations shown in the comparisons in table 2.2. Research suggests that, on average, mothers tend to be more invested in and skilled at child care than fathers, and that mothers are more apt than fathers to engage in the kinds of child-care activities that appear to be particularly crucial to children's cognitive, emotional, and social development.[96] Analogously, in these studies of matched lesbian and heterosexual couples, women in every category—heterosexual birth mother, lesbian birth mother, nonbiological lesbian social mother—all score about the same as one another but score significantly higher than the men on measures having to do with the care of children.[97]

In our view, these patterns reflect something more than a simple "gender effect," however, because sexual orientation is the key "exogenous variable" that brings together parents of same or different genders. Thus, sexual orientation and gender should be viewed as *interacting* to create new kinds of family structures and processes—such as an egalitarian division of child care—that have fascinating consequences for all of the relationships in the triad and for child development.[98] Some of the evidence suggests that two women co-parenting may create a synergistic pattern that brings more egalitarian, compatible, shared parenting and time spent with children, greater understanding of children, and closeness and communication between parents and children. The genesis of this pattern cannot be understood on the basis of either sexual orientation or gender alone. Such findings raise fruitful comparative questions for future research about family dynamics among two parents of the same or different gender who do or do not share similar attitudes, values, and behaviors.

We know little thus far about how the sexual orientation of nonresidential fathers may be related to their relationships with their children (the fourth panel of table 2.2) and even less about that for custodial fathers. The Jerry J. Bigner and R. Brooke Jacobsen studies find similarity in parenting and in father–child relations among heterosexual nonresidential fathers and gay nonresidential fathers.[99] Frederick W. Bozett found that in a small sample of children with gay fathers, most children had very positive feelings toward their fathers, but they also worried that peers and others might presume that they, too, had a gay sexual orientation (Bozett did not include a control group of children with heterosexual fathers).[100]

PARENTAL FITNESS

The bottom panel of table 2.2 demonstrates that evidence to date provides no support for those, such as Wardle, who claim that lesbian mothers suffer greater levels of psychological difficulties (depression, low self-esteem) than do heterosexual mothers.[101] On the contrary, the few differences observed in the studies suggest that these lesbian mothers actually display somewhat higher levels of positive psychological resources.

Research on a more diverse population, however, might alter the findings of difference and similarity shown in table 2.2. For example, the ethnographic evidence suggests that people of color with homoerotic practices often value racial solidarity over sexual solidarity. Keith Boykin, director of the National Black Gay and Lesbian Leadership Forum, cites a 1994 University of Chicago study which found that among people who engage in homoerotic activity, whites, urbanites, and those with higher education were more likely to consider themselves gay or lesbian.[102] If, as it appears, racial/ethnic solidarities deter disproportionate numbers of people of color from coming out, they might suffer greater psychological and social costs from living in the closet or, conversely, might benefit from less concern over their sexual identities than do white gay parents. We also do not know whether lesbian couples of different racial/ethnic and social class contexts would display the same patterns of egalitarian, compatible co-parenting reported among the white lesbian couples.

NO DIFFERENCES OF SOCIAL CONCERN

The findings summarized in tables 2.1 and 2.2 show that the "no differences" claim does receive strong empirical support in crucial domains. Lesbigay parents and their children in these studies display no differences from heterosexual counterparts in psychological well-being or cognitive functioning. Scores for lesbigay parenting styles and levels of investment in children are at least as "high" as those for heterosexual parents. Levels of closeness and quality of parent–child relationships do not seem to differentiate directly by parental sexual orientation, but indirectly, by way of parental gender. Because every relevant study to date shows that parental sexual orientation per se has no measurable effect on the quality of parent–child relationships or on children's mental health or social adjustment, there is no evidentiary basis for considering parental sexual orientation in decisions about children's "best interest." In fact, given that children with lesbigay parents probably contend with a degree of social stigma, these similarities in child outcomes suggest the presence of compensatory processes in lesbigay-parent families. Exploring how these families help children cope with stigma might prove helpful to all kinds of families.

Most of the research to date focuses on social-psychological dimensions of well-being and adjustment and on the quality of parent–child relationships. Perhaps these variables reflect the disciplinary preferences of psychologists who have conducted most of the studies, as well as a desire to produce evidence directly relevant to the questions of "harm" that dominate judicial and legislative deliberations over child custody. Less research has explored questions for which there are stronger theoretical grounds for expecting differences—children's gender and sexual behavior and preferences. In fact, only two studies generate much of the baseline evidence on potential connections between parents' and child's sexual and gender identities.[103] Evidence in these and the few other studies that focus on these variables does not support the "no differences" claim. Children with lesbigay parents appear less traditionally gender-typed and more likely to be open to homoerotic relationships. In addition, evidence suggests that parental gender and sexual identities interact to create distinctive family processes whose consequences for children have yet to be studied.

HOW THE SEXUAL ORIENTATION OF PARENTS MATTERS

We have identified conceptual, methodological, and theoretical limitations in the psychological research on the effects of parental sexual orientation and have challenged the predominant claim that the sexual orientation of parents does not matter at all. We argued instead that despite the limitations, there is suggestive evidence and good reason to believe that contemporary children and young adults with lesbian or gay parents do differ in modest and interesting ways from children with heterosexual parents. Most of these differences, however, are not causal, but are indirect effects of parental gender or selection effects associated with heterosexist social conditions under which lesbigay-parent families currently live.

First, our analysis of the psychological research indicates that the effects of parental gender trump those of sexual orientation.[104] A diverse array of gender theories (social learning theory, psychoanalytic theory, materialist, symbolic interactionist) would predict that children with two same-gender parents, and particularly with co-mother parents, should develop in less gender stereotypical ways than would children with two heterosexual parents. There is reason to credit the perception of lesbian co-mothers in a qualitative study that they "were redefining the meaning and content of motherhood, extending its boundaries to incorporate the activities that are usually dichotomized as mother and father."[105] Children who derive their principal source of love, discipline, protection, and identification from women living independent of male domestic authority or influence should develop less stereotypical symbolic, emotional, practical, and behavioral gender repertoires. Indeed, it is the claim that the gender mix of parents has no effect on their children's gender behavior, interests, or development that cries out for sociological explanation. Only a crude theory of cultural indoctrination that posited the absolute impotence of parents might predict such an outcome, and the remarkable variability of gender configurations documented in the anthropological record readily undermines such a theory.[106] The burden of proof in the domain of gender and sexuality should rest with those who embrace the null hypothesis.

Second, because homosexuality is stigmatized, selection effects may yield correlations between parental sexual orientation and child development that do not derive from sexual orientation itself. For example, social constraints on access to marriage and parenting make lesbian parents likely to be older, urban, educated, and self-aware—factors that foster several positive developmental consequences for their children. On the other hand, denied access to marriage, lesbian co-parent relationships are likely to experience dissolution rates somewhat higher than those among heterosexual co-parents.[107] Not only do same-sex couples lack the institutional pressures and support for commitment that marriage provides, but qualitative studies suggest that they tend to embrace comparatively high standards of emotional intimacy and satisfaction.[108] The decision to pursue a socially ostracized domain of intimacy implies an investment in the emotional regime that Giddens terms "the pure relationship" and "confluent love."[109] Such relationships confront the inherent instabilities of modern or postmodern intimacy, what Beck and Beck-Gersheim term "the normal chaos of love."[110] Thus, a higher dissolution rate would be correlated with but not causally related to sexual orientation, a difference that should erode were homophobia to disappear and legal marriage be made available to lesbians and gay men.

Most of the differences in the findings discussed previously cannot be considered deficits from any legitimate public policy perspective. They either favor the children with lesbigay parents, are secondary effects of social prejudice, or represent "just a difference" of the sort democratic societies should respect and protect. Apart from differences associated with parental gender, most of the presently observable differences in child "outcomes" should wither away under conditions of full equality and respect for sexual diversity. Indeed, it is time to recognize that the categories "lesbian mother" and "gay father" are historically transitional and conceptually flawed, because they erroneously imply that a parent's sexual orientation is the decisive characteristic of her or his parenting. On the contrary, we propose that homophobia and discrimination are the chief reasons why parental sexual orientation matters at all. Because lesbigay parents do not enjoy the same rights, respect, and recognition as heterosexual parents, their children contend with the burdens of vicarious social stigma. Likewise, some of the particular strengths and sensitivities such children appear to display, such as a greater capacity to express feelings or more empathy for social diversity, are probably artifacts of marginality and may be destined for the historical dustbin of a democratic, sexually pluralist society.[111]

Even in a utopian society, however, one difference seems less likely to disappear: the sexual orientation of parents appears to have a unique (although not large) effect on children in the politically sensitive domain of sexuality. The evidence, while scanty and underanalyzed, hints that parental sexual orientation is positively associated with the possibility that children will be more likely to attain a similar orientation—and theory and common sense also support such a view. Children raised by lesbian co-parents should and do seem to grow up more open to homoerotic relationships. This may be partly due to genetic and family socialization processes, but what sociologists refer to as "contextual effects" not yet investigated by psychologists may also be important. Because lesbigay parents are disproportionately more likely to inhabit diverse, cosmopolitan cities—Los Angeles, New York, and San Francisco—and progressive university communities—such as Santa Cruz, Santa Rosa, Madison, and Ann

Arbor[112]—their children grow up in comparatively tolerant school, neighborhood, and social contexts, which foster less hostility to homoeroticism. Sociology could make a valuable contribution to this field by researching processes that interact at the individual, family, and community level to undergird parent–child links between gender and sexuality.

Under homophobic conditions, lesbigay parents are apt to be more sensitive to issues surrounding their children's sexual development and to injuries that children with nonconforming desires may experience, more open to discussing sexuality with their children, and more affirming of their questions about sexuality.[113] It therefore seems likely, although this has yet to be studied, that their children will grow up better informed about and more comfortable with sexual desires and practices. However, the tantalizing gender contrast in the level of sexual activity reported for sons versus daughters of lesbians raises more complicated questions about the relationship between gender and sexuality.

Even were heterosexism to disappear, however, parental sexual orientation would probably continue to have some impact on the eventual sexuality of children. Research and theory on sexual development remain so rudimentary that it is impossible to predict how much difference might remain were homosexuality not subject to social stigma. Indeed, we believe that if one suspends the heteronormative presumption, one fascinating riddle to explain in this field is why, even though children of lesbigay parents appear to express a significant increase in homoeroticism, the majority of all children nonetheless identify as heterosexual, as most theories across the "essentialist" to "social constructionist" spectrum seem (perhaps too hastily) to expect. A nondefensive look at the anomalous data on this question could pose fruitful challenges to social constructionist, genetic, and bioevolutionary theories.

We recognize the political dangers of pointing out that recent studies indicate that a higher proportion of children with lesbigay parents are themselves apt to engage in homosexual activity. In a homophobic world, antigay forces deploy such results to deny parents custody of their own children and to fuel backlash movements opposed to gay rights. Nonetheless, we believe that denying this probability capitulates to heterosexist ideology and is apt to prove counterproductive in the long run. It is neither intellectually honest nor politically wise to base a claim for justice on grounds that may prove falsifiable empirically. Moreover, the case for granting equal rights to nonheterosexual parents should not require finding their children to be identical to those reared by heterosexuals. Nor should it require finding that such children do not encounter distinctive challenges or risks, especially when these derive from social prejudice.

The U.S. Supreme Court rejected this rationale for denying custody when it repudiated discrimination against interracially married parents in *Palmore v. Sidoti* in 1984: "Private biases may be outside the reach of the law, but the law cannot, directly or indirectly, give them effect."[114] Inevitably, children share most of the social privileges and injuries associated with their parents' social status. If social prejudice were grounds for restricting rights to parent, a limited pool of adults would qualify.

One can readily turn the tables on a logic that seeks to protect children from the harmful effects of heterosexist stigma directed against their parents. Granting legal rights and respect to gay parents and their children should lessen the stigma that they now suffer and might reduce the high rates of depression and suicide reported among closeted gay youth living with heterosexual parents. Thus, while we disagree with those who claim that there are no differences between the children of heterosexual parents and children of lesbigay parents, we unequivocally endorse their conclusion that social science research provides no grounds for taking sexual orientation into account in the political distribution of family rights and responsibilities.

It is quite a different thing, however, to consider this issue a legitimate matter for social science research. Planned lesbigay parenthood offers a veritable "social laboratory" of family diversity in which scholars could fruitfully examine not only the acquisition of sexual and gender identity, but the relative effects on children of the gender and number of their parents as well as of the implications of diverse biosocial routes to parenthood. Such studies could give us purchase on some of the most vexing and intriguing topics in our field, including divorce, adoption, step parenthood, and domestic violence, to name a few. To exploit this opportunity, however, researchers must overcome the heteronormative presumption that interprets sexual differences as deficits, thereby inflicting some of the very disadvantages it claims to discover. Paradoxically, if the sexual orientation of parents were to matter less for political rights, it could matter more for social theory.

NOTES

This chapter was originally published in *American Sociological Review* 66 (2001): 159–83 and is reprinted here by permission. We are grateful for the constructive criticisms on early versions of this article from Celeste Atkins, Amy Binder, Phil Cowan, Gary Gates, Adam Green, David Greenberg, Oystein Holter, Celia Kitzinger, Joan Laird, Jane Mauldon, Dan McPherson, Shannon

Minter, Valory Mitchell, Charlotte Patterson, Anne Peplau, Vernon Rosario, Seth Sanders, Alisa Steckel, Michael Wald, and the reviewers and editors of *ASR*. We presented portions of this work at UCLA Neuropsychiatric Institute Symposium on Sexuality; the Feminist Interdisciplinary Seminar of the University of California, Davis; and the Taft Lecture Program at the University of Cincinnati.

1. Debb Price, "Middle Ground Emerges for Gay Couples," *Detroit News*, October 4, 1999, p. 9(A).
2. Compare Michael Wald, "Same-Sex Couples: Marriage, Families, and Children. An Analysis of Proposition 22, The Knight Initiative" (Stanford Institute for Research on Women and Gender, Stanford University, Stanford, California, December 1999)
3. Lynn D. Wardle, "The Potential Impact of Homosexual Parenting on Children," *University of Illinois Law Review* 1997 (1997): 833–919.
4. Leslie Cooper, ACLU gay family rights staff attorney, personal communications, September 27, 2000.
5. Robert Lerner and Althea K. Nagai, "Out of Nothing Comes Nothing: Homosexual and Heterosexual Marriage Not Shown to Be Equivalent for Raising Children" (paper presented at the Revitalizing the Institution of Marriage for the 21st Century conference, Brigham Young University, Provo, Utah, March 2000).
6. Lerner and Nagai, "Out of Nothing Comes Nothing," 3.
7. Maggie Gallagher, "The Gay-Parenting Science," *New York Post*, March 30, 2000, p. 3.
8. Including Wardle, "Potential Impact"; Lerner and Nagai, "Out of Nothing Comes Nothing"; and ourselves.
9. Wardle, "Potential Impact."
10. See, for example, Paul Cameron and Kirk Cameron, "Homosexual Parents," *Adolescence* 31 (1996): 757–76; Paul Cameron, Kirk Cameron, and Thomas Landess, "Errors by the American Psychiatric Association, the American Psychological Association, and the National Educational Association in Representing Homosexuality in Amicus Briefs about Amendment 2 to the U.S. Supreme Court," *Psychological Reports* 79 (1996): 383–404.
11. David Cantor, *The Religious Right: The Assault on Tolerance and Pluralism in America* (New York: Anti-Defamation League, 1994); Gregory M. Herek, "Bad Science in the Service of Stigma: A Critique of the Cameron Group's Survey Studies," in *Stigma and Sexual Orientation: Understanding Prejudice against Lesbians, Gay Men, and Bisexuals*, ed. G. M. Herek (Thousand Oaks, Calif.: Sage, 1998), 223–55; Gregory M. Herek, "Paul Cameron Fact Sheet" (copyright 1997–2000 by G. M. Herek) at psychology.ucdavis.edu/rainbow/html/facts_cameron_sheet.html (accessed January 2000).
12. Robin Woodruff, testimony regarding "Subcommittee Meeting to Accept Empirical Data and Expert Testimony Concerning Homosexual Foster Parents," Hearing at the Office of the Attorney General, Little Rock, Ark.: September 9, 1998 (available from the authors on request).
13. Wardle, "Potential Impact."

14. In *J.B.F. v. J.M.F.* (Ex parte J.M.F. 1970224, So. 2d 1190, 1988 Ala. LEXIS 161 [1998]), for example, Alabama's Supreme Court quoted Wardle's (1997) essay ("Potential Impact") to justify transferring custody of a child from her lesbian mother to her heterosexual father.

15. Wardle, "Potential Impact."

16. David Popenoe, "American Family Decline, 1960–1990: A Review and Appraisal," *Journal of Marriage and the Family* 55 (1993): 527–41; David Popenoe, *Life without Father* (New York: Free Press, 1996).

17. David Blankenhorn, *Fatherless America: Confronting Our Most Urgent Social Problem* (New York: Basic, 1995).

18. Barbara Dafoe Whitehead, "Dan Quayle Was Right," *Atlantic Monthly* 271 (April 1993): 47–50.

19. Wardle, "Potential Impact:" 860.

20. The extrapolation is "inappropriate" because lesbigay-parent families have never been a comparison group in the family structure literature on which these authors rely. See Douglas B. Downey and Brian Powell, "Do Children in Single-Parent Households Fare Better Living with Same-Sex Parents?" *Journal of Marriage and the Family* 55 (1993): 55–72; Sara S. McLanahan, "Family Structure and the Reproduction of Poverty," *American Journal of Sociology* 90 (1985): 873–901.

21. Blankenhorn, "Fatherless America."

22. Cameron et al., "Errors by the American Psychiatric Association."

23. Herek, "Bad Science in the Service of Stigma."

24. Diana Baumrind, "Commentary on Sexual Orientation: Research and Social Policy Implications," *Developmental Psychology* 31 (1995): 130–36.

25. Patrick J. Falk, "The Gap between Psychosocial Assumptions and Empirical Research in Lesbian-Mother Child Custody Cases," in *Redefining Families: Implications for Children's Development*, ed. A. E. Gottfried and A. W. Gottfried (New York: Plenum, 1994), 151.

26. Judith Rich Harris, *The Nurture Assumption: Why Children Turn Out the Way They Do* (New York: Free Press, 1998).

27. Daryl J. Bern, "Exotic Becomes Erotic: A Developmental Theory of Sexual Orientation," *Psychological Review* 103 (1996): 320–35.

28. In March 2000, Norwegian sociologist Oystein Holter (personal communication) described Helmut Stierlin's "delegation" theory (published in German)— that children take over their parents' unconscious wishes. Holter suggests this theory could predict that a child who grows up with gay parents under homophobic conditions might develop "contrary responses." We are unfamiliar with this theory but find it likely that under such conditions unconscious wishes of heterosexual and nonheterosexual parents could foster some different "contrary responses."

29. G. Dorsey Green and Frederick W. Bozett, "Lesbian Mothers and Gay Fathers," in *Homosexuality: Research Implications for Public Policy*, ed. J. C. Gonsiorek and J. D. Weinrich. (Newbury Park, Calif.: Sage, 1991), 197–214; Celia Kitzinger and Adrian Coyle, "Lesbian and Gay Couples: Speaking of Difference,"

Psychologist 8 (1995): 64–69; Charlotte J. Patterson, "Children of Lesbian and Gay Parents," *Child Development* 63 (1992): 1025–42.

30. Charlotte J. Patterson, "Families of the Lesbian Baby Boom: Parents' Division of Labor and Children's Adjustment," *Developmental Psychology* 31 (1995):115–23; Gillian A. Dunne, "Opting into Motherhood: Lesbians Blurring the Boundaries and Transforming the Meaning of Parenthood and Kinship," *Gender and Society* 14 (2000): 11–35.

31. Celia Kitzinger, *The Social Construction of Lesbianism* (London: Sage, 1987); Celia Kitzinger, "Liberal Humanism as an Ideology of Social Control: The Regulation of Lesbian Identities," in *Texts of Identity*, ed. J. Shotter and K. Gergen (London: Sage, 1989), 82–98.

32. Victoria Clarke, "Sameness and Difference in Research on Lesbian Parenting" (working paper of Women's Studies Research Group, Department of Social Sciences, Loughborough University, Leicestershire, U.K., 2000), 28, paraphrasing Celia, "Should Psychologists Study Sex Differences? Editor's Introduction: Sex Differences Research: Feminist Perspectives," *Feminism and Psychology* 4 (1994): 501.

33. Kitzinger and Coyle, "Lesbian and Gay Couples."

34. Clarke, "Sameness and Difference."

35. These estimates derive from an extrapolation of Kinsey data claiming a roughly 10 percent prevalence of homosexuality in the adult male population. Interestingly, Michael et al.'s (Robert T. Michael, John H. Gagnon, Edward O. Laumann, and Gina Bari Kolata, *Sex in America: A Definitive Survey* [Boston: Little Brown, 1994]) revisiting of Kinsey (Alfred C. Kinsey, Wardell B. Pomeroy, and Clyde E. Martin, *Sexual Behavior in the Human Male* [Philadelphia: W. B. Saunders, 1948]; Alfred C. Kinsey, Wardell B. Pomeroy, Clyde E. Martin, and Paul H. Gebhard, *Sexual Behavior in the Human Female* [Philadelphia: W. B. Saunders, 1953]) suggests that Kinsey himself emphasized that different measures of sexual orientation yield different estimates of individuals with same-sex sexual orientations in the population. Had scholars read Kinsey differently, they might have selected his figure of 4 percent of the men in his sample who practiced exclusive homosexual behavior from adolescence onward, rather than the widely embraced 10 percent figure. In fact, the 10 percent number is fundamentally flawed: Kinsey found that of the 37 percent of the white men in his sample who had at least one sexual experience with another man in their lifetimes, only 10 percent of them (i.e., 3.7 percent of the entire white male sample) had exclusively same-sex sexual experiences for any three-year period between ages sixteen and fifty-five. Also see Patterson, "Children of Lesbian and Gay Parents" and "Lesbian and Gay Parents and Their Children," in *The Lives of Lesbians, Gays, and Bisexuals: Children to Adults*, ed. R. C. Savin-Williams and K. M. Cohen (Fort Worth, Tex.: Harcourt Brace College Publishers, 1996), 274–304.

36. Charlotte J. Patterson and Lisa V. Freil, "Sexual Orientation and Fertility," in *Infertility in the Modern World: Biosocial Perspectives*, ed. G. Bentley and N. Mascie-Taylor (Cambridge, England: Cambridge University Press, 2000).

58   *Judith Stacey and Timothy J. Biblarz*

37. Edward O. Laumann, John H. Gagnon, Robert T. Michael, and Stuart Michaels, *National Health and Social Life Survey, 1992 [MRDF]* (Chicago: University of Chicago and National Opinion Research Center [producer]; Ann Arbor, Mich.: Inter-university Consortium for Political and Social Research [distributor], 1995).

38. This assumes that the ratio of number of dependent children to total offspring among current lesbigay parents will be roughly the same as that for all parents and children. See James Sweet and Larry Bumpass, "The National Survey of Families and Households—Waves 1 and 2: Data Description and Documentation," Center for Demography and Ecology, University of Wisconsin, Madison, 1996, at www/ssc.wisc.edu/nsfh/home.htm (accessed January 2000).

39. U.S. Census Bureau, "Population Estimates Program," *Population Division* (Washington, D.C.: 1999) at www.census.gov/population/estimates/nation/intfile2-l.txt, and natdoc.txt (accessed January 5, 2000).

40. Also see M. V. Lee Badgett, "The Economic Well-Being of Lesbian, Gay, and Bisexual Adults' Families," in *Lesbian, Gay and Bisexual Identities in Families: Psychological Perspectives*, ed. C. J. Patterson and A. R. D'Augelli (New York: Oxford University Press, 1998), 231–48; Dan A. Black, Hoda R. Maker, Seth G. Sanders, and Lowell Taylor, "The Effects of Sexual Orientation on Earnings" (working paper of Department of Economics, Gatton College of Business and Economics, University of Kentucky, Lexington, 1998).

41. Vie Groze, "Adoption and Single Parents: A Review," *Child Welfare* 70 (1991): 321–32; Joan F Shireman, "Single Parent Adoptive Homes," *Children and Youth Services Review* 18 (1996): 23–36.

42. Kinsey et al., *Sexual Behavior in the Human Male*; Kinsey et al., *Sexual Behavior in the Human Female*; Michael et al., *Sex in America*; Edward O. Laumann, John H. Gagnon, Robert T. Michael, and Stuart Michaels, *The Social Organization of Sexuality: Sexual Practices in the United States* (Chicago: University of Chicago Press, 1994).

43. Henning Bech, *When Men Meet: Homosexuality and Modernity* (Chicago: University of Chicago Press, 1997), 211.

44. Jonathan Ned Katz, *The Invention of Heterosexuality* (New York: Dutton, 1995); Steven Seidman, *Difference Troubles: Queering Social Theory and Sexual Politics* (New York: Cambridge University Press, 1997).

45. Jerry J. Bigner and R. Brooke Jacobsen, "Parenting Behaviors of Homosexual and Heterosexual Fathers," *Journal of Homosexuality* 18 (1989): 73–86; Jerry J. Bigner and R. Brooke Jacobsen, "Adult Responses to Child Behavior and Attitudes toward Fathering: Gay and Nongay Fathers," *Journal of Homosexuality* 23 (1992): 99–112.

46. The field is now in a position to take advantage of new data sources. For example, the 1990 U.S. census allowed (albeit imperfectly) for the first time the identification of gay and lesbian couples, as will the 2000 census (Dan A. Black, Gary Gates, Seth Sanders, and Lowell Taylor, "Demographics of the Gay and Lesbian Population in the United States: Evidence from Available Systematic Data Sources," *Demography* 37 (2000): 139–54). From 1989 to the present, the *U.S.*

General Social Surveys (www.icpsr.umich.edu/GSS/index.html) have also allowed for the identification of the sexual orientation of respondents, as does the *National Health and Social Life Survey* (Laumann et al., *Social Organization of Sexuality*).

47. Frederick W. Bozett, "Gay Fathers: A Review of the Literature," in *Homosexuality and the Family*, ed. F. W. Bozett (New York: Haworth Press, 1989), 137–62; Patterson and Freil, "Sexual Orientation and Fertility"; Ester D. Rothblum, "'I Only Read About Myself on Bathroom Walls': The Need for Research on the Mental Health of Lesbians and Gay Men," *Journal of Consulting and Clinical Psychology* 62 (1994): 213–20.

48. Keith Boykin, *One More River to Cross: Black and Gay in America* (New York: Anchor, 1996); Lionel Cantu, "Entre Hombres/Between Men: Latino Masculinities and Homosexualities," in *Gay Masculinities*, ed. P. Nardi (Thousand Oaks, Calif.: Sage, 2000), 224–46; Joseph Carrier, "Miguel: Sexual Life History of a Gay Mexican American," in *Gay Culture in America: Essays from the Field*, ed. G. Herdt (Boston: Beacon, 1992), 202–24; Beverly Greene and Nancy Boyd-Franklin, "African-American Lesbians: Issues in Couple Therapy," in *Lesbians and Gays in Couples and Families: A Handbook for Therapists*, ed. J. Laird and R. J. Green (San Francisco: Jossey-Bass, 1996), 251–71; William Hawkeswood, *One of the Children: Gay Black Men in Harlem* (Berkeley: University of California Press, 1997); F. R. Lynch, "Nonghetto Gays: An Ethnography of Suburban Homosexuals," in *Gay Culture in America: Essays from the Field*, ed. G. Herdt (Boston: Beacon, 1992), 165–201; John Peterson, "Black Men and Their Same-Sex Desires and Behaviors," in *Gay Culture in America: Essays from the Field*, ed. G. Herdt (Boston: Beacon, 1992), 147–64.

49. Laura Benkov, *Reinventing the Family: Lesbian and Gay Parents* (New York: Crown, 1994).

50. Amy E Bourne, "Mothers of Invention," *San Francisco Daily Journal*, May 21, 1999, pp. 1, 9.

51. Raymond W. Chan, Risa C. Brooks, Barbara Raboy, and Charlotte J. Patterson, "Division of Labor among Lesbian and Heterosexual Parents: Associations with Children's Adjustment," *Journal of Family Psychology* 12 (1998): 402–19; David K. Flaks, Ilda Ficher, Frank Masterpasqua, and Gregory Joseph, "Lesbians Choosing Motherhood: A Comparative Study of Lesbian and Heterosexual Parents and Their Children," *Developmental Psychology* 31 (1995): 105–14.

52. The twenty-one studies considered in tables 2.1 and 2.2 are, in date order, Beverly Hoeffer, "Children's Acquisition of Sex-Role Behavior in Lesbian-Mother Families," *American Journal of Orthopsychiatry* 51 (1981): 536–44; Sally L. Kweskin and Alicia S. Cook, "Heterosexual and Homosexual Mothers' Self-Described Sex-Role Behavior and Ideal Sex-Role Behavior in Children," *Sex Roles* 8 (1982): 967–75; Judith Ann Miller, R. Brooke Jacobsen, and Jerry J. Bigner, "The Child's Home Environment for Lesbian vs. Heterosexual Mothers: A Neglected Area of Research," *Journal of Homosexuality* 7 (1982): 49–56; Catherine Rand, Dee L. R. Graham, and Edna I. Rawlings, "Psychological Health and Factors the Court Seeks to Control in Lesbian Mother Custody Trials," *Journal of Homosexuality* 8 (1982): 279–83; Mary

E. Hotvedt, and Jane Barclay Mandel, "Children of Lesbian Mothers," in *Homosexuality, Social, Psychological, and Biological Issues*, ed. W. Paul (Beverly Hills: Sage, 1982), 275–91; Susan Golombok, Ann Spencer, and Michael Rutter, "Children in Lesbian and Single-Parent Households: Psychosexual and Psychiatric Appraisal," *Journal of Child Psychology and Psychiatry* 24 (1983): 551–72; Richard Green, Jane Barclay Mandel, Mary E. Hotvedt, James Gray, and Laurel Smith, "Lesbian Mothers and Their Children: A Comparison with Solo Parent Heterosexual Mothers and Their Children," *Archives of Sexual Behavior* 15 (1986): 167–84; Mary B. Harris and Pauline H. Turner, "Gay and Lesbian Parent," *Journal of Homosexuality* 12 (1986): 101–13; Bigner and Jacobsen, "Parenting Behaviors"; Sharon L. Huggins, "A Comparative Study of Self-Esteem of Adolescent Children of Divorced Lesbian Mothers and Divorced Heterosexual Mothers," in *Homosexuality and the Family*, ed. F. W. Bozett (New York: Haworth, 1989), 123–35; Alisa Steckel, "Psychosocial Development of Children of Lesbian Mothers," in *Gay and Lesbian Parents*, ed. F. W. Bozett (New York: Praeger, 1987), 75–85; Bigner and Jacobsen, "Adult Responses"; Carole Jenny, Thomas A. Roesler, and Kimberly Poyer, "Are Children at Risk for Sexual Abuse by Homosexuals?" *Pediatrics* 94 (1994): 41–44; Charlotte J. Patterson, "Children of the Lesbian Baby Boom: Behavioral Adjustment, Self-Concepts and Sex Role Identity," in *Lesbian and Gay Psychology: Theory, Research, and Clinical Applications*, ed. B. Green and G. M. Herek (Thousand Oaks, Calif.: Sage, 1994), 156–75; J. Michael Bailey, David Bobrow, MarilynWolfe, and Sarah Mikach, "Sexual Orientation of Adult Sons of Gay Fathers," *Developmental Psychology* 31 (1995): 124–29; Flaks et al., "Lesbians Choosing Motherhood"; A. Brewaeys, I. Ponjaert, E. V. Van Hall, and S. Golombok, "Donor Insemination: Child Development and Family Functioning in Lesbian Mother Families," *Human Reproduction* 12 (1997): 349–59; Fiona L. Tasker and Susan Golombok, *Growing Up in a Lesbian Family* (New York: Guilford, 1997); Raymond W. Chan, Barbara Raboy, and Charlotte J. Patterson, "Psychosocial Adjustment among Children Conceived via Donor Insemination by Lesbian and Heterosexual Mothers," *Child Development* 69 (1998): 443–57; Chan et al., "Division of Labor"; and Kevin F. McNeill, Beth M. Rienzi, and Augustine Kposowa, "Families and Parenting: A Comparison of Lesbian and Heterosexual Mothers," *Psychological Reports* 82 (1998): 59–62.

53. Mike Allen and Nancy Burrell, "Comparing the Impact of Homosexual and Heterosexual Parents on Children: Meta-Analysis of Existing Research," *Journal of Homosexuality* 32 (1996): 19.

54. Allen and Burrell, "Comparing the Impact."

55. We chose to display the specific findings in each of the quantitative studies, rather than to conduct a meta-analysis, because at this stage of knowledge not enough studies are targeted to the same general "outcome" to enable a meta-analysis to reveal systematic patterns. The single meta-analysis that has been done (Allen and Burrell, "Comparing the Impact,") reached the typical "no difference" conclusion, but its conclusions were hampered by this very problem. The small number of studies available led Allen and Burrell to pool studies focused on quite different parent and child "outcomes," heightening the risk that findings in one direction effectively offset findings in another.

56. Flaks et al. "Lesbians Choosing Motherhood."

57. Brewaeys et al. "Donor Insemination."

58. Chan et al., "Psychosocial Adjustment among Children Conceived via Donor Insemination," 443–57.

59. Chan et al., "Division of Labor."

60. Green et al., "Lesbian Mothers and Their Children."

61. Tasker and Golombok, *Growing Up in a Lesbian Family.*

62. Green et al., "Lesbian Mothers and Their Children."

63. Belcastro et al. (Philip A. Belcastro, Theresa Gramlich, Thomas Nicholson, Jimmie Price, and Richard Wilson, "A Review of Data-Based Studies Addressing the Affects [*sic*] of Homosexual Parenting on Children's Sexual and Social Functioning," *Journal of Divorce and Remarriage* 20 [1993]: 105–22) point out that R. Green et al. ("Lesbian Mothers and Their Children") did not successfully match heterosexual and lesbian single-mother families on the dimension of household composition. While 39 of R. Green et al.'s 50 lesbian single-mother households had a second adult residing in them by one-plus years postdivorce, only 4 of the 40 heterosexual single mothers did so. R. Green et al. (1986) note this difference, but do not discuss its implications for findings; nor do Belcastro et al. (1993).

64. Tasker and Golombok, *Growing Up in a Lesbian Family.*

65. Green et al., "Lesbian Mothers and Their Children."

66. Hotvedt and Mandel, "Children of Lesbian Mothers."

67. Steckel, "Psychosocial Development of Children of Lesbian Mothers."

68. Green et al., "Lesbian Mothers and Their Children."

69. Many of these studies use conventional levels of significance (e.g., \t\ > 1.96, p < .05, two-tailed tests) on minuscule samples, substantially increasing their likelihood of failing to reject the null hypothesis. For example, Hoeffer's (Hoeffer, "Children's Acquisition of Sex-Role Behavior") descriptive numbers suggest a greater preference for masculine toys among boys with heterosexual mothers than those with lesbian mothers, but sampling only ten boys in each group makes reaching statistical significance exceedingly difficult. Golombok, Spencer, and Rutter's (Golombok et al., "Children in Lesbian and Single-Parent Households," table 8) evidence of a greater average tendency toward "femininity" among daughters raised by heterosexual mothers than those raised by lesbian single mothers does not reach statistical significance in part because their tabular crosscutting leads to very small cell counts (to meet conventional criteria the differences between groups would have to be huge in such cases). Single-difference tests that maximize cell counts (e.g., the percentage of children—male or female—in each group who report gender-role behavior that goes against type) might well yield significant results. Recent research on model selection shows that to find the best model in large samples, conventional levels of significance need to be substantially tightened, but that for very small samples conventional levels can actually be too restrictive (see Adrian E. Raftery, "Bayesian Model Selection in Social Research [with Discussion]," *Sociological Methodology* 25 [1995]:111–95). Also see R. Green et al. (1986) in note 59 and Steckel (1987) in note 66.

62 Judith Stacey and Timothy J. Biblarz

70. Much qualitative work, particularly by lesbian feminist scholars, has been exploring these issues. For example, Wells (Jess Wells, *Lesbians Raising Sons*, Los Angeles: Alyson Books, 1997) argues that, unlike what she refers to as "patriarchal families," lesbian co-mother families rear sons to experience rather than repress emotions and instill in daughters a sense of their potential rather than of limits imposed by gender. From a quantitative perspective, this is a "testable" hypothesis that has sizeable theoretical implications but that researchers in the field do not seem to be pursuing.

71. Green et al., "Lesbian Mothers and Their Children."

72. The R. Green et al. (1986) research was conducted in a context in which custody cases often claimed that lesbian motherhood would create gender identity disorder in children and that lesbian mothers themselves were unfit. It is understandable that their summary reassures readers that the findings point to more similarities than differences in both the mothers and their children. See R.Green et al., "Lesbian Mothers and Their Children," 167.

73. Brewaeys et al., "Donor Insemination," table 4.

74. Brewaeys et al., "Donor Insemination," 1356.

75. Tasker and Golombok, *Growing Up in a Lesbian Family*.

76. Tasker and Golombok, *Growing Up in a Lesbian Family*.

77. Susan Golombok and Fiona Tasker, "Do Parents Influence the Sexual Orientation of Their Children? Findings from a Longitudinal Study of Lesbian Families," *Developmental Psychology* 32 (1996): 3–11.

78. Golombok and Tasker, "Do Parents Influence the Sexual Orientation?" 8.

79. J. Michael Bailey, David Bobrow, MarilynWolfe, and Sarah Mikach, "Sexual Orientation of Adult Sons of Gay Fathers," *Developmental Psychology* 31 (1995): 124–29.

80. Tasker and Golombok, *Growing Up in a Lesbian Family*.

81. Patterson (Charlotte J. Patterson, "Children of the Lesbian Baby Boom: Behavioral Adjustment, Self-Concepts and Sex Role Identity," in *Lesbian and Gay Psychology: Theory, Research, and Clinical Applications*, ed. B. Green and G. M. Herek [Thousand Oaks, Calif.: Sage, 1994], 156–75) found that children ages four to nine with lesbian mothers expressed more stress than did those with heterosexual mothers, but at the same time they also reported a greater sense of overall well-being. Patterson speculates that children from lesbian-mother families may be more willing to express their feelings—positive and negative—but also that the children may actually experience more social stress at the same time that they gain confidence from their ability to cope with it. Also see table 2.1.

82. Tasker and Golombok, *Growing Up in a Lesbian Family*; Bozett, "Gay Fathers,"148; Valory Mitchell, "The Birds, the Bees . . . and the Sperm Banks: How Lesbian Mothers Talk with Their Children about Sex and Reproduction," *American Journal of Orthopsychiatry* 68 (1998): 400–409.

83. The only empirical evidence reported is Tasker and Golombok's (1997) finding of no differences in unemployment rates among young adults that are associated with their parents' sexual orientations. However, some of the children

studied were still in school, and the authors provide no information on occupations attained to assess differences in long-term occupational achievements.

84. Kweskin and Cook, "Heterosexual and Homosexual Mothers."

85. Hoeffer, "Children's Acquisition of Sex-Role Behavior," 536.

86. Hoeffer, "Children's Acquisition of Sex-Role Behavior," table 4.

87. Diana Baumrind, "Parental Disciplinary Patterns and Social Competence in Children," *Youth and Society* 9 (1978): 239–75; Diana Baumrind, "New Directions in Socialization Research," *American Psychologist* 35 (1980): 639–52.

88. Brewaeys et al.,"Donor Insemination."

89. Flaks et al., "Lesbians Choosing Motherhood."

90. Brewaeys et al., "Donor Insemination."

91. Brewaeys et al., "Donor Insemination."

92. Chan et al., "Psychosocial Adjustment among Children."

93. Chan et al., "Psychosocial Adjustment among Children."

94. Tasker and Golombok, *Growing Up in a Lesbian Family*. Mitchell, "Birds, the Bees," 407.

95. So do Brewaeys et al., "Donor Insemination"; Chan et al., "Division of Labor"; Flaks et al., "Lesbians Choosing Motherhood."

96. Frank F. Furstenberg Jr. and Andrew J. Cherlin, *Divided Families* (Cambridge, Mass.: Harvard University Press, 1991); Ronald L. Simons and Associates, *Understanding Differences between Divorced and Intact Families: Stress, Interactions, and Child Outcome* (Thousand Oaks, Calif.: Sage, 1996).

97. Chan et al. ("Division of Labor," 415) make interesting connections between these kinds of findings and the theoretical perspectives developed in Chodorow (Nancy Chodorow, *The Reproduction of Mothering: Psychoanalysis and the Sociology of Gender* [Berkeley: University of California Press, 1978]) and Gilligan (Carol Gilligan, *In a Different Voice: Psychological Theory and Women's Development* [Cambridge, Mass.: Harvard University Press, 1982]).

98. Gillian A Dunne, "What Difference Does 'Difference' Make? Lesbian Experience of Work and Family Life," in *Relating Intimacies*, ed. J. Seymour and P. Bagguley (New York: St. Martin's, 1999), 189–221; Dunne, "Opting into Motherhood"; Patterson, "Families of the Lesbian Baby Boom."

99. Bigner and Jacobsen, "Parenting Behaviors"; "Adult Responses."

100. Frederick W. Bozett, "Children of Gay Fathers," in *Gay and Lesbian Parents*, ed. F. W. Bozett (New York: Praeger, 1987), 3–22, 39–57; Bozett, "Gay Fathers."

101. Wardle, "Potential Impact."

102. Boykin, *One More River*, 36.

103. R. Green et al., "Lesbian Mothers and Their Children"; Tasker and Golombok, *Growing Up in a Lesbian Family*.

104. Brewaeys et al., "Donor Insemination"; Chan et al., "Division of Labor"; Chan et al., "Psychosocial Adjustment among Children"; Flaks et al., "Lesbians Choosing Motherhood."

105. Dunne, "Opting into Motherhood," 25.

106. Nancy Bonvillain, *Women and Men: Cultural Constructs of Gender*, 2d ed. (Upper Saddle River, N.J.: Prentice Hall, 1998); Caroline B. Brettell and Carolyn F.

Sargent, *Gender in Cross-Cultural Perspective*, 2d ed. (Upper Saddle River, N.J.: Prentice Hall, 1997); Sherry Ortner and Harriet Whitehead, *Sexual Meanings: The Cultural Construction of Gender and Sexuality* (Cambridge, England: Cambridge University Press, 1981).

    107. Alan P. Bell and Martin S. Weinberg, *Homosexualities: A Study of Diversity among Men and Women* (New York: Simon and Schuster, 1978); Jeffrey Weeks, Brian Heaphy, and Catherine Donovan, *Same Sex Intimacies: Families of Choice and Other Life Experiments,* (Cambridge, England: Cambridge University Press, 2001).

    108. Dunne, "Opting into Motherhood"; Maureen Sullivan, "Rozzie and Harriet?: Gender and Family Patterns of Lesbian Coparents," *Gender and Society* 10 (1996):747–67; Weeks et al., *Same Sex Intimacies.*

    109. Anthony Giddens, *The Transformation of Intimacy: Sexuality, Love and Eroticism in Modern Societies* (Stanford, Calif.: Stanford University Press, 1992).

    110. Ulrich Beck and Elisabeth Beck-Gersheim, *The Normal Chaos of Love* (London: Polity, 1995).

    111. Mitchell, "The Birds, the Bees"; Ann O'Connell, "Voices from the Heart: The Developmental Impact of a Mother's Lesbianism on Her Adolescent Children," *Smith College Studies in Social Work* 63 (1994): 281–99.

    112. Black et al., "Demographics of the Gay and Lesbian Population."

    113. Mitchell, "The Birds, the Bees"; Tasker and Golombok, *Growing Up in a Lesbian Family.*

    114. Nancy D. Polikoff, "This Child Does Have Two Mothers: Redefining Parenthood to Meet the Needs of Children in Lesbian-Mother and Other Nontraditional Families," *Georgetown Law Journal* 78 (1990): 569–70.

3

The Politics of Child Sexual Abuse Research

Janice Haaken and Sharon Lamb

In July 1998, *Psychology Bulletin* published a meta-analysis of the long-term impact of child sexual abuse on college students.[1] The article sought to debunk a belief that had gained widespread currency in mental health culture: that childhood sexual abuse was inevitably traumatic and inevitably led to later mental health problems. Most controversial was its suggestion that a morally neutral term such as "adult–child" sex might be used as the broadest rubric of investigation in this area, because child sexual abuse implies a particular and inevitable negative outcome. The authors argued that the mental health field has been governed by a bias toward viewing intergenerational sexual contact as inherently pathogenic, and that this bias has produced a highly narrow understanding of the association between child abuse and adult psychopathology.

The controversy that erupted in response to this article has been most frequently framed as a dispute between science and public morality. On the one hand, there are various professionals, victims-rights advocates, and moral conservatives casting Bruce Rind, Philip Tromovitch, and Robert Bauserman—the authors of the now infamous study—as recklessly neglectful of public morality. On the other hand, equally pious investigators are coming to their defense, insisting on the political and moral autonomy of science. Much like the polarized debate over the reliability of recovered memories of childhood sexual abuse in psychotherapy, neither position captures the complexity of the issues.

In this essay, we "unpack" the findings of the Rind et al. study, exploring key issues raised and placing them within a wider cultural context. While scientific inquiry is always embedded in a cultural and political framework, research that engages in redefining sexual boundaries is particularly rife with potential for arousing what has been termed "moral panic." Whether the issue is homosexuality, teenage sexuality, abortion, or rape, sexuality seems to carry surplus freight as a combustible topic. In recognizing that there is an element of hysteria associated with public outrage to the Rind et al. article, we do not mean to imply that there is no basis for criticism of this study. Indeed, there are legitimate bases for criticism. But our primary focus here is on what forces, historically and in the present, contribute to the sub-currents of this debate which are so easily obscured by the turbulence.

We agree, in part, with those critics, including Raymond Fowler, president of the American Psychological Association (APA), who have argued that scientists must be sensitive to the social implications of research findings and that taking care in explaining controversial findings need not imply censorship. In the last two decades, incest and other forms of sexual abuse have been at the forefront of the women's and children's rights movements. Sexual violations have acquired tremendous social symbolic power in American political culture so that any challenge to the gains of these movements is perceived to be a threat to victims. But the controversy over the Rind et al. article stirs deeper uncertainties over the place of child sexual abuse in politics, the place of sexuality in children's lives, our understanding of trauma and recovery, the boundary between childhood and adolescence, and the place of scientific inquiry in adjudicating moral questions. We address each of these issues, attempting to steer a middle ground between a social constructionist or culturally relative position on sexuality on the one hand and an approach that emphasizes universal principles of justice and care on the other.

A STUDY OF STUDIES

Some of the controversy associated with the Rind et al. study involves hierarchies within science. Most social scientific studies are modest in what they can claim. They are bound by the populations from which subjects are drawn, by the limitations of their measures, and by various additional methodological constraints. The power of the meta-analytical method lies in its capacity to rise above the terrain of a particular field and to assess the overall strength of findings from a series of studies. It is, in effect, a study of studies, "meta" suggesting a more encompassing viewpoint, a higher level of analysis than that produced by the limited vantage point of a single investigation.

When performing a meta-analysis, researchers collect none of their own data, but sort through the data collected by others. In the Rind et al. meta-analysis, the researchers selected a sample of studies done on college students that addressed the issue of outcome from sexual abuse. In choosing which studies to include, they required that each study used in the meta-analysis meet certain minimal criteria such as adequate sample size, use of a control group, and a reporting on one of eighteen symptoms they had identified. Previously, Rind and Tromovitch had performed a meta-analysis of community studies that showed that the effect size with regard to long-term adjustment is small.[2] This means that, in community samples, those people who had been sexually abused as children were, over time, only slightly worse off psychologically than those who had not been sexually abused.

This newer meta-analysis of fifty-nine studies of college students who had been sexually abused as children suggests that not all of them were still wounded by adulthood, and not all of them were traumatized as children. While child sexual abuse (CSA) was associated with poorer adjustment, the magnitude of the effect, as in the community study, was small, and, in the authors' words, "the negative potential of CSA for most individuals who have experienced it has been overstated."[3] They also found that two-thirds of male CSA experiences and almost a third of female CSA were reported not to have been negative at the time of the abuse. Three of every eight male experiences and one of every ten female experiences were even experienced as positive at the time. When the long-term outcome was negative, it was difficult for the authors to figure out why because of so many confounding variables. In fact, family environment was found to be confounded with and to account for current adjustment in college students more than CSA.

The article was published in July 1998 with little incident. It had gone through two revisions and two sets of reviewers before *Psychological Bulletin* saw fit to publish it. The drama that ensued drew its emotional strength from two primary sources: one was politically and religiously conservative anxiety over sexuality, and particularly homosexuality; and the other was psychology's professional concerns with maintaining social legitimacy.

It is not uncommon for fringe groups to seek out support for their causes in the scientific literature. Like the Bible, the scientific literature is vast enough to support a wide range of opinions and viewpoints. So, it was not surprising that the North American Man-Boy Love Association, on its website, seized this research as supporting its members' idealized view of the man–boy sexual relationship. Just as predictable was the moral panic of conservatives, gripped by the fear that homosexual pedophiles would, en masse, tear down legal and cultural sanctions against adult–child sex. Talk-show hosts such as Laura Schlessinger as well as the Christian Coalition and the Family Research Council (a fundraising group for conservative causes) began to rail against the article on the air. Matt Salmon, a Republican congressman from Arizona, denounced the article along with Florida Republican Dave Weldon at a press conference hosted by the Family Research Council.

Conservative organizations routinely monitor sexual research, looking for signs of relaxing sexual mores—signs that become associated with the weakening of social boundaries between the "good" and the "bad" elements of society. Sexual control becomes associated with social and moral order, but sexuality also becomes a domain where more diffuse social anxieties are imported. Public problems such as the widening of the income gap, the growth of poverty among youth, and the excesses of consumer culture (problems the political right is highly resistant to addressing), are masked by the moral righteousness of sexual crusades. Indeed, one of the most important aspects of the meta-analysis was its finding that the effects of poverty and other broad indicators of family well-being outweighed sexual abuse as a factor associated with mental health problems in adulthood. But the heat of sexual hysteria readily obscures these less dramatic forms of "abuse." Poverty and neglect of children do not mobilize the same moral outrage in American society as does the specter of weakening sexual taboos.

Anxious about appearing "lax" on moral issues, the American Psychiatric Association eventually joined conservative organizations in calling for the APA to retract the article. Matt Salmon even introduced a resolution to condemn the article in Congress, and the House voted, almost unanimously (14 abstained), to condemn the article on the grounds that it gave a green light to pedophiles. After initially supporting the scientific validity of the article,[4] Raymond Fowler, the president of the APA, retracted his support and in June wrote a letter to Congress denouncing it, saying that the article included opinions inconsistent with the APA's views. He also set up a board to review future articles that have the potential to raise public concern.

In support of Fowler and the APA, Patricia Kobor, director of science and policy at the APA, argues that psychologists are

participants in a social contract with Congress and the public: if we don't work with them to explain how and what we are about, they can and will assume the worst and act on it. If psychological scientists value public support and federal funding for research, if they hope to be of some service to the common welfare, then we have to work with members of Congress and other groups, and we have to safeguard a reputation for straight talk and fair play.[5]

Funding of psychological research is increasingly governed by a more conservative mood in the nation, rather than on more liberal principles of "common welfare." Both psychology and psychiatry have a long history of dependence on the state, and particularly on its conservative wing. These professions gained initial prominence during World War I, with the testing and treatment of soldiers, and made monumental gains with the funding of training programs and research again after subsequent wars. Since the 1980s, an increasingly conservative political agenda dominates the funding of research, emphasizing biological over social causes and individual mental health over social change. While a cause such as child sexual abuse unites politicians and psychologists, declaring one's opposition to child sexual abuse is a risk-free stance; indeed, only highly marginal organizations such as the North American Man-Boy Love Association defend such practices that others might call abuse.

It would be misleading to conclude, however, that all of the criticisms of the Rind et al. study emanated from a conservative political agenda. Some criticisms come from child welfare advocates fearful of a cultural swing in the direction of minimizing the impact of sexual abuse, just as there was a previous tendency in the mental health community toward overstating sexual abuse as a single causal determinant of adult distress. The *APSAC Advisor* (a newsletter of the American Professional Society on the Abuse of Children) published a commentary[6] responding to the uproar by pointing out that those in the sexual abuse research community have actually known for some time that a significant number of sexually abused children have no measurable long-term negative outcomes.[7] That does not negate, they argue, the responsibilities of clinicians to treat those who have been harmed. Taking issue with the interpretation of "small effect size," they point out the well-known fact that we accept that smoking causes lung cancer while the effect size for this association is small and comparable to that of child sexual abuse to long-term psychological problems. These authors also point out that the meta-analysis only looks at one kind of outcome, mental health, and that there are other outcomes that may be measured as indicators of long-term trauma (for example, quality of life, successful adjustment, capacity for pleasure).

One of the more problematic critiques leveled at the meta-analysis is that victims may not be a reliable source of data on the effects of their abuse experiences. The authors of the APSAC critique argue that an abused child may learn from the abuser that such experiences are normal and positive and accept the abuser's view of such events to his or her own detriment. They suggest that when considering outcomes, the idea that a child learns that adult–child sex is acceptable is, in and of itself, a poor outcome.[8] This is an interesting critique because it brings up important issues of believability as well as multiple perspectives on the truth. Ironically, Rind et al. seem to be advocating "believing the child" (or, rather, believing the college student's perspective) when they argue that perhaps the term *child sexual abuse* should not be used to describe all forms of "adult–child" sex.

And, while Rind et al. argue that, on the one hand, college students are telling us that some acts we consider child sexual abuse may not be abusive, they also argue that "the findings of the current review should not be construed to imply that CSA never causes intense harm for men or women—clinical research has well documented that in specific cases it can."[9] And although they embrace these two perspectives, they reveal their own bias for a single cause or a single perspective by stating, "Classifying a behavior as abuse simply because it is generally viewed as immoral or defined as illegal is problematic, because such a classification may obscure the true nature of the behavior and its actual causes and effects."[10] This notion that there is an "essential" reality that empirical investigation has the power to uncover belies their strongest argument: that sexual experiences are open to multiple meanings and interpretations.

SEXUAL ABUSE RESEARCH IN HISTORICAL CONTEXT

During the first wave of research on incest and child sexual abuse in the 1970s and 1980s, researchers routinely pointed out the relative paucity of literature on incest or child sexual abuse. Influenced by the children's rights and women's movements of that period, sexual abuse researchers had a sense of venturing into culturally forbidden territory, of finding what previous researchers and clinicians were not inclined to see.

Having won this ground, researchers and professionals on the forefront of the sexual abuse awareness movement have been understandably wary of assessing the costs of the victory. But there were costs, some of which emerged in zealous campaigns to ferret out histories of sexual abuse, whether in day care cases or in the history of psychotherapy patients. The mere suspicion or question of a history of sexual abuse seemed definitive evidence because the general thinking in the field throughout the 1980s was that the effects of a history of sexual abuse were denied, minimized, or otherwise concealed and that the risk of "false positives" was negligible. It seemed counterintuitive that children or adults would produce, or could be led to produce, disturbing sexual scenes or memories not based on actual abuse incidences. By the late

1980s, child sexual abuse had achieved a tremendous cultural potency as a primary cause of adult psychopathology, particularly for women.

Although in basic agreement about the trauma of sexual abuse, there was a tension between child welfare advocates who situated child sexual abuse as a family problem and feminists who described it as a product of a history of patriarchal oppression. The writing of child welfare proponents focused on public health, which tends to emphasize prevention and protection as well as therapy. Sometimes lumped together with issues of physical abuse and neglect, mothers as well as fathers were examined as perpetrators, and mother blaming was acceptable practice in this literature. Mothers became the focus of blame for sexual abuse for "not knowing" and thus not protecting their daughters. While feminist responses were also concerned with protection of children and especially girls, the focus became the maniacal male, which produced an easy target for women's anger. Both feminists and child welfare advocates, however, were united in their use of the long list of symptoms from trauma to argue for greater child protection, more insurance benefits, and therapy for victims.

The rise of sexual abuse as a moral crusade coincided with changes in the mental health community and institutions as well. Women entered the field in growing numbers during the 1970s and 1980s, creating a more responsive mental health culture to female concerns. The expansion of the field and the growing public acceptance of psychotherapy meant that issues of happiness and well-being were taken seriously as mental health issues. But by the 1980s, restrictions on mental health coverage contributed to the movement to focus on trauma; extreme indicators of psychological distress displaced this earlier focus on "strains and stresses."[11]

It could be argued that women's interest in child sexual abuse and the discovery of the commonality of abuse in women's histories paved the way for their greater voice and professionalization of therapy for abuse and victimization. But with the decline of an activist women's movement during the 1980s, the struggle of women against patriarchal control took on a more individualistic cast. The social problem of exploitation of women and girls was increasingly defined as a mental health problem.[12]

With the decline of the broad-based social movements of the 1960s and 1970s, the mental health issue of child sexual abuse emerged as a unifying issue around which health professionals, women's organizations, and conservatives alike could organize. Right-wing conservatives were frightened by sex, whereas leftists and feminists were critical of the patriarchal family. As we noted earlier, it has been much harder to win the struggle against poverty, inequality, or even nonsexual physical abuse of children than it has the struggle against pornography and child sexual abuse. The child advocacy movement and the growing cadre of psychotherapists, psychologists, and social workers as well as feminist activists found unity around the conviction that child sexual abuse was not only wrong, but that it had devastating effects on the lives of children, on women as a group, and on the mental health of women and girls in this society. This conviction certainly had support from the devastated lives of many victims. Clinical histories and consciousness-raising groups were rife with stories of such damage. But it is important to recognize how abuse stories may be mobilized for multiple political ends and that some stories gain more political currency than others.[13]

WOMEN ANGELS, CHILD INNOCENTS

Narratives and research on child sexual abuse that emerged out of this postactivist era positioned women as innocent and simultaneously damaged. Middle-class women were able to rebel against patriarchal controls and break from familial entanglements through the position of innocent child-victim, in a way that was more difficult to achieve from the perspective of more morally ambiguous and conflicted adult sexuality. There is a long history of cultural splitting between the portrait of evil temptress, on the one hand, and virtuous maiden on the other. During periods of broad-based activism, women have been able collectively to resist these narrow and repressive images, refusing the positions of either "angel of the house" or evil temptress. But during periods when feminist gains seem more precarious, the ideal of female moral purity assumes a more central social symbolic position in the movement for women's rights.

Just as casting women as the "angels in the house" concealed deeper currents of female rebellion during the late nineteenth century, casting children as innocents obscures the more complex reality of their lives. The romanticizing of childhood in nineteenth-century Western culture took place during an era of massive child labor and of displaced children in the growing urban areas of the country. During this same period, the family was portrayed as a womblike refuge from the ravaging effects of industrial life. This fantasy of the family as a "haven in a heartless world," shielding children from adult life, was itself a reaction to the harshness of industrial life. And it was a cultural fantasy that thrived in an era when childhood was becoming increasingly dangerous for the children in the working classes. Protection of children from wanton influences became the hallmark of nineteenth-century moral reformers.

Similarly today, the debate over "protecting" children from adult sexual predators is symptomatic of a broader range of concerns over children and "loss of innocence." This has been a period of shifting cultural borders: the borders of gender, sexuality, and normative conceptions of family life. Protections and supports for families have declined, even as the rallying cry for protection of the "sexual innocence" of children becomes more strident. The movement to increase social awareness of child sexual abuse signified both the vital advances of feminism and the limited terrain of its victories by the 1980s. No paid parental leave policy, no national health insurance, and no subsidized child care existed. Disparities in income widened and child poverty rates grew. Women were working more hours than ever, still carrying the lion's share of housework and child care within the family. Set against these defeats were notable victories in the area of sexual rights: the legalization of abortion and the passage of sexual harassment and reformed rape laws were among the main gains of this era in addition to removing discriminatory barriers in employment.

Child sexual abuse acquired symbolic importance as a social problem—as the "epidemic" of the late 1980s and early 1990s—because it registered many concerns that unified women. Protection of children is an area in which women have been granted and have assumed authority in most societies, but it is also an area in which "failures" fall particularly harshly on women as mothers. Child sexual abuse more often implicated men as fathers, shifting the axis of mother blaming. In a sense, it was a historical redistribution of guilt—a collective project of coming out from under the load of unequal social responsibilities for the adult fate and happiness of children.

CONTEMPORARY SEXUAL POLITICS

The sexual politics of second-wave feminism—the women's movement that emerged in the 1970s—was organized around sexual liberation and emancipation from traditional constraints. Debate about the role of patriarchy centered on the repression of female desire—the inhibitions and constraints imposed on women by the law of the father—rather than on the legacy of overt violations. Yet, as the movement achieved significant advances and women entered public life and the professions in historically unprecedented numbers, there was a significant shift in the sexual politics that took hold within the movement. At the same time, sadomasochism, queer politics, and feminist pornography became more publicly visible.

But these developments lacked a popular base in feminist informed practice, for instance, in the mental health field, social services, or crisis services. While there has been greater public discussion of sexuality, greater tolerance for diverse sexual practices among adults, and greater use of sex for commercial purposes, the idea of protecting children from sexuality is still quite salient. Many states still restrict sex education programs from speaking about sexual intercourse in any way that does not support abstinence. And although advertisers dress up children to portray sexual images on television and in magazines, the majority of the public believes that children are not sexual beings. One study of mental health professionals indicates that psychologists generally believe that two 8-year-olds exposing their genitals to each other is "wrong."[14]

One of the important issues raised in the Rind et al. meta-analysis, obscured in the heat of moral outrage, is that child sexual abuse has widened to encompass so many experiences and degrees of abuse that it loses any discriminative power as a concept. A recent trend in the child advocacy literature illustrates this trend, with the profile of the perpetrator shifting to youth—with a high percentage of perpetrators identified as adolescent boys—and a focus on sexual acts committed between children. Since children are understood to be asexual, it is assumed that sexual explorations in childhood are either initiated by adult perpetrators or are part of some cycle of abuse whereby adults enact sexual acts with children who then compulsively reenact them with peers their own age or younger.

Two critiques are missing in this mental health literature on child perpetrators. The first is one that explains the effects of adolescent boys growing up in a culture that supports male sexual entitlement and group denigrating of girls. This critique focuses on the socialization of gender roles—a socialization process that places adolescent sex offenders on a continuum of dominating behaviors of males toward females and their acts as somewhat normative in male socialization. The finding in the Rind et al. study that the first sexual experience of girls is more often described as negative than positive suggests that the boundary between the normative sexuality and abuse for girls is a murky one. The second missing critique focuses on "normal" childhood sexuality.

Freud's theory of infantile sexuality was among his most radical "discoveries," a perspective that incensed Victorian romantic portraits of the asexuality of children. Of course, adult fantasies are perpetually projected onto children: the creation of an imagined oasis of childhood innocence and purity, which must be defended against predatory adult incursions, expresses anxieties on the part of adults over their own sexual impulses and desires.

The uproar over whether sex between adults and children is abusive or not stems from the idea that any kind of adult–child sex is abuse, no matter what the outcome and no matter what the feelings of the child or the adult. It is important to recognize, however, that children can never be equal participants in relation to adults and sex, and by imagining they could we leave open the way to exploitation. The moratorium of adolescence speaks to this issue of equality, saying that children are a special category because of their vulnerability to being exploited, and that adolescence is a time of transition. But this kind of categorization does not necessarily need to mean that before adolescence children are asexual or innocent.

Anthropological work not only reveals enormous variation in sexual activity in children but also many cultures that encourage children's "hands-on" learning of sex. In our own country research has shown that children as young as age three can reach orgasm and that in latency-aged children, mutual sexual play is quite common. Sexual activities of children do not, as Freud suggested, decline in the latency years, but continue with increasing frequency throughout childhood.

In spite of this evidence of common childhood sexuality, we hold onto an image of the child as a sexual innocent. And what seems particularly hypocritical in the moral outrage over the Rind et al. study is that children who are not enclosed in this imaginary enchanted space of childhood innocence in American society are routinely discarded. Once children cross the threshold, leaving childhood behind, they increasingly lose this sentimental veil of adult protection. There are three notable examples: adolescent perpetrators of sexual abuse; teen mothers; adolescents who kill. In each of these cases, children are treated as if they were adults. How can we send adolescents to prison and adult court for murder and also say that an adolescent boy who seeks to have sex with an adult can give no consent? Are children only to be protected when they fit our fantasy of innocence and passivity?

SCIENCE AND SEXUAL ABUSE

In order to understand the heat generated by the meta-analysis, we also need to think through the relationship between politics and science. For many trained in the procedural rules of science, professional identity is based on the ideal of social distance and objectivity. From this perspective, the scientist takes his or her inquiry wherever it leads, with a dispassionate commitment to results uncontaminated by subjectivity. There is something to be said for this tradition—for seeking out evidence contrary to one's assumptions or hypothetical propositions about the world. But this ideal has come in for considerable scrutiny over the years, as critics have pointed out how embedded research is in cultural assumptions and subjective factors.

Deciding on the primary causes of human suffering is a cultural process as much as it is a scientific one. Indeed, it is often difficult, if not impossible, to disentangle the two. It is very difficult to separate, for example,

how much of the trauma associated with rape is the result of the sexual
violence and how much results from cultural beliefs that women who are
raped are damaged goods. Human acts operate within a meaning system
that provides interpretations, including the right to feel violated and to demand redress.

The uproar over the Rind et al. study is also affiliated with a history of
struggle on the part of women in resisting male control of science. There
is understandable suspicion of science among people who are more apt
to be objects of study than participants in deciding on the terms of inquiry. Furthermore, some areas of feminism exhibit wariness toward science because so many aspects of women's lives are not readily open to
empirical verification. In the aftermath of the contemporary feminist
movement, the distresses women began to articulate focused largely on
events in private life, behind closed doors and beyond the reaches of the
observational methods of science. Women moved into the professions,
as scientists and mental health practitioners, with a commitment to reveal
formerly concealed truths and to confronting resistance within the professions to investigating women's concerns. This emphasis on the moti-
vational side to science and the understanding that it has a close affinity
with powerful social interests was a central galvanizing insight behind establishing women's studies as an academic discipline.

In *Whose Science? Whose Knowledge?* the scientist Sandra Harding addresses the issue of a feminist epistemology with regard to women entering
scientific fields.[15] Her use of the phrase "standpoint theory" was intended to
show that there is a way of doing science that might set aside objectivity and
begin from an individual perspective, and, as she puts it, the dailiness of
women's lives. In honoring this perspective, women researchers have ex-
alted women's individual experiences as an equal and viable source of
knowledge to empirical inquiry, not only because empiricism is fraught
with biases and often in the hands of men but because empiricism can
never answer some questions that are vital to women's lives.

It is with this understanding that we question the use of the phrase
"true nature" in reference to the sexual acts described. The victim advocates who responded in the *APSAC Advisor* questioned whether we can
trust that a positive response to adult–child sex is a "true" response or
one conditioned by the abuser. We take the position that there may not
be a "true" nature to these acts, even if there are important reasons to
view them in certain ways over others.

Let's examine masturbation, which is introduced by Rind et al. in discussing the historical determinants of sexual taboos. The culture no
longer believes that masturbation is an evil that produces blindness. And

yet Jocelyn Elders was fired from her position as surgeon general because she suggested that school sex education programs might introduce this as an educational topic and as an alternative to sexual intercourse in the high school years. This is all to say that although we have changed in our opinion of the effects of masturbation, it is still an area of social control over youth. While science can debunk the belief that masturbation produces blindness, social prohibitions make it less likely that research would generate findings that masturbation is associated with increased mental health or with the enhancement of later sexual relationships.

There is no universal boundary between normative and pathological sexuality, nor are there precise definitions of any of these acts. Furthermore, definitions are contested because of conflicting values and ideas in the culture that affect how they are framed and interpreted. Broader patterns of cultural influence and positions of power structure the effects of various social encounters. Men are not treated as if they are damaged goods when abused. Rather, men who cross "authorized" sexual boundaries are more apt to be viewed as adventurous.

Statistical analysis of competing data sets do not do justice to what is at stake in the battle over the status of child sexual abuse as a cause of adult suffering, and particularly women's suffering. We need an alternative means of entering into the psychological and social meaning of these accounts and of understanding why and how they came to carry such import for vast numbers of contemporary women.

Likewise, we need an alternative means of entering into an understanding of children's agency and sexuality. Ironically, it may be that a general change in our attitudes toward children that allows them their sexuality and some capacity for consent would work better to prevent sexual abuse, in the same way that sex education works to prevent teen pregnancy. But whether we refer to CSA as adult–child sex or not, we are not released from the moral dilemmas, from working through moral questions about appropriate behavior toward children, about their exploitation, and about their care. Conservative responses that make facile statements issuing zero tolerance in the area of sex and sexual abuse ignore the broader issues of poverty and poor education that both compound the effects of sexual violations and are far more chronic and pervasive in American society.

There are many good reasons for adults not to have sex with children that do not require a romanticized picture of children that casts them as true innocents, easily damaged, or unable to give consent. Common morality should argue against sexual exploitation of children and for a duty or obligation of every adult to protect and care for children. From a feminist perspective, we might expect that the loosening of such boundaries, before there is equality among the sexes, would most certainly lead to greater misuse of young girls, and greater misuse of them in their own homes. And we need to take into consideration that we live in a culture that still equates sexuality with shame, where parents do not routinely tickle the genitals of their children (as they do in some cultures) but have routinely beaten their bare bottoms.

Science has much to offer, and yet scientifically produced knowledge cannot, in and of itself, answer questions of morality or questions about the relative value of subjective experience of such events. To say that women and men who have been abused as children do not necessarily suffer longstanding trauma is not the same as saying that abuse is fine. To say that children might experience abuse as pleasurable sex is not to say that abuse is acceptable. All of these claims require a deeper exploration of abuse and sexuality, an exploration that has been limited by the anxieties often evoked in talk about sex. All of these ideas are worth further investigation, further debate.

NOTES

This chapter originally appeared in *Society* 37, no. 4 (May/June 2000) in a symposium entitled: "Classifying Sexual Behavior," and is reprinted here by permission.

1. Bruce Rind, Philip Tromovitch, and Robert Bauserman, "A Meta-Analytic Examination of Assumed Properties of Child Sexual Abuse Using College Samples," *Psychological Bulletin* 124, no.1 (July 1998): 22–53.
2. Bruce Rind and Philip Tromovitch, "A Meta-Analytic Review of Findings from National Samples on Psychological Correlates of Child Sexual Abuse," *Journal of Sex Research* 34, no. 3 (1997): 237–55.
3. Rind et al., " Meta-Analytic Examination," 42.
4. Rind, personal communication, 1999.
5. Patricia Kobar, "On Behalf of Science: Science, Politics, and Pedophilia." *Psychological Science Agenda: APA Science Directorate* 12 (September/October 1999): 1–2.
6. Steven J. Ondersma, Mark Chaffin, and Lucy Berliner, "Comments on the Rind et al. Meta-Analysis Controversy," *APSAC Advisor* 12 (1999): 1–3.
7. Kathleen Kendall-Tackett, Linda M. Williams, and David Finkelhor, "Impact of Sexual Abuse on Children: A Review and Synthesis of Recent Empirical Studies," *Psychological Bulletin* 113, no.1 (1993): 164–80.
8. Ondersma et al., "Comments," 1.
9. Rind et al., "Meta-Analytic Examination," 42.
10. Rind and Tromovitch, "A Meta-Analytic Review," 45.

11. Janice Haaken, *Pillar of Salt: Gender, Memory, and the Perils of Looking Back* (New Brunswick, N.J.: Rutgers University Press, 1998).

12. See Sharon Lamb, *The Trouble with Blame: Victims, Perpetrators, and Responsibility* (Cambridge, Mass.: Harvard University Press, 1996); and Sharon Lamb, "Constructing the Victim: Popular Images and Lasting Labels," in *New Versions of Victims: Feminists Struggle with the Concept*, ed. Sharon Lamb (New York: New York University Press, 1999): 108–38.

13. See Lamb, ed., *New Versions of Victims: Feminists Struggle with the Concept* (New York: New York University Press, 1999), and Janice Haaken, *Pillar of Salt*.

14. William N. Friedrich, Patricia Grambsch, Linda Damon, and Sandra K. Hewitt, "Child Sexual Behavior Inventory: Normative and Clinical Comparisons," *Psychological Assessment* 4 (1992): 303–11.

15. Sandra Harding, *Whose Science? Whose Knowledge? Thinking from Women's Lives* (Ithaca, N.Y.: Cornell University Press, 1991).

4

Defense Mechanisms: Using Psychoanalysis Conservatively

Cynthia Burack

THE CHILD WAS LOST, BUT NOW SHE IS FOUND

In 1984, political theorist Jean Bethke Elshtain published an essay entitled "Symmetry and Soporifics: A Critique of Feminist Accounts of Gender Development." In that essay, Elshtain calls attention to "the missing child" in feminist theory and notes that she had considered calling this critique of feminist theories of gender development "The Case of the Missing Child."[1] Of course, the absence of children from social and political theory has never been limited to feminist thought, which has repeatedly mounted its own critique of the "missing children" in mainstream social thought.[2] In any case, by the 1990s, injunctions such as Elshtain's to theorize about, and from the perspective of, children are answered by theorists of many ideological complexions, including feminists and social conservatives.

However, feminists and social conservatives tend to respond to the challenge to take children into account in quite different ways. Many feminists make children and children's well-being central in analyses of children's development and of the political economy. Social conservatives make children central to their analyses of a wide range of social, moral, and political issues—including authority, gender roles, sexuality, first amendment issues, and separation of church and state. It is not surprising that feminists and social conservatives usually end up on opposing sides of political debates. What is more intriguing than this raw political fact is the way that children's needs themselves are under contention. The child is not so much missing as she is a locus of vigorous disagreement. Feminists are concerned about what it means for children to be "found" by social theorists and policy analysts: how children and their

81

needs are represented and—a deeply historically and philosophically related issue—how adult women fare in the wake of these representations.

As a theorist, Elshtain does not specialize in psychological approaches
to social and political life, but she is interested in the role that psychoanalysis might play in helping us understand "human complexity and
moral agency." And she makes the strong claim that "a rejection of psychoanalytic theory is fatal for feminism and . . . for all contemporary social thought."[3] I agree with Elshtain that psychoanalysis can provide an
indispensable set of tools for liberation movements to think with, but so-
cial-theoretical uses of psychoanalysis also invite scrutiny. Psychoanalysis is a multivocal set of discourses whose many practitioners represent
cultural differences as well as quite distinct theoretical perspectives that
conceptualize selfhood and relationality in markedly different ways.
Moreover, theories—and psychoanalytic theories are no exception—do
not speak for themselves but must be interpreted, and these interpretations can be more or less careful, astute, or honest. Particular care must
be taken when authors use theoretical arguments to underwrite particular social and political arrangements to which they are already committed. Unfortunately, this concern with interpretation is not always in evidence.

A recent work that demonstrates a pattern of ideological deployment
of psychoanalytic arguments is that of Elshtain's colleague at the Institute
for American Values. David Blankenhorn's *Fatherless America: Confronting Our Most Urgent Social Problem*[4] can be situated in the New
Right discourse on families as a work of advocacy dedicated to articulat-
ing the effects of family structure on children. *Fatherless America* is an
interesting work because the text makes explicit many of the psychological claims and assumptions that ground social conservative writings on
families. I begin by surveying Blankenhorn's own arguments in support
of his critique of contemporary U.S. norms and attitudes about fatherhood. Then, I offer a series of skeptical readings of Blankenhorn's scholarly appropriations of psychoanalytic theory to support his claims on behalf of nature and what I shall call the "fundamental family." A critical
reading of Blankenhorn's psychoanalytic choices and interpretations
helps to clarify the ideological agenda that is at stake in social conservative critiques of family life and "fatherlessness." Blankenhorn claims of
his critics, feminists as well as nonfeminist "cultural elites," that they seek
to undermine fatherhood and displace fathers. But Blankenhorn's fatherhood and masculinity are themselves ideological constructions. As such,
they are intended to displace all visions of fatherhood and masculinity
that are not consistent with social conservative values and goals.

CONSCRIPTING FATHERS AND PSYCHOANALYSTS

Central to New Right discourse about families and gender roles are assumptions about the naturalness of heterosexuality, the nuclear family, and distinct gender roles, a bundle of assumptions that make up the fundamental family. Social conservative thinkers are quite critical of feminist and other critiques of heterosexual masculinity, as well as of arguments for androgyny or even diminished sex role differentiation.[5] They argue that children need the different "qualities" that sex-differentiated male and female heterosexual parents bring to parenting, that these differences are biologically based, and that efforts to encourage fathers to be more nurturing (and thus more like mothers) are deleterious to children as well as to society as a whole.[6] Families must be based upon biological relations, sex role differentiation, and heterosexual marriage. Finally, it is useful for understanding this family model to note the spiritual dimension of the masculine role that Blankenhorn clarifies in other writing. Noting that men are "taller when they bow," he concludes:

> I believe that . . . a root-and-branch moralization of male behavior can finally be understood only in spiritual terms—as potential fruit of a spiritual sensibility or calling, or perhaps even better, as grace, a spiritual gift. The core mystery of fatherhood is that a bare biological act yields such a transforming spiritual reality. Such a mystery is best understood as a calling to men to participate with God in creation.[7]

One reason that Blankenhorn, George Gilder, and other social conservatives give for opposing lessened sex role differentiation is that the family is the social institution that performs the task of harnessing aggressive and antisocial male sexuality. Blankenhorn makes it clear that the constraints of family life come more naturally to women than they do to men.

> Obligating fathers to their children is less a matter of biology than of culture. Compared to mothers, fathers are less born than made. As a social role, fatherhood is less the inelastic result of sexual embodiment than the fragile creation of cultural norms. . . . In a larger sense, the fatherhood story is the irreplaceable basis of a culture's most urgent imperative: the socialization of males. More than any other cultural invention, fatherhood guides men away from violence by fastening their behavior to a fundamental social purpose.[8]

According to Blankenhorn, men must be "conscripted" into responsible fatherhood. He leaves no doubt that, left to their own devices, men will constitute more of a danger to society than a boon to it. By withholding sex until marriage and then consenting to sex role–differentiated marriage, it is women's task to conscript men into fatherhood. Without the institution of heterosexual marriage, cemented by the obligation of biological paternity, men are unattached and dangerous. Sex role–differentiated fatherhood is necessary to control the naturally aggressive tendencies of men, who would otherwise be left unsupervised and unconstrained by cultural control.[9]

Blankenhorn's method is worth noting. He presents *Fatherless America* as empirical social science—a dispassionate and nonpartisan presentation of data and arguments that make the author's case for alarm regarding the plight of families and society. Blankenhorn carefully avoids labeling the various positions on family life either "liberal" or "conservative" and, thus, positions his own argument as beyond ideology. Blankenhorn's "fathers" are abstractions: "the main character in this book is not a real person."[10] An ideal type analysis permits Blankenhorn to use social science data and argument in the service of an affirmation of the abstract "main character," "the Good Family Man." For Blankenhorn, the Good Family Man fulfills the maximal, rather than minimal, dimensions of "good-enough fatherhood" and contrasts with the "New Father." If the Good Family Man represents the aspirations of average American fathers, the New Father is a creature of cultural elites, a threat to the well-being of children, and a sign of cultural confusion.

Unlike the social theory of the midcentury Old Right, New Right arguments increasingly do not call for women's subordination to men.[11] Likewise, Blankenhorn does not explicitly call for the maintenance of gender inegalitarian practices and institutions. Even so, the fundamental family arrangements solicited by New Right social and political theorists support and reinforce gender hierarchy.[12] I am less concerned in this chapter with these effects themselves, however, and more interested in the form of the argument that glosses these effects through appeals to particular kinds of authoritative data and argument. Invoked throughout *Fatherless America* are psychoanalytic arguments that Blankenhorn calls into use to frame—both positively and negatively—the thesis of the decline of fatherhood. The difficulty for Blankenhorn is that his interpretations of these texts do not withstand critical examination. Rather, these interpretations expose the extent to which Blankenhorn's arguments are ideologically predetermined and the authorities he cites merely expedient window dressing.

(ANNA) FREUD KNOWS BEST

Blankenhorn explicitly calls upon psychoanalysis to perform a number of services in his argument about fatherlessness and child well-being. Of these, his resort to Anna Freud is troubling because the partial appropriation of her arguments both misrepresents her work and is so unmistakably consistent with his own purposes. Blankenhorn uses Anna Freud and Dorothy Burlingham's *War and Children* and *Infants without Families* in support of his arguments for gender-differentiated parenting.[13] Both of these texts are concerned with issues of child care and child development stemming from Freud's and Burlingham's work with children in WWII England.

Freud and Burlingham founded the Hampstead War Nurseries in 1940 as a refuge for London children separated from their parents as a result of war-time exigencies. They meant for the nurseries to provide not only physical protection and sustenance but also psychological care and an opportunity to study the psychological needs of children, especially in extreme conditions.[14] Blankenhorn relies upon Freud and Burlingham's observations on war-time father absence—and occasional father presence—to make one argument that is central to his case for the contemporary dilemma of "fatherlessness": the argument for the existence of a particular kind of distinctive and essential fatherhood role. To this end, he cites Freud and Burlingham on the differences between the behavior of visiting fathers and mothers in the war nurseries, quoting Freud and Burlingham's observations that fathers were more "awkward" than mothers and less able to take up, however intermittently, their accustomed roles with their children. He notes the very different contexts in which children were likely to seek, and miss, solicitude from parents, as when children cried for mothers more frequently in periods of emotional distress and only occasionally for fathers, and then more in moments of physical fear.[15]

To the extent that Blankenhorn uses Freud and Burlingham's work on father absence to document his own concerns with fatherlessness he is on relatively safe ground. Freud and Burlingham do assume the sex role–differentiated parenting patterns that Blankenhorn understands as natural and desirable. Even here, however, care must be taken with Blankenhorn's normative reading of Freud and Burlingham. Much in their texts is descriptive; the authors theorize about the children's psychological needs and the effects of various kinds of provisioning and deprivation in the context of the actual family lives from which children were removed as a result of war-time bombing. Thus, for example, although Blankenhorn suggests that the children's relatively greater accommodation to father absence than mother absence is the result of natural and transhistorical differences in mothers' and fathers' relationships with children, Freud and Burlingham note this distinctive response as a function of different *actual* relationships: "Fathers are treated better in this respect. The children were always more or less used to their coming and going and not dependent on them for their primitive gratifications. Consequently, parting from them is no real shock and their memory remains more undisturbed."[16]

As is true of numerous other examples, Freud and Burlingham do not suggest that such patterns of care and emotional connection are the only way that family life can, or should, be organized. They do not, for example, argue that fathers cannot, or should not, provide the "primitive gratifications" that are more frequently associated with mothers, only that most children's fathers at the time did not and that it could reasonably be assumed that these children's fathers had not. On the other hand, Freud and Burlingham do undermine Blankenhorn's arguments in a way that he does not acknowledge. Besides commenting on the consequences of gender role–differentiated parenting in ways that Blankenhorn notes, the psychoanalysts engaged in a project of testing the boundaries of children's adaptability to institutional life. They did this by encouraging attachments to particular nurses and caregivers and to particular groups of children—by deliberately creating what they called "artificial families." Freud and Burlingham experimented with the formation of artificial families to relieve children of some of the stresses and deprivations particularly associated with institutional life. Finding that institutions were unable to provide many forms of nurturance and stimulation required for healthy development, Freud and Burlingham set out to construct small consistent groupings of nurses and children that might mimic some of the patterns of care, nurturance, and stimulation to be found in family life.

As the authors elaborate in their texts, they are surprisingly successful in their quest to use artificial families to fulfill many psychological needs of the children in their care. The psychoanalysts find that the formation of artificial families quickly precipitates "the emotional reactions of children in a natural family setting," including positive attachments, moral concern, linguistic development, and facial expressiveness, as well as the more negative—but developmentally predictable—responses of sibling rivalry, possessiveness, and anxieties about loss.[17] Even in the negative reactions to their "substitute mothers" Freud and Burlingham find reason for satisfaction, as children require not only pleasurable experiences related to attachment for their emotional growth, but also must grapple with the frustrations related to emotional attachment in order to "learn to love."[18]

Despite the fact that the artificial families constituted in the Hampstead War Nurseries are discussed at length in both *War and Children* and *Infants without Families*, Blankenhorn does not mention them. There is good reason for this omission. Blankenhorn's argument about "fatherlessness" is not merely an argument in favor of the active presence of fathers; indeed, the New Father that he criticizes at length is a father who is both overinvolved with his children and involved in the wrong ways; that is, he is a father who is more like a mother than a proper father. Blankenhorn's argument is, rather, for a particular kind of fatherhood that is twice grounded in biology. First, the tasks of fatherhood, like those of motherhood, are grounded in role differentiation based on the parent's biological sex; second, fatherhood mirrors motherhood in requiring a biological relation to a child. Despite obvious problems with this conclusion, it appears from Blankenhorn's reading of Freud and Burlingham that they empirically and normatively endorse the kind of fundamental family that Blankenhorn sets out to find in their work.

Whether domesticating male violence, predisposing men to the financial support of their offspring, or revealing the minimal natural "role" of men with regard to nurturance, biological connection to children occupies an indispensable place in Blankenhorn's account of fatherhood. Although Blankenhorn argues strenuously in support of the "natural" role of men in families, he largely assumes the biological substrate of maternity, maternal nurturance, and the mother–child bond. The indispensability of biological mothers is taken for granted at the same time that it bolsters Blankenhorn's case for a biological fatherhood that is represented by the figures of the Old Father and the Good Family Man. Unfortunately, Freud and Burlingham give little comfort to this biologistic project.

The consequence of the artificial family for a project like Blankenhorn's is not, as Freud and Burlingham might hope, reassurance for the possibilities of child provisioning in the absence of parental care. It is, rather, a threat to an ideological story about the boundaries of biologically mandated parenting roles. Blankenhorn's reading of Anna Freud is purposive and selective. More, it prefigures his appropriations of psychoanalysts who, even more than Anna Freud, represent concerns with psychological attachment and the consequences of attachments that fail.

THE POLITICAL IDEOLOGY OF ATTACHMENT

Perhaps the most predictable appropriation of psychoanalytic theory for a defense of the fundamental family is the use of John Bowlby's work on attachment. Invocations of Bowlby appear to ground Blankenhorn's concern with child care and the consequences of its absence. Bowlby remains a central theorist of attachment phenomena in children and in adults and is associated even today with influencing contemporary ideas about children's emotional needs. Bowlby defines *attachment theory* as "a way of conceptualizing the propensity of human beings to make strong affectional bonds to particular others and of explaining the many forms of emotional distress and personality disturbance, including anxiety, anger, depression, and emotional detachment, to which unwilling separation and loss give rise."[19]

Bowlby's concern with bonding and bond disruption is certainly concerned with young children, and particularly with the effects, emotional and social, of poor or interrupted bonding. However less remarked, it is also a theory of life-span development. Central to attachment theory is the principle that "neither love nor grief is felt for just *any* other human being, but only for one, or a few, particular and individual human beings. The core of what I term an 'affectional bond' is the attraction that one *individual* has for another *individual*."[20]

Bowlby emphasizes the mother–child bond in his writings on attachment. Yet, Blankenhorn calls on Bowlby for a different purpose than to reinforce the infant need for human attachment to specific caregivers— either biological mothers or less desirable others. Blankenhorn's agenda is to emphasize the very different kinds of love and attachment of which mothers and fathers are capable. Blankenhorn argues:

> A father's love is qualitatively different from a mother's love. This difference takes us to the heart of the matter. Compared to a mother's love, a father's love is frequently more expectant, more instrumental, and significantly less conditional. . . . Compared to the mother's love, the father's love must frequently be sought after, deserved, earned through achievement.[21]

Bowlby writes of the first attachment figure for infants as "the mother," "a mother-figure," "a preferred figure," and a "care-giving figure." But Blankenhorn's ideological purposes will not tolerate this lack of clarity about caregiving roles. For Blankenhorn, the sexual division of labor is both natural *and* the result of a fragile cultural "script."

Ultimately, the division of parental labor is the consequence of our biological embodiment as sexual beings and of the inherent requirements of effective parenthood.

. . . we can endeavor, however imperfectly, to incorporate men as they are into family life, in part by giving them distinctive, gendered roles that reflect, rather than reject, *inherent masculine norms*—such as, for example, the breadwinner role.[22]

In the end, what is perhaps most interesting about Blankenhorn's recourse to Bowlby's attachment theory as support for his arguments about nature and gender differentiation is not what Blankenhorn concludes about children but what he concludes about adult men. Bowlby and other attachment theorists take pains to emphasize not only the needs of children and the ways in which these needs may be thwarted to terrible effect, but also the continued attachment needs of adults. In contrast, Blankenhorn's male "nature"—like that described by other social conservatives such as George Gilder—is either unresponsive to attachment needs or destructively attached. When Blankenhorn writes that the "cultural invention" of fatherhood "guides men away from violence," he propounds a view of men as naturally connecting to others not through love, trust, or empathy (the domain of mothers, and of women more generally), but through aggression and violence. Such a depiction of men and masculinity is, in fact, more consistent with what Bowlby and other attachment theorists refer to as "disrupted attachment," an early developmental failure. Indeed, Blankenhorn also argues that violence in males is one consequence of early developmental failures (read: fatherlessness). Discussing "hypermasculinity," or "protest masculinity," Blankenhorn states that "the weight of evidence increasingly supports the conclusion that fatherlessness is a primary generator of violence among young men."[23] It is not clear which argument Blankenhorn intends to make: are men naturally prone to violence in the absence of the constraints of the fatherhood role, or do predispositions to violence result from failed families? The answers to both of these questions appear to be "yes."

John Bowlby's work on attachment usefully complicates Blankenhorn's project. But Bowlby's is not the only version of attachment theory. Blankenhorn also appears to borrow from the object relations psychoanalysis of Donald Winnicott, albeit in a more tenuous manner and without explicit attribution, in his notion of the "good-enough father." Blankenhorn may actually be unaware of the provenance of the terminology that he borrows, but it a meaningful provenance nonetheless. Blankenhorn's good-enough father, closely linked with his preferred ideal type—the Good Family Man—can easily be read through the lens of Winnicott's thought and concerns.[24]

Bowlby and Winnicott were colleagues in the British Psycho-Analytical Society and, more than that, were central figures in the "Middle Group" that represented compromise between the warring factions of child analysts Melanie Klein and Anna Freud in the British Society at midcentury. Bowlby's work of the early 1950s in attachment theory was frequently read to require the virtually constant presence of mothers with their children in the first years of children's lives. Winnicott provided an explicit corrective to this conception of attachment, writing for popular and scholarly audiences alike of "good-enough mothering" and the "good-enough mother."[25] Indeed, some scholars have suggested that Winnicott was "the great liberator" from the mothering requirements that attachment theory appeared to espouse.[26] Other scholars have noted that the stringent mothering requirements that made their appearance after WWII were in no small part ideological, requiring as they did women's presence at home at a time when men were returning home after the war to reclaim jobs from women. As one of Winnicott's biographers sums up this trend, "In British psychoanalysis after the war there was not so much a return to Freud . . . as a return to Mother."[27]

Winnicott's conception of the good-enough mother (which he sometimes refers to as a broader phenomenon—the "facilitating environment") is one of his most lasting contributions to psychoanalysis and family thought.[28] Like Blankenhorn, Winnicott was concerned with child development and neglect as well as with larger social issues, such as juvenile delinquency, that he believed could be linked to emotional deprivation and the pathology of primary caregivers. Winnicott's elucidation of the good-enough mother served multiple purposes. One of these was to soothe women's concerns about their knowledge and fitness for child care even at the same time that he gave remarkably detailed instructions about the emotional and physiological processes that accompanied early childhood development. A large measure of Winnicott's success as an early childhood expert was due the fact that he could simultaneously reassure mothers that they were "naturally" able to do what was required for their baby's emotional health and explain to them what they needed to do to achieve desirable outcomes. Passages such as the following, addressed directly to mothers, illustrate these dual purposes at work: "This is so simple that I think it will appeal to you as a natural sequence, and therefore a good basis for the study of the way you hold your infant. This is all very obvious, but the trouble is that if you do not know these things you may easily let your immense skill get wasted."[29] Although it relies upon commonly held assumptions of the natural mothering processes of women, the pedagogical function of the work of postwar child experts cannot be underestimated.

Yet another purpose for the detailed elucidation of the contours of good-enough mothering was to establish the particular childhood emotional needs that were to be met by mothering and the consequences of failures to meet these needs. Central among the tasks of the good-enough mother were "holding" (or "containing") infantile feelings, negotiating the child's needs for illusion and disillusionment (also known as creating "transitional space"), and avoiding emotional intrusiveness toward the child that might result in the child's creation of a "false self."[30] Without investigating these tasks in detail, it is sufficient to note that, notwithstanding his soothing responses to actual mothers, Winnicott understood them to require significant emotional labor and emotional health on the part of the caregiver. A mother need not understand or be able to articulate her processes as she undertook them, but neither were they the simple consequences of either female role requirements or, as Blankenhorn suggests, female embodiment.

As a result, the shift from "good-enough mother" to Blankenhorn's "good-enough father" is not a simple move from one set of natural attributes and processes to another set that complements the first. Neither did Winnicott mean to exempt fathers from the emotional tasks associated with the construction of the child's self. Instead, he acknowledges the importance of mothers' more significant presence in the lives of most children. When Winnicott points out that due to childbirth and breast feeding fathers will necessarily "come a little later," he nonetheless points out with regard to good-enough mothering that "this includes fathers, but fathers must allow me to use the term maternal to describe the total attitude toward babies and their care."[31]

In fact, with regard to the actual study of childhood emotional needs Winnicott gives virtually no support to the gender role differentiation demanded by Blankenhorn, either by validating the idea that early childhood needs are "naturally" provided by mothers or by validating Blankenhorn's insistence that fathers cannot and should not engage in these early forms of provisioning. With regard to the psychoanalytic theorists of attachment, Blankenhorn's readings are political ideology, not child development science.

Having constructed the idea of the good-enough father and the ideal types of the Old Father and the Good Family Man, Blankenhorn positions contemporary feminists in opposition to them. For example, Blankenhorn situates Jessica Benjamin's analysis of failures of mutual recognition in childhood psychodynamics and adult relationships as a specific "assault" on the Old Father. Blankenhorn's Old Father, the father of the 1950s, is his favored representative of paternal authority, an authority that Blankenhorn represents throughout as natural and benign, if fragile and embattled. "[Jessica] Benjamin's and [Judith] Lorber's essentialist, feminist critique of paternity represents our cultural script's most radical assault against the Old Father. At the same time, the animating core of this critique—deep suspicion of paternal authority—is widespread and spreading in our society, especially within elite culture."[32]

Although Blankenhorn acknowledges that "much of [this feminist critique] is accurate," he avers that such critique advances a dangerous agenda. While the Old Father is not perfect, those who criticize him are encouraging hostility to fatherhood as an institution and to "the idea of paternal authority."[33] Not surprisingly, the Old Father is racially unmarked, so Blankenhorn is not moved to confront the ways in which white paternal authority in the 1950s was implicated in a range of racist— as well as sexist—customs, institutions, and sociopolitical arrangements.

CONCLUSION

As much as it decries "fatherlessness," *Fatherless America* expresses anxieties about the loss of a "natural" and benign masculine authority. For Blankenhorn, feminists and others who find fault with the ideal of the fundamental family are guilty of undermining social order by attempting to replace traditional fatherhood with other forms of fatherhood. Unfortunately, this argumentative strategy does not just exclude contemporary, revisionist, and/or speculative psychoanalytic contributions to debates about families. The strategy also flattens, simplifies, and sometimes utterly misrepresents the contributions of those whose orthodoxy is read in selective and one-dimensional terms. More important for the role of evidence in political debates, such a strategy establishes respected theorists of the past as unambiguous and unambivalent allies in important contemporary social and political debates.

In the end, psychoanalysis is often not easily co-opted for the ideological project at hand. Even when the project is one that purports to demonstrate natural forms of familial relations and unimpeachable tenets of child well-being, it is nonetheless true that the rich text of psychoanalysis can be "either friend or foe, depending on its alliances."[34] Returning to a psychoanalysis that predates contemporary feminist challenges and scholarship does not alter this theoretical dilemma. As many critics of psychoanalysis know, even orthodox, nonfeminist versions of psychoanalysis both assume and challenge traditional forms of authority.

NOTES

I am grateful to Laree Martin and Jyl J. Josephson for their comments on drafts of this chapter. An early version of this chapter was delivered at the annual meeting of the Association for the Psychoanalysis of Culture and Society in Atlanta, Georgia, in November 1998.

1. Jean Bethke Elshtain, *Real Politics: At the Center of Everyday Life* (Baltimore: Johns Hopkins University Press, 1997), 196.
2. See, for example, Susan Moller Okin, *Justice, Gender, and the Family* (New York: Basic, 1989); Jyl J. Josephson, "Liberal Justice and the Political Economy of Children's Well-being," *New Political Science* 23, no. 3 (2001): 389–406; Valerie Lehr, *Queer Family Values: Debunking the Myth of the Nuclear Family* (Philadelphia: Temple University Press, 1999).
3. Elshtain, *Real Politics,* 166.
4. David Blankenhorn, *Fatherless America: Confronting Our Most Urgent Social Problem* (New York: Basic, 1995). Blankenhorn is a writer and lecturer, as well as the founder and president of the Institute for American Values, a think tank devoted to research and education on family issues.
5. Blankenhorn, *Fatherless America,* 90–92; Elshtain, *Real Politics,* 229–48.
6. George Gilder, *Men and Marriage* (Gretna, La.: Pelican, 1992).
7. David Blankenhorn, "Fatherhood Uprooted: A Sociologist Looks at Fatherlessness and Its Causes," *Institute for American Values* 2001, at www.american values.org/html/touchstone.shtml (accessed February 25, 2002).
8. Blankenhorn, *Fatherless America,* 65.
9. As Blankenhorn puts it, "The ideal of paternal breadwinning encultures male aggression by directing it toward a prosocial purpose." Blankenhorn, *Fatherless America,* 116.
10. Blankenhorn, *Fatherless America,* 4.
11. See Sara Diamond, *Not by Politics Alone: The Enduring Influence of the Christian Right* (New York: Guilford, 1998); Susan Friend Harding, *The Book of Jerry Falwell: Fundamentalist Language and Politics* (Princeton, N.J.: Princeton University Press, 2000).
12. Jyl J. Josephson and Cynthia Burack, "The Political Ideology of the Neo-Traditional Family," *Political Ideologies* 3, no. 2 (1998): 213–31.
13. Anna Freud and Dorothy Burlingham, *War and Children* (Westport, Conn.: Greenwood, 1943); Anna Freud and Dorothy Burlingham, *Infants without Families: The Case For and Against Residential Nurseries* (New York: International University Press, 1944).
14. Freud and Burlingham, *War and Children,* 12–13.
15. Blankenhorn, *Fatherless America,* 55.
16. Freud and Burlingham, *War and Children,* 54.
17. Freud and Burlingham, *Infants without Families,* 53–64.
18. Freud and Burlingham, *Infants without Families,* 61.

19. John Bowlby, *The Making and Breaking of Affectional Bonds* (London: Tavistock, 1979), 127.

20. Bowlby, *Making and Breaking*, 67, emphases in the original.

21. Blankenhorn, *Fatherless America*, 219. The phrase "less conditional" in the previous sentence should read "more conditional," as this would be consistent with the meaning of what follows.

22. Blankenhorn, *Fatherless America*, 122, 117, emphasis added.

23. Blankenhorn, *Fatherless America*, 31.

24. For other appropriations of Winnicott see, for example, the popular work of R. D. Laing (R. D. Laing, *The Divided Self* [London: Penguin,1969]). The concept of "good enough" has also been borrowed from Winnicott to describe the ministrations of the "good enough parent" (Bruno Bettelheim, *A Good Enough Parent: A Book on Child-Rearing* [New York: Knopf, 1987]), the "good enough therapist" (Michael Eigen, *The Electrified Tightrope* [Northvale, N.J.: Jason Aronson, 1993]), and the adoption of the "good enough enemy" (Howard Stein, *Developmental Lives, Cultural Space* [Norman: University of Oklahoma Press, 1987]).

25. Donald Woods Winnicott, *Playing and Reality* (London: Tavistock, 1971).

26. Jeremy Holmes, "Attachment Theory: A Secure Base for Policy?" in *The Politics of Attachment: Towards a Secure Society*, ed. Sebastian Kramer and Jane Roberts (London: Free Association Books, 1996), 27–42.

27. Adam Phillips, *Winnicott* (Cambridge, Mass.: Harvard University Press, 1988), 10.

28. For discussion of the facilitating environment, see Donald Woods Winnicott, *The Maturational Processes and the Facilitating Environment* (New York: International Universities Press, 1965).

29. Donald Woods Winnicott, *Babies and Their Mothers* (Reading, Mass: Addison-Wesley, 1987), 19.

30. Winnicott, *Maturational Processes*; Winnicott, *Playing and Reality*.

31. Winnicott, *Playing and Reality*, 141.

32. Blankenhorn, *Fatherless America*, 92.

33. Blankenhorn, *Fatherless America*, 93.

34. Mari Jo Buhle, *Feminism and Its Discontents: A Century of Struggle with Psychoanalysis* (Cambridge, Mass.: Harvard University Press, 1998), 338.

5

A Liberal Dose of Conservatism: The "New Consensus" on Welfare and Other Strange Synergies

Jenrose Fitzgerald

In 1996, the Personal Responsibility and Work Opportunity Reconciliation Act (PRWORA) significantly restructured redistributive welfare programs in the United States. Those who oppose this legislation often point to it as a prime example of Republican-drafted conservative social policy. However, when analyzed in the context of the legislative history of the PRWORA, distinctions between "liberals" and "conservatives" are not so easily drawn. A good deal of the policy research supporting the "end of welfare" over the last two decades has been decidedly conservative—  usually marked by libertarian or paternalistic sentiments. However, in the 1980s and 1990s, a "new consensus" was forged between liberals and conservatives: that welfare is primarily a problem of dependency and family breakdown *rather than* of systemic inequality or structural economic change. Despite its conservative associations, this line of thinking—in one form or another—has come to dominate welfare thinking across the political spectrum.

How has such a synergy been achieved? It can be attributed in large part to the particular ways welfare policy research has evolved over the last thirty years. During this period, poverty researchers have steadily shifted focus away from structural problems of unemployment, low wages, discrimination, and economic restructuring toward the measurement and evaluation of so-called social indicators such as dependency, out-of-wedlock birth rates, or family dysfunction. Even though some may make the argument that structural economic shifts and an unequal distribution of opportunity *impact* trends in family structure, work, education, and welfare taking, the basic unit of analysis is nevertheless the work and family "behavior" of the welfare population. Indeed, a fundamental flaw in both conservative and liberal strategies for reforming welfare can be found in the methodological constraints of policy researchers on the topic—social scientists who, in one way or another, measure and evaluate the behavior of low-income citizens. Thus, even when structural factors are taken into account, they are incorporated into a behavioral research paradigm that is incapable of seriously engaging them.

In *Words of Welfare*, Sanford Schram notes that this trend is not entirely new to the 1990s:

> From the income maintenance experiments of the 1960s to the workfare demonstrations of the 1990s—that is, from liberal-minded experiments about a guaranteed income to conservative-minded programs requiring work for benefits—welfare policy research has been implicated in a pernicious but pervasive logic: the poverty of poor people is a mysterious thing, attributable in good part to their individual behavior, worthy of being medicalized in terms of experimental interventions that are designed to test the viability of various schemes for changing their behavior.[1]

However, in the last two decades this behavioral focus has taken new forms, and the structural elements that *were* once partially integrated into poverty research have now fallen out of the discourse of welfare. Based on examination of congressional hearings on welfare reform in the 1980s and 1990s, I show how the emergent categories of dependency and family breakdown transformed welfare policy debates and further entrenched behavioral models of poverty research.[2] I then show how this research paradigm has contributed to the scapegoating of low-income women (particularly single mothers) for all of the problems associated with postindustrial poverty. My goal is not to deconstruct or refute specific findings or claims by specific policy researchers; there has by now emerged an excellent body of social science literature to this end. Instead, I consider the overall impact of behavioral research models and framings on welfare policy *debates*. Even when researchers are doing their jobs very responsibly, the constraints of the objectivist and individualizing behavioral research paradigms within which they operate often allow their work to be co-opted and used to rationalize grossly irresponsible policies.[3]

Furthermore, I consider the role liberals have played in this transformation, despite the association of recent welfare reform efforts with right-wing Republican "social conservatism." I pay particular attention to the legacy of Daniel Patrick Moynihan and other Democrats who moved the "liberal" line on poverty analysis considerably toward the right, even as they fought against what they claimed was a "conservative assault" on necessary social programs in the 1980s and 1990s. The move to a behavioral model of reform represents both a misguided methodological approach *and* a failed political strategy that has backfired dramatically, leaving those who did wish to challenge punitive and draconian welfare policies unable to do so effectively. Indeed, rather than helping welfare recipients move above the poverty level in the long run, the reforms of the 1990s have obliterated the safety net while simultaneously blaming poor, single mothers for every imaginable societal ill. Ultimately, in order for the problems of "postindustrial poverty" to be addressed, policy researchers and reformers must shift their focus from the so-called behaviors of dependency and illegitimacy to the more tangible and concrete problems of poverty, economic stratification, and structural economic change. In the process, I hope to muddy any tidy assumptions readers might have of the boundaries of what counts as "social conservatism"— not because such boundaries are not useful, but because they are complex and hence must be continually remapped and redrawn.

BEYOND VILLAINS AND HEROES: THE MOYNIHAN LEGACY

In 1965, Daniel Patrick Moynihan wrote a controversial report on poverty called *The Negro Family: The Case for National Action*. This report has received so much attention that it is referred to simply as "the Moynihan report" by policymakers, historians, feminist scholars, and others. The controversy surrounding the report was by all counts predictable— Moynihan broke with popular wisdom when he suggested that "Negro poverty" was no longer primarily a problem of male unemployment, but was linked to a "matriarchal" family structure that he called a "tangle of pathology." This argument angered many because it appeared to blame poor black families for their own poverty. President Lyndon Johnson's administration distanced itself from this report as a result of the controversy and quietly went about the business of waging the War on Poverty, while Moynihan took considerable heat for his research and his framing of the problem.

In 1987, twenty-two years after Moynihan's report had been rejected as racist, a curious thing happened. In the intervening years, welfare rolls had grown, economic inequality had intensified, and poverty had made its way onto the national agenda once again. Senator Moynihan held a series of welfare reform hearings, which culminated in the Family Support Act of 1988 (FSA)—the first major national welfare reform since the

War on Poverty. But this time Moynihan was not viewed as the villain; instead, he emerged as a hero.[4] Over and over, those who testified prefaced their remarks by praising Moynihan's efforts and declaring him vindicated. This sentiment was neatly summed up by Sander Levin (D-MI) in a 1987 hearing: "For many years, you were a voice in the wilderness, and now there is a rather large chorus . . . the numbers have grown. And I think it is interesting to ask why."[5]

It is particularly interesting to ask why this "rather large chorus" included so many self-identified liberals, given the neoconservative nature of Moynihan's thesis. By the late 1980s, "family breakdown" and "welfare dependency" were the primary issues being addressed by policymakers and poverty researchers, and Moynihan's leadership and research were absolutely central to this shift.[6] The "new consensus" of the 1980s was that poverty was not caused by male unemployment, low wages, or minority disenfranchisement but by changing patterns of family and work behavior. There were some partisan differences, of course. Conservatives insisted that recipients must become self-sufficient through mandatory work, while liberals stressed that work requirements were only viable if a range of supportive services were in place that could enable people to transition into jobs.[7] Conservatives wanted to restrict eligibility for unmarried mothers, while liberals wanted to discourage out-of-wedlock births by expanding the opportunities available to young women. Indeed, the hearings of 1987–1988 show that despite the talk of a new consensus, liberals and conservatives disagreed with each other as much as they agreed. But both Democrats and Republicans took Moynihan's most basic theses about dependency and family breakdown as their points of departure. They ultimately passed the FSA in 1988, which increased work requirements for recipients, expanded transitional services (including child care and education and training programs), and established tougher child support enforcement—all of which were supposed to strengthen families and reduce dependency.

The FSA was the result of a consensus that Moynihan had been right about the relationship between family breakdown and welfare dependency. Given this narrative, and Moynihan's reputation as a neoconservative Democrat, one might expect that he would be thrilled that these categories of analysis carried over into reform efforts leading up to the PRWORA of 1996. In welfare hearings in the mid-1990s, however, another curious thing happened. Moynihan started to express frustration, even outrage, at the direction welfare reform was taking. He found much of the PRWORA both punitive and in conflict with the spirit of the FSA—legislation he still supports. And Moynihan was not alone: Mary Jo Bane and David Ellwood, the top policy researchers on welfare under the Clinton administration, were also outraged at how their research had been appropriated. Indeed, several researchers under the Clinton administration resigned over the PRWORA. Apparently, different players meant very different things by "ending dependency" through "strengthening families." What exactly did the "new consensus" of the 1980s entail? And if there was a consensus, why are Moynihan and others scratching their heads and denouncing legislation their research has been so influential in defining? I take this conundrum as my point of departure into what turns out to be a much more complicated story than I once imagined. Ultimately, Moynihan emerges not as a hero, but not as the unidimensional neoconservative villain that has been characterized in so many accounts either. Instead, he emerges as a highly troubling figure for those who wish to draw sharp distinctions between liberal and conservative positions on welfare.

FROM "TANGLE OF PATHOLOGY" TO "FAMILY BREAKDOWN"

Moynihan's 1965 "tangle of pathology" thesis was not only racially charged, but highly gendered as well. He argued that a decline in unemployment among nonwhite men emerged alongside an increase in welfare taking among nonwhite families, suggesting that unemployment was no longer the primary cause of poverty. Instead, he said, the problem seemed to be correlated with family structure. Thus, he wrote: "In essence, the Negro family has been forced into a matriarchal structure which, because it is so out of line with the rest of American society, seriously retards the progress of the group as a whole, and imposes a crushing burden on the Negro male and, as a consequence, on a great many Negro women as well."[8]

Given this diagnosis, his solution was to remove barriers to the assimilation of black families to a more patriarchal structure and to the family wage system in which men were primary breadwinners and women were primary caretakers of children. Although this model of family life didn't fit the reality of most families even in the 1960s, it was nevertheless the dominant vision and model of the ideal nuclear family.

Moynihan did not blame the problems of black families entirely on "behavior" in his 1965 report. These problems were seen as effects of larger systemic realities, from the legacy of slavery to changing labor markets to migration patterns related to a changing economy. He also pointed to racial discrimination and consequent un- or underemployment as contributing

factors to the emasculation of black men and the putative decline of the "Negro family." Furthermore, he argued that the wages available to low-skilled men were often inadequate for supporting families, and that this was a serious barrier to those who were trying to break out of cycles of "dependency" by reinstating the family wage system. Consider: "Because the father is either not present, is unemployed, or makes such a low wage, the Negro woman goes to work. . . . This dependence on the mother's income undermines the position of the father and deprives the children of the kind of attention, particularly in school matters, which is now a standard feature of middle-class upbringing."[9]

In short, Moynihan did acknowledge that the family wage system itself *might* be flawed given the wage structure—this "middle-class" ideal wouldn't necessarily be realizable for all families, even for those who *did* wish to embrace it. However, this nod did not stop him from concluding that, in general, the best strategy for dealing with "Negro poverty" was to focus *not* primarily on problems of unemployment or economic structure, but on the family.

By the 1980s, this family discourse had changed dramatically. As more women (including mothers) entered the workforce, the expectation that both parents would work outside the home became commonplace. Furthermore, it was clear that many of the families on AFDC were single-parent families. This reality challenged the basic premise of the family wage system on which the welfare system was built. This premise had led to the exemption of primary caretakers of children from work requirements, for example, on the basis that their role was to raise and socialize their children rather than to be breadwinners. But by the 1980s, Moynihan and others had declared an "earthquake" in family structure, indicating that the welfare requirements regarding work and family "behavior" had to change as well. Recipients previously exempted from work requirements (such as single mothers) had to be redefined as employable. In a 1983 hearing, Judith Gueron (vice president of the Manpower Demonstration Research Corporation) argued that public opinion on welfare mothers' exemption had shifted due to an increase in Aid to Families with Dependent Children (AFDC) rolls coupled with the increase in nonwelfare mothers who had entered the labor force. "Persistent questions arose," according to Gueron, "as to why some individuals, including mothers of school-aged and preschool children, should work and pay taxes while others *didn't have to contribute to their support*."[10] Women raising children alone, in other words, were no longer seen as contributing anything if they weren't working outside the home as well as acting as primary caretakers.

Women were not the only targets of reform. Child support enforcement also became a centerpiece of the reform efforts of the 1980s, largely in response to the increase in divorce rates over the 1970s and 1980s. This was often used to make the case that welfare policy would be more "equalizing," such that absent fathers would have to bear as much of the burden of caring for their families as present mothers.[11] Although child support enforcement was framed in the 1987–1988 hearings as an attempt to ease financial burdens on mothers, however, the actual goal was to reduce the government's burden of providing for children and return this burden to families. Income from work and child support enforcement was introduced not as a means for increasing the income of custodial parents, but as a way of extracting that income from custodial parents and absent fathers *rather than* from government budgets. In a 1987 hearing,[12] Professor Irwin Garfinkel explained: "The route to both greater independence and greater economic well-being for poor single mothers is the *replacement* of income from welfare with income from earnings and child support."[13] In other words, in the face of the breakdown of the family wage system, policymakers simply revised that system to include virtual families. In the process, poor single mothers' dependence on welfare was pathologized while their dependence on men (present or absent, real or imagined) was introduced as cure.[14]

Underlying all of these analyses was a version of Moynihan's thesis about "Negro poverty"—but with a significant revision. Instead of "race" or "culture," or even "gender," the rubrics that came to dominate welfare debates were the seemingly more neutral rubrics of "children" and "families." Moynihan had argued (and now, he thought, confirmed) that while industrial poverty might have been caused primarily by racial discrimination, blocked opportunities, and unemployment, changing child-rearing norms and "family breakdown" were at the heart of the *new* poverty. If families could just take "personal responsibility" for themselves and their children, so the story went, means-tested antipoverty programs should only be necessary in rare and extreme circumstances. Such a thesis was far less controversial when put in the terms of "family" and "child dependency" than it had been when framed in more overtly racialized or even gendered terms. In the process, unfortunately, the few "structural" elements of Moynihan's previous theories about poverty—which had initially included *some* critique of racial inequality, low wages, and of the devaluation of women's child-rearing activities—had fallen away. Now the problem fell squarely in the realm of "behavior" and, as such, would result in legislation aimed at changing behavior more than at alleviating poverty.

Of course, not all attempts to change work and family "behaviors" are created equal. While I am emphasizing the considerable overlap between liberal and conservative researchers here, it is important to reiterate that not all of these players were up to the same thing—even when they were using the same language, methods, and categories of analysis. The FSA, for example, for all of its limitations, was far more committed to providing services to low-income families than is the 1996 legislation. Most importantly, it was committed to providing education and training, as well as services such as child care, that might help low-income women eventually secure jobs above the minimum wage. Furthermore, the FSA favored incentives over punishment, while the PRWORA is more directly punitive. Indeed, these are among the reasons why Moynihan and others so vehemently oppose the PRWORA—and why they believe it will fail. However, they contributed to and further entrenched a behavioral diagnosis of poverty, even as they sought to protect transitional services and minimize punitive or draconian measures.

In what follows, I consider two hearings from the 1990s that demonstrate the failure of this strategy. The first focuses on creating better "indicators of dependency" to measure the effects of the FSA and to better understand what Moynihan calls "post-industrial poverty." The second focuses on the relationship between welfare and out-of-wedlock births. In each case, we can see how those who were attempting to include a structural diagnosis of the conditions that lead to increased poverty and reliance on means-tested programs were overridden by others who wished to severely cut these programs and who blamed single mothers for every societal ill. These debates demonstrate that the behavioral paradigm was so entrenched by the 1990s that it became almost impossible to make the argument that individuals should not be blamed for their own poverty. They further show how objectivist policy research can get co-opted in the process of policy debates and put in the service of those controlling the process—regardless of whether their views or policy proposals match the empirical findings of the research used to justify them.

DIAGNOSTICS OF DEPENDENCY

In the early 1990s, as a new series of hearings was held to evaluate the results of the Family Support Act, debates over how this reform should proceed intensified. On February 27, 1991, Senator Moynihan announced in a press release that two hearings would be held the following week to discuss the problem of *welfare dependency*. Moynihan stressed: "These hearings will help us develop a set of indicators that will tell us whether we are succeeding, whether child poverty is going up or down, whether welfare dependency is increasing or decreasing." He went on to argue that while they had successfully developed measures for *industrial* society, these measures were no longer applicable to the *postindustrial* age. This was the purpose of the hearing—to come up with a new set of indicators for postindustrial poverty.[15]

Those who discussed these measures framed them in a progressive, nonpunitive light. Martin Gerry, assistant secretary of planning and evaluation for the U.S. Department of Health and Human Services, stressed the importance of the development of new *social indicators for dependency* in an effort to counteract the ostensibly conservative assault on welfare:

> A clear policy link would be established between the status of today's children and the social and economic independence or dependence of tomorrow's families. Such a link would assist greatly in rejecting the disempowering notions, both of pathologizing the poor and routinely professionalizing the solutions to the problems of the poor which have dominated much of the social policy discussions of the last two decades.[16]

Gerry did not frame himself or other well-meaning researchers as integral players in pathologizing or professionalizing efforts, but rather as oppositional dissenters. He expressed frustration over the "variety of university and think-tank based pundits" who had offered "rationales to justify the failure . . . of Government programs to end welfare dependency among children." Indeed, he argued that "all of them . . . can be described in one way or the other as pathologizing children."[17] Significantly, both Gerry and Moynihan supported the development of social indicators at least in part because they wanted to draw attention to the negative effects of inadequate social policy on poverty rates; while others were making the case that "recipients can do better," they attempted to argue that policymakers could and should do better to serve the poor and "end dependency." The indicators project was an attempt to measure and record these trends.[18]

So, what did Moynihan et al. expect these numbers to accomplish? And how were they any different from the "university and think tank pundits" with their "disempowering notions"? Most puzzling of all, how could they possibly have imagined themselves as dissenters in an otherwise pathologizing, politically biased, *conservative* attack on the poor? These 1991 hearings suggest that liberals were indeed attempting on some level to counter interpretations and data sets that blamed all social problems on welfare or on the poor rather than on the inability of social policy to solve the problem of postindustrial poverty. The development of "indicators of dependency" was at least in part an attempt to counter the views of extremists on the right. However, the framing of these measures as "indicators of dependency" reinforced the notion that dependency was more of a problem than poverty or economic structure. The framing and "reading" of these data, as well as the categories of analysis employed (what is being measured, for example), have a significant impact on policy debates.

The extent to which these indicators framed welfare as a behavioral issue is illustrated in the testimony of William Gorham, then president of the Urban Institute in Washington, D.C., Gorham claimed that basic social science research could provide the same kind of predictive and preventive knowledge base for social problems that basic biomedical research provided for understanding and preventing disease. In his testimony, he told the story of Jim Shannon, a great success story for biomedical science: "We have to talk about building a better establishment of behavioral scientists. . . . Jim Shannon created a bio-medical miracle in the period when I was in government. . . . He did so by persuading the Congress that there was a link between basic bio-medical research and disease prevention and cure. Jim Shannon built a science."

Gorham went on to suggest that the social sciences had not enjoyed this type of support, because they had not yet persuaded Congress that they could provide the information necessary for the prevention and cure of problems associated with poverty:

> I just do want to underline that cellular biology has been the great science story of the past 25 years—cellular biology and genetics. And it is not impossible to conceive that the next leap forward is going to be in *behavioral understanding*. Much of the equipment to do it is in place now. What remains is for the Jim Shannon of human behavior to step forward and say it can be done and ask that it be done.[19]

Gorham's medical analogy underscores the pathologizing nature of the behavioral approach to welfare policy research. This analytical bias constrains policy researchers—liberal and conservative—and works to significantly limit the range of debates about the causes of and cures for poverty. These behavioral framings do not interrogate the decline in jobs paying a living wage, the rapid increase in part-time and temporary employment, a declining and grossly underfunded public education system, the mismatch between available jobs and the skills of the unemployed, or other factors that could contextualize the disparities that structure inequality. Indeed, it is a bit peculiar that, while the primary policy researchers on welfare since the 1960s have been economists, the thing they are most incapable of analyzing is the impact of a changing economy on all "working families"—and especially within low-income communities.

Recall that the opening remarks for this 1991 hearing call for postindustrial poverty measures because industrial measures no longer work to explain trends in welfare taking. The statement's underlying assumption about the "postindustrial" condition is that unemployment, low wages, or other structural barriers are no longer central causes of poverty. Indeed, Moynihan had argued numerous times that if unemployment was the central problem of the industrial era, "dependency" was becoming the defining feature of the postindustrial era. Whatever Moynihan understood by "dependency," the rhetorical move was a devastating one—it played right into the hands of Newt Gingrich and others who wanted to end entitlement programs altogether. What such framings consistently and systematically ignored, furthermore, was the growing literature by left and liberal economists and feminists insisting that the postindustrial economy creates considerable structural barriers for low-skilled workers. The jobs that pay a "family wage" do not exist for single mothers and other primary caretakers who are expected to simultaneously raise their children, attend school training programs, and work for wages to support their families.[20] These considerations were integrated into the "indicators of dependency" project only to the extent that employment and wage levels were measured for people at different skill and education levels. However, the framing of these measures in terms of postindustrial dependency trends and behaviors undermines any effort to read them as possible evidence of fundamentally flawed strategies for economic restructuring, or of the family wage system. This strategy for framing postindustrial poverty easily lent itself to the view that the central cause of postindustrial economy was the irresponsible work and reproductive "behaviors" of single mothers.

ILLEGITIMACY AND SOCIAL SCIENCE

The first "finding of the Congress" framing the PRWORA reads: "Marriage is the foundation of a successful society."[21] The remaining "findings" associate low test scores, intergenerational poverty, crime rates among youth, drug and alcohol abuse, and a host of other "social problems" with "illegitimacy" rates. The final finding suggests that, due to these correlations, the reduction of illegitimacy rates should be a primary goal of welfare legislation. While many liberals and conservatives alike agreed on such a goal, however, the punitive means by which it was pursued in this legislation revealed a decidedly conservative, paternalistic stamp. This was not quite what Gerry, Moynihan, and Gorham had in mind when they argued for the creation of "indicators of dependency."

The most heated debate about the relationship between welfare and out-of-wedlock births occurred at a 1994 hearing chaired by Harold Ford. The question at hand was: does the availability or size of welfare benefits encourage illegitimacy? The majority of experts who testified answered with a resounding "no." They insisted that poverty, not welfare, was the root of the problem—and they had numbers to prove it. The first economist to testify at this hearing was Greg Duncan, professor of economics from the University of Michigan. Duncan argued:

> The weight of scientific evidence does not suggest that reducing or eliminating benefits for teen mothers would have a substantial impact on the number of out-of-wedlock births, especially among blacks. On the other hand, research does suggest that reductions in the family incomes of children have a detrimental impact on the cognitive development and academic attainment of children.[22]

Duncan went on to say that *heightened poverty* caused by reductions in benefit levels for AFDC, food stamps, and Medicaid could account for the rise in out-of-wedlock births, especially among teens. To further support his claim, he cited the following statement signed by sixty-seven prominent researchers: "The best social science research suggests that welfare programs are not among the primary reasons for the rising number of out-of-wedlock births. . . . We strongly urge the rejection of any proposal that would eliminate the safety net for poor children born outside of marriage. Such policies would do more harm than good."[23] This view was later corroborated by Robert Greenstein, executive director of the Center on Budget and Policy Priorities.[24]

Charles Murray, the next economist to testify, offered a very different interpretation of the same data. First, he argued that the correlation between welfare and illegitimacy was understated by Duncan. Murray admitted that some studies showed a stronger correlation than others; however, he argued that this was due to the fact that the studies measured results in relation to, at most, a 10 percent reduction in welfare benefits. In his view, all this showed was that "very little can be expected of a 10-percent change in welfare benefits. It also implies that a 100-percent change in welfare benefits would have a very large effect."[25] It is a cruel irony that Murray was able to twist the findings of these researchers to suggest that rather than increasing benefits to improve conditions for single mothers, the best solution would be to cut them off entirely. However, this line of argument was not surprising coming from a libertarian neoclassical economist whose research claims are guided by the assumption that the behavioral decisions of individuals are primarily a simple result of rational economic calculus. Murray's *Losing Ground,* published at the height of Reagan's presidential career, is used by conservatives to argue that welfare and other social programs only intensify social problems. Despite the fact that Murray's argument is dismissed by most social scientists, he has not altered his view. Indeed, in a tenth-anniversary edition of *Losing Ground* (printed in 1994), Murray said he would change nothing about his book because, to his mind, his findings had only been proven *right* in the interim.[26] Similarly, in this hearing, Murray suggested that liberal biases clouded the truths in the data: "Greg [Duncan] is sitting over there listening to me, and he is thinking about going back to his computers when he gets back to Michigan and running the numbers, he can find out. There is progress to be made on this. I am afraid we are more obfuscating it than clarifying it here this morning."[27]

What do debates over illegitimacy reveal about the efficacy of policy science in the arena of welfare reform? First, it is clear that there was much disagreement over the interpretation of data. Second, despite the fact that Duncan had the weight of sixty-seven respected researchers behind his claim that poverty, not welfare, was the problem to be addressed, this research was easily appropriated to make the opposite argument. Third, by restricting debates to arguments over who had the least-biased data on welfare and illegitimacy, researchers and policymakers left unchallenged the necessarily political and value-laden character of the dominant analytical frame—that is, the focus on individual responses to a limited set of "incentives." As Michael Katz points out, the poverty research economists rarely "examine[d] their assumptions about the role of market incentives on human behavior or the limits of market models as the basis for public social obligations. In the process, they either ignored or belittled the few alternative frames proposed."[28] Even when alternative interpretations were proposed, debate was limited by these methodological biases. The outrage and frustration of Moynihan et al. at the direction reform was taking rested on the denial of their own participation in a discursive system that blamed poverty on the poor. As Schram points out, "Research findings on such topics are presented in the language of objective social science, leaving them open to appropriation by interpreters who use them for various political ends."[29]

CONCLUSION

Debates staged between "liberals" and "conservatives," Democrats and Republicans, gained so much attention throughout the political process of staging the successes and failures of welfare reform that a significant fact has been too often overlooked: neither side offered a coherent structural critique of poverty. It is tempting to see the "end of welfare as we know it" as a conservative assault on necessary liberal social programs, a Republican policy resulting from a Republican-controlled Congress. Indeed, many liberals made this argument in expressing dissatisfaction with the direction of reform in the 1990s. However, the behavioral focus of both liberal and conservative reformers contributed to this outcome. For women raising children alone, this logic is especially pernicious, as their "behavior" is cited as the *cause* of a host of problems that are systemic and beyond their individual control. Yet, neither the conservative nor the liberal approach has attempted in a concerted way to support single mothers; rather, both worked to coerce those mothers to adapt to the demands of a changing economy that has little to offer them in return. As Nancy Fraser has pointed out, "In effect, [such approaches] decree simultaneously that these women must be and yet cannot be normative mothers."[30]

This turn of events, in which it is increasingly difficult to distinguish between liberals and conservatives on the issue of welfare reform, seems to confirm Fraser's diagnosis that a neoliberal political imaginary has emerged that supports a vision of justice-as-formal-equality that leaves low-income families behind. Toward the beginning of Clinton's tenure, Fraser wrote: "The most chilling prospect of all is the possible cooptation of significant elements of progressive social movements in such a post-Fordist, neoliberal hegemony."[31] However much the Clinton administration differed from the Reagan and both Bush administrations on other policy matters, its approach to welfare reform suffered from many of the same fundamental methodological flaws as those of its conservative counterparts. Systemic disparities that structure inequality in the current economic and political climate have been ignored or underplayed for too long by both political parties. Until researchers and policymakers shift their focus from trends in recipients' reproductive and work "behavior" to an analysis that can account for larger societal disparities in the distribution of income and opportunity—that is, until a coherent structural analysis of poverty and *systemic* inequality replaces the narrow behavioral analysis of "dependency"—the real roots of postindustrial poverty will not be addressed.

NOTES

1. Sanford Schram, *Words of Welfare: The Poverty of Social Science and the Social Science of Poverty* (Minneapolis: University of Minnesota Press, 1995), 6.

2. For a close examination of the 1987–1988 hearings, see Nancy Naples, "The 'New Consensus' on the Gendered 'Social Contract': The 1987–1988 U.S. Congressional Hearings in Welfare Reform," *Signs* 22, no. 4 (1997): 907–45.

3. See Schram, *Words of Welfare.*

4. In his own account in *Miles to Go,* Moynihan said: "The findings were denounced, rejected, seen as refuted. A period of calm followed—say a quarter of a century. Whereupon, a new generation came along, and the findings were accepted." See Daniel P. Moynihan, *Miles to Go: A Personal History of Social Policy* (Cambridge, Mass.: Harvard University Press, 1996), 160.

5. U.S. Senate, *Welfare: Reform or Replacement? (Work and Welfare), Hearings before the Subcommittee on Social Security and Family Policy Senate Finance Committee* (February 23, 1987), 133. This sentiment was repeatedly expressed in these hearings. For John Rockefeller's (D-WV) testimony, see U.S. Senate, *Work and Welfare* (1987), 137.

6. Moynihan chaired all of the congressional hearings in 1987–1988 leading up to the FSA.

7. In one 1987 hearing, Moynihan described the new consensus thus:

In the last ten years, liberals and conservatives have found common ground on the issue of work and welfare. Simply put, poor adults who are able should be helped to work. Conservatives have persuaded liberals that there is nothing wrong with obligating able-bodied adults to work. Liberals have persuaded conservatives that most adults want to work and need some help to do so. (U.S. Senate, *Work and Welfare* [1987], 4)

8. Daniel P. Moynihan, *The Negro Family: The Case for National Action* (Washington, D.C.: U.S. Department of Labor, Office of Policy Planning and Research, 1965), 29.

9. Moynihan, *Negro Family,* 25.

10. U.S. House, *Review of Employment and Employability in the Food Stamp Program and Related Welfare Programs, Hearing before the Subcommittee on Domestic Marketing, Consumer Relations, and Nutrition, House Committee on Agriculture,* September 28, 1983, 5.

11. U.S. Senate, *Welfare: Reform or Replacement? (Child Support Enforcement) Hearings before the Subcommittee on Social Security and Family Policy, Senate Finance Committee* (January 23; February 2, 1987), 74.

12. This hearing was one in a series of hearings titled "Welfare: Reform or Replacement?" in which, under the leadership of Moynihan, policymakers called for "welfare *replacement* rather than welfare reform." U.S. Senate, *Child Support Enforcement* (1987), 360. The underlying message was that, if all parents took responsibility for their children, AFDC would no longer be necessary.

13. U.S. Senate, *Child Support Enforcement* (1987), 360.

14. For a discussion on gendered aspects of child support policies, see Jyl J. Josephson, *Gender, Families, and State: Child Support Policy in the United States* (Lanham, Md.: Rowman & Littlefield, 1997).

15. See U.S. Senate, *Welfare Dependency, Hearings before the Subcommittee on Social Security and Family Policy, Senate Finance Committee* (March 4 and 8, 1991), 3.

16. U.S. Senate, *Welfare Dependency* (1991), 7.

17. U.S. Senate, *Welfare Dependency* (1991), 7.

18. See Sanford Schram, *After Welfare: The Culture of Postindustrial Social Policy* (New York: New York University Press, 2000).

19. U.S. Senate, *Welfare Dependency* (1991), 53.

20. For a discussion of structural economic analyses of postindustrial poverty, see Alice O'Connor, *Poverty Knowledge: Social Science, Social Policy, and the Poor in Twentieth-Century U.S. History* (Princeton, N.J.: Princeton University Press, 2001): 260–65.

21. U.S. House, *H.R. Rep. No. 651. Personal Responsibility and Work Opportunity Reconciliation Act of 1996, Committee on the Budget,* 2d session (1996), 15.

22. U.S. House, *Welfare Reform Proposals, Including H.R. 4605, the Work and Responsibility Act of 1994, Part 2, Hearings before the Subcommittee on Human Resources, House Ways and Means Committee* (July 29, August 9, and August 16, 1994), 833.

23. U.S. House, *Welfare Reform Proposals* (1994), 834.

24. U.S. House, *Welfare Reform Proposals* (1994), 850–52.

25. U.S. House, *Welfare Reform Proposals* (1994), 844.

26. See O'Connor, *Poverty Knowledge,* 247–50.

27. U.S. House, *Welfare Reform Proposals* (1994), 868.

28. Michael Katz, *The Undeserving Poor: From the War on Poverty to the War on Welfare* (New York: Pantheon, 1989): 121–22.

29. Schram, *Words of Welfare,* 9.

30. Nancy Fraser, *Unruly Practices: Power, Discourse and Gender in Contemporary Social Theory* (Minneapolis: University of Minnesota Press, 1989), 153.

31. Nancy Fraser, "Clintonism, Welfare, and the Antisocial Wage: The Emergence of a Neoliberal Political Imaginary," *Rethinking Marxism* 6 (1993): 9–23.

II

INTIMATE POLITICS: GENDER, FAMILIES, AND SEXUALITY

6

Reading the Rhetoric of "Compassionate Conservatism"

Nancy D. Campbell

Self-declared "compassionate conservatives" have rewritten the history of U.S. social policy since the mid- to late 1980s. Compassionate conservatism delegitimates the welfare state by displacing blame from the differential effects of social structure and public policy onto individual attitudes, beliefs, and decisions about family formation and configuration, sexual and reproductive practices, and employment. The deflection from public to private, from macro to micro, from social to personal responsibility is useful to the project of restructuring the neoliberal state by scaling back social provision while expanding the penetrating reach of the carceral state.[1] This "deflection dynamic" forms part of an interlocking set of assumptions that I call "governing mentalities" that can be read as characterizing the "crisis" to which compassionate conservatives respond.[2] When compassionate conservatives partake in "family values" crisis talk, they are anxiously responding to large-scale structural and cultural transformations of "hypercapitalism."[3] Their concern is especially audible in struggles over whether social policy should become more directive or "compassionately coercive" toward badly behaved citizens.[4]

REWRITING THE HISTORY OF THE U.S. WELFARE STATE

Compassionate conservatism is neither truly compassionate nor conservative. "Rallying the armies of compassion" mobilizes a nostalgic response to changing modes of social reproduction.[5] Nostalgia, however, is always about the present. The neoconservative rewriting of the past, now underway for the better part of two decades, lends ideological

113

justification for the restructuring of the present along neoliberal lines. Compassionate conservatives argue that individuals should absorb more and more of the costs of social reproduction as they seek to implement what amounts to domestic "structural adjustment." The burning question of social policy is, who should absorb the costs of social reproduction? The neoliberal reallocation of public resources has occurred with little more than ideological assertion at base. For instance, Lawrence Mead argues that the United States is a nation of individualists who will not accept more generous social policies. As citizen-subjects, we supposedly avoid "dependency" on the state because we fear we will become "addicted" to it and lose our motivation, our entrepreneurial spirit, or our national pride.

Advanced by Democrats in the wake of Walter Mondale's defeat and misnamed "passionate conservatism,"[6] the "compassionate conservative movement" consisted of a motley crew of politicians, officials such as William J. Bennett, and quasi-academic writers such as those whose work I scrutinize here. One of its most articulate progenitors was Governor Pete Wilson (R-CA), who called for "compassion" in arenas ranging from drug treatment to his "preventive approach to government" in speeches from the late 1980s through 1992.[7] Wilson argued Republicans should take the lead in "bettering conditions that shape children's lives. That's why we turn to solutions that are compassionate but conservative." The solutions he had in mind attacked the "deficits that bedevil us at every level of government [which] represent another kind of deficit throughout society—a deficit in personal and parental responsibility." Despite the rhetorical appeal of compassionate conservatism, it might not have become a household keyword were it not for the election of George W. Bush in 2000.

The Bush administration's implementation of the new White House Office of Faith-Based and Community Initiatives attests to the currency and practicality of exercises in "historical semantics."[8] These programs are exactly those for which compassionate conservatives have argued— they are the first step toward building a conservative social and human services delivery infrastructure modeled along the lines of the very effective conservative philanthropy and "research" think tanks assembled in the last twenty years.[9] Why should this move concern any feminists besides those who are concerned with maintaining the separation of church and state?

Compassionate conservatism responds to an actual rather than an imaginary crisis—not an ideological crisis in "family values" but a material crisis in social reproduction.[10] The outcome of this struggle, which concerns how social reproduction will take place and the role of the state within it, has great significance for women's lives because of women's overresponsibility for absorbing the costs of social reproduction within gendered, racialized, and sexualized "structures of constraint" that limit potential individual and collective resistance to this form of extraction. As a nation, we are in a remarkably deep state of denial about the toll this takes.

Women's unpaid labors remain the "hidden cost" of social reproduction.[11] There is a "double whammy" at work in that women are also "made poor" by labor markets structured to shunt them into low-security, low-wage service work. Racial and sexual discrimination—combined with women's "underinvestment" in human capital—places most women in states of economic and social vulnerability relative to most men. Compassionate conservatives' palpable fear that women will refuse to carry out "their childcare responsibilities" runs deeper than their fear that women will shift "their" burdens to the state. It is a full-scale fear that women will refuse to behave as good women should. Such fears betray pervasive suspicion toward the long-term impacts of structural change upon social relations. Will women refuse to play our part in the social arrangements that subordinate women to men, women of color to white women, and single, lesbian, or bisexual women to the minority of women who inhabit so-called nuclear family configurations? Attempts to control women—or at least to contain their power and harness it to state-sanctioned projects—arose in the wake of successful mass movements to expand civil rights, sexual and reproductive rights, and women's rights.

Small wonder that one of the founding fathers of compassionate conservatism, Marvin Olasky, blames the flaws of what he calls the "postmodern welfare state" on feminists.[12] According to him, the government antipoverty programs of the late 1960s took a "feminist-flawed approach" because feminist social workers infiltrated and hijacked the welfare system. Feminists sought to deemphasize the role of religion and bend the state to their secular agenda especially by encouraging poor women to think "marriage is not the answer."[13] While compassionate conservatives correctly see feminism and "secular humanism" as encroaching on the "traditional" cultural values they seek to restore, they attribute more success to the liberal feminist project of harnessing the power of the state to feminist goals than sober reflection can provide.[14]

Compassionate conservatives put Olasky forward as a hero because he advocates not reform but complete abolition of the social safety net, based on a rationale that combines elements of cultural conservatism, moral absolutism, and neoliberal social policy. He dates postmodernity to 1960s welfare rights struggles:

Attitudes changed during that decade, however, as a postmodern welfare system emerged alongside a postmodern cultural system. Postmodernism in welfare meant, in theory, that there was no right way to act. In practice, it meant a war on the biblical understandings that still underlay even New Deal governmental welfare—for example, that able-bodied people should work.[15]

He argued that antipoverty programs will fail as long as separation of church from state prevails and as long as the "War on Poverty [is] a war on God." His historical narrative traces the rise of a professionalized form of "new-style compassion" that increased governmental obligations to single mothers while decreasing marital obligations through no-fault divorce and the devaluation of the marriage contract. Like many, he forgets that no-fault divorce law reform was a conservative rather than a liberal reform, and that feminists had little to do with the move to unilateral, on-demand divorce.[16] The "devaluation of marriage" had more to do with the sad state of heterosexual relations pressured by the large-scale social and economic conditions of a highly stratified society than any assault on religion. This is but one example of how compassionate conservatives tether their political and cultural agenda to their historical storytelling.

Feminist revisionist histories of the U.S. welfare state have expanded our understanding of how integral race, gender, and class stratification has been to the evolution of institutions that respond to large-scale economic shifts.[17] The feminist critique has yielded a fine-grained knowledge about how social programs reinscribed women's subordination and racial stratification by setting benefits low and maintaining tight eligibility requirements, to say nothing of the degradation and humiliation that accompanied welfare receipt in the twentieth century. Still these criticisms and the wealth of detailed historical data upon which they were based were made in the spirit of enabling the state to provide material assistance in more equitable and universal ways. It is thus with a sense of irony and alarm that I approach another set of revisionist histories produced by compassionate conservatives in order to tease out the specific historical claims upon which the project to dismantle the welfare state is now being instituted.

FROM OLD-STYLE COMPASSION
TO "HURLING MONEY AT THE NEEDY"

Compassionate conservatives argue for a return to nineteenth-century forms of social provision through charitable organizations that they claim worked to mitigate poverty. Their task is to buttress the negative comparison to welfare state programs, which they believe not only failed to relieve poverty but paradoxically produced it. Today's compassionate conservatives cast the U.S. welfare state as a failure, typically by citing rising rates of addiction, homicide, illiteracy, female-headed households, and father absence. Increases in these "moral pathologies" are linked not to the social processes, structures, and misguided policies that have actually produced them but to individual behavior, decisions, attitudes, beliefs, and values. Obsessed with the growth of female-headed households and increasing crime and illicit drug use, they have used the cultural figures of drug-using and impoverished women as condensed symbols in a political shorthand that anxiously encodes notions of social decay, disease, and disorder.

Rewriting history into this framework has been Olasky's chief project since he catapulted to national prominence when Newt Gingrich commended *The Tragedy of American Compassion* in his first speech as the speaker to the House of Representatives on January 4, 1995: "Olasky goes back for 300 years and looked [sic] at what has worked in America, how we have helped people rise beyond poverty and how we have reached out to save people. He may not have the answers, but he has the right sense of where we have to go as Americans." The intellectual founding father of compassionate conservatism, as George W. Bush calls him, Olasky has published many books of a pseudohistorical nature that emphasize biblical values, cultivate an aura of authentic academic research, and serve the present-day purposes of right-wing Christian cultural conservatives.

Additionally, Olasky carries over his politically engaged scholarship and "lived research" into his personal life. He and his wife adopted a biracial child and founded an antiabortion Crisis Pregnancy Center to put into practice his pro-life strategy to contain abortion by extending personal compassion grounded in moral absolutism.[18] His book *Abortion Rites* contains two chapters titled "Compassion Coming of Age" and "The New Compassion" that argue antiabortion efforts should take as their model the effort to roll back and contain Communism. The book contains the nascent germ of compassionate conservatism—"contain[ing] abortion by extending compassion."[19] He derived this idea from late-nineteenth-century voluntary charitable organizations, which, according to Olasky, created "anti-abortion refuges" staffed by volunteers who extended "compassion—personal care and challenge, not just the offering of money" to disgraced mothers of illegitimate children.[20] Compassionate individuals opened their homes to women who become pregnant out-of-wedlock and "help[ed] them do what was right."[21]

Feminists who have detailed the history of reproductive and sexual practices have produced a body of scholarship based on evidence that contests
conservatives' repetitive inaccuracies in several ways.[22] Homes for unwed
mothers organized by charitable organizations attached behavioral strings
through oppressive policies directed toward residents and barred African
American women. An exhaustive history of abortion in nineteenth-century
Chicago found such "refuges" hardly welcoming: "Maternity homes expected mothers to repent and required them to stay long periods of time,
perform domestic tasks, and participate in religious services."[23] Women
sought maternity homes largely as a last resort after failing to obtain abor-
tions.[24] By counterpoising thoroughly documented feminist histories constructed on the basis of primary sources to Olasky's work, I mean not only
to draw attention to the shortcomings of his scholarship but to shift the context in which we seek to understand his efforts. One of the few serious academic responses to Olasky's work has been David Hammack's review of
The Tragedy of American Compassion.[25] The stakes in this struggle over the
effectiveness of religious organizations is not so much accuracy or profes-
sionalism but a contest over how Americans use narratives about their past
to generate and attribute meaning to their present. Thus, it is not narrow
"debunking" of specific claims in which we need to engage, but broad, diverse, and public intellectual engagement on this historical terrain.

Debunking is of limited utility in public engagement directed toward
shifting political semantics because it reinforces the view of a "true" story
to which the false one contrasts. The charge that Olasky "abuses" history
could be made but this is not my intent. Rather, I want to discern the political uses to which Olasky's claims are put, which are more important
and telling than those he himself makes. For example, articles that adopt
Olasky's story about the shift from "old-style" voluntary compassion to
"new-style" professional social work assume that his mythic retelling of
the success story of heroic faith-based "poverty fighters" is an accepted
historical narrative.[26]

> As late as the early 20th century, a new plethora of Protestant, Catholic and
> Jewish groups were spearheading a comprehensive assault on poverty and
> its causes. Such groups, aided by a dedicated corps of volunteers at the
> grass-roots level, were immersed in nearly every facet of life—trade
> schools, housing, savings banks, street outreach, Bible teaching and char-
> acter education, medical and legal aid societies, visiting nurse services, em-
> ployment offices, job training, small businesses and farming.[27]

"Success" is adduced with little evidence.[28] The article "Learn the Basics"
attributed the end of the first era of "community-based" activity to the
New Deal, the creation of "what has been deemed the welfare state."

Suggesting there is something suspect about even the appellation "welfare state," Liben echoes the following neoconservative logic: "Despite almost $7 trillion of Great Society spending, child poverty persisted while every form of social pathology rose dramatically." Reiterating the assertion that "few experts denied the past successes of faith-based groups in this arena," the article constructed charity work as based on treating individuals as diverse in their particularity in contrast to the government's "one-size fits all" approach. Given extreme regional variation in social provision, it is difficult to grant credence to this claim, but it is important to recognize its form. By colonizing the ground of difference, conservatives deflect criticisms that they seek to proselytize and so homogenize those they serve. They thereby escape the charge that they are blaming individual character defects: "Poverty sometimes has behavioral causes, such as substance abuse, but government resembles the rich father who gives money to his children in place of love and attention, discipline and responsibility. In contrast, faith-based organizations devoted their attention to the entire needs of the individual including the need to be held accountable for one's actions."[29]

Substance abuse is invoked directly in the construction of social provision as enabling addiction.[30] Liben writes, "FDR himself warned against what could follow: 'Continued dependence . . . induces a spiritual and moral disintegration. . . . To dole out relief in this way is to administer a narcotic, a . . . destroyer of the human spirit.'" Addiction is always on tap to signal compulsion without control and failures of individual behavior or "bad choices." Addiction is a potent metaphor for social decline that has been especially useful to compassionate conservatives, who regularly conflate drug dependency with "welfare dependency": "Crack babies in inner-city hospitals trembled and twitched uncontrollably. Teenage mothers, alone with squalling children, fought the impulse to strike out. Men in their twenties called job holders 'chumps' and went on a rampage in Los Angeles. Women in their thirties, abandoned by husbands, waited in welfare offices for their numbers to be called."[31] Addiction signals an "out of control" way of life that conservatives would like to control by heaping a new set of obligations on the poor and people they see as badly behaved.

"Learn the Basics" advances another of Olasky's claims about the merits of "old-style charities," which is that such groups recognized that people do not change without behavioral incentives, standards, and demands to do so. In contrast, the welfare state simply "hurl[ed] cash at the needy," thereby introducing what is called Gresham's Law: "Bad charities—government programs without strings—drive out good ones—faith-oriented programs which demand accountability and tackle human needs holistically." William J. Bennett, a key figure in the compassionate conservative movement first in his capacity as "drug czar," illustrated Gresham's Law: "'Families, churches, and community groups have been forced to surrender . . . to bureaucratic experts. Fathers were replaced by welfare checks; private charities were displaced by government spending; religious volunteers were dismissed as 'amateurs'; whole communities were demolished in slumclearance.'" Liben continues, "Finally, institutions of faith succeed in empowering the poor because they believe that redemption is possible, that people can change dramatically if they are challenged to commit to worthy goals outside of themselves."[32] Ironically, in light of their continued construction of social policy as "hurling cash at the needy," compassionate conservatives lament that lack of resources held religious groups back from eradicating poverty long ago. The problem with this story, of course, is that it makes very little historical sense. The successes of charitable organizations were not and have not been documented. Indeed, there is much historical evidence to suggest that by the early twentieth century, charitable organizations were frustrated with the increase in adult dependency and lacked effective means to address it.[33]

"Old-style" compassion worked, Olasky claimed, because "poorly paid but deeply dedicated professional managers" and optimistic volunteers "suffered with" the needy by adopting hard-to-place babies, providing shelter, and working one-on-one to produce sorrow for past misdeeds.[34] The "empire-building of so-called poverty pimps" then displaced the older values-driven compassion with money.[35] Thus, Charles Murray would argue that "writing checks will not end the problems of the underclass" because poverty, a condition of most human societies since the dawn of history, was not the problem.[36] The problem lay in our efforts to relieve it.

Forgetting that the New Deal was in many ways a defeat for the left, the compassionate conservatives argue that the left wanted "new compassion" to be nothing more than income transfer: "If utopia could be attained through mass redistribution, personal compassion was unnecessary. Compassion could become synonymous with sending a check or passing redistributionist legislation."[37] By the 1930s, Olasky argues, the "new compassion" was translated into professionally run government programs of "material transfer" based on a "social universalistic impulse"—rather than "old-style" volunteerism, personal challenge, spiritual concern, and individual responsibility. They counterpoised liberal Democratic "materialism" to the spiritual and moral solutions that prevailed under "old-style compassion." The "current impasse" of U.S. social policy, as Olasky called it, derived from throwing money at social problems through complex bureaucracies. His answer is to stop writing checks and to dismantle the modern welfare state because "true" compassion simply cannot be mobilized within it.

If New Dealers, Fair Dealers, and liberal social workers got it wrong, what, then, are the root problems of poverty according to compassionate conservatives? Poor parenting, the decline in traditional marriage, and broken social bonds are their most consistent answers. As Murray puts it, "Some substantial proportion of women play their role of mother appallingly badly, leaving the children unnurtured, undisciplined, sometimes unfed and unwashed."[38] According to him, food is there for malnourished children, but, "too often, a competent mother is not": "More money is not going to make competent mothers of incompetent ones, nor conscientious mothers of irresponsible ones. More money is not going to bring fathers back to the children they have sired and then abandoned."[39] Poverty, Murray and Olasky agree, has been part of the human condition since the "dawn of history"—but today's poor are cast as more pathological than yesterday's poor. Gingrich argues antipoverty efforts condemn "too many of our fellow citizens to lives of despair" and do more damage than the Vietnam War:

> When we look at the murder rate among young black men, at the cocaine and heroin and crack addiction among young Americans of all races, at the illiteracy rate, at the number of children who have never known their father or had any father figure, at the devastation of our inner cities, we can see clearly that America's approach to helping the poor is doing great damage and that it is in urgent need of replacement. This means replacing a culture of poverty and violence with a wholly different culture of productivity and safety—not just helping the poor or focusing on the inner cities, but actually replacing one culture with another.[40]

The sustained academic critique of the "culture of poverty" thesis would seem to have fallen on willfully deaf ears.[41] Cultural displacement takes the form of an experience of religious conversion that will "peel . . . away the whole culture, revealing a better one."[42] Social conservatives feel this process is best accomplished "outside of government"—as the trappings of cultural difference are peeled away, the federal safety net will wither. A monoculture of productivity and safety will displace the "multiculture" of poverty and violence, and effectively restore inner cities, Indian reservations, and West Virginia Appalachian neighborhoods to a state of health.[43] The comparison to Alcoholics Anonymous (AA) is not idle, for conservatives figure "liberal social provision" as "not unlike an addictive drug" or an "emotional narcotic."[44]

Liberals themselves are cast as "arrogant elitists" whose impure and even corrosive forms of compassion reproduced a "lesser or deprived class" insulated from the "freedom to fail."[45] Such "social engineering" destroyed the personal incentive, self-esteem, risk, and responsibility essential to a "free market" system by sapping the "vigor and strength of the nation."[46] Conservatives argue their policies "will inflict less harm on mankind" because conservatives are humble, cautious, mature, and realistic. They believe that "complete attainment" of racial integration, an end to sex discrimination, universal health insurance coverage, or an end to poverty are but impossible, immature, unconstrained liberal dreams.[47]

CONCLUSION

Compassionate conservatives seek to reauthorize the masculine power of the state over the distribution of public resources by making them contingent upon private behavior. If the burning question of social policy is, "who should absorb the costs of social reproduction," much of U.S. social policy assumes that social problems would be solved if individuals did everything "we" want them to do. In Margaret Thatcher's words, "You get a responsible society when you get responsible individuals."[48] Compassionate conservatives valorize individual choice and responsibility, yet self-sovereignty has always been both an illusion for most and a technique of the self available to few. Cultural conservatives do not want individuals to have too much self-sovereignty—then they might "choose" to engage in unhealthy habits or behaviors. They want to direct individuals to the "right" choices, much as parents rely on judicious doses of "choice" and coercion to compel children to behave in socially acceptable ways.

The translation of behavioral models into policy depends on each of us internalizing a belief in our self-sovereignty while at the same time accepting that some (other) people will be the target of directive interventions. Behavioral models downplay the systemic effects of location within social structure, obscuring the uneven distribution of the privilege, knowledge, and resources that it takes to realize individual agency. They seek to "empower" individuals through an ideology of choice and personal responsibility that is not supported by the redistribution of the actual means to exercise agency from within a structure. The effect is that many of us then live between a rock and a hard place.

Redefining coercion as a compassionate form of discipline and control over the behavior and decisions of poor citizens is one of the chief mechanisms by which what I call postmodern Progressivism proceeds.[49] Like its modern predecessor, postmodern Progressivism centers on conforming individual behavior to normative constructs based on the behavior of an ideal-typical individual abstracted from the culturally dominant group. Progressive individualist policies effectively shift blame to individuals for what might otherwise be seen as the cumulative effects of policy decisions, social change, and structural phenomena. However, postmodern Progressivism differs from the maternalist ethos of the early twentieth century, for it is undercut by the neoconservative hegemony constructed in the 1980s. The ultimate outcome of postmodern Progressivism is both paternalist and privatizing—authority without infrastructure, a behavioral mandate without redistributive mechanisms, coercion without due process.

NOTES

1. The concept of the "carceral" system as a mark of the punitive functions of the state was developed by Michel Foucault in *Discipline and Punish: The Birth of the Prison* (New York: Vintage Books, 1979). Restructuring takes many forms, among them forms of public divestment usefully designated as domestic "neoliberalism." The expansion of the carceral state must be seen in relation to the retraction of other more supportive forms of social provision.

2. See Nancy D. Campbell, *Using Women: Gender, Drug Policy, and Social Justice* (New York: Routledge, 2000). "Compassionate coercion" showed up early in debates in the drug treatment arena during the maternal crack-cocaine crisis of the late 1980s. See also Sanford F. Schram, *Praxis for the Poor* (New York: New York University Press, 2002).

3. See Ruth Colker, *American Law in the Age of Hypercapitalism: The Worker, the Family, and the State* (New York: New York University Press, 1998).

4. See remarks on the need for compassionate coercion made before the U.S. Congress. Senate Subcommittee on Children, Family, Drugs, and Alcoholism of the Committee on Labor and Human Resources. *Falling through the Crack: The Impact of Drug-Exposed Children on the Child Welfare System* (101st Cong., 2d sess., Washington, D.C., March 8, 1990), 14.

5. Remarks of George W. Bush, "Bush Names New Faith-Based Director," in *TOOLLINE* 2 (February 2002). Welcoming the second director of the White House Office of Faith-Based Initiatives, Bush stated, "My job is to unify our country around common, big goals, and there is nothing more important than to help the hopeless see hope, to help the addicted see a better life, to help the collective will of our country to have a better tomorrow and realize its potential."

6. John Herbers, "Party Looks Inward for Ways to Regain Majority," *New York Times,* November 8, 1984, p. B1. The article incorrectly rendered a remark of Representative James R. Jones (D-OK), who urged the Democratic National Commit-

tee to be "fiscally conservative without losing [its] commitment to the needy and . . . redirect our policy in that direction." The Democrats interviewed were not suggesting spending cutbacks but seeking to appeal to the "white majority."

7. Robert B. Gunnison, "Wilson Calls for Compassion," *San Francisco Chronicle,* August 20, 1992, p. A10.

8. Raymond Williams, *Keywords,* rev. ed. (Oxford: Oxford University Press, 1983); Nancy Fraser and Linda Gordon, "A Genealogy of Dependency: Tracing a Keyword of the U.S. Welfare State," *Signs* 19, no. 2 (winter 1994): 309–36.

9. See *New York Times,* Sunday, May 20, 2001, on conservative philanthropies and think tanks. Close to one-third of current fellows from such programs went into Bush administration jobs.

10. See Stephanie Coontz, *The Way We Never Were* (New York: Basic, 1992).

11. See Nancy Folbre, *Who Pays for the Kids? Gender and the Structures of Constraint* (New York: Routledge, 1994).

12. Olasky is a one-time Jewish communist who converted to Christianity and became a professor of journalism at the University of Texas at Austin. See Marvin Olasky, *The Tragedy of American Compassion* (Washington, D.C.: Regnery Gateway, 1992), 22.

13. Olasky, *Tragedy of American Compassion,* 9.

14. For a comparative assessment of feminists' relative successes that outlines the limits of the U.S. experience, see Carol Bacchi, *Same Difference: Feminism and Sexual Difference* (New York: Allen & Unwin, 1990).

15. This argument and those that follow are based on Olasky, *Tragedy of American Compassion,* 71-75.

16. See J. Herbie DiFonzo, *Beneath the Fault Line: The Popular and Legal Culture of Divorce in America* (Charlottesville: University Press of Virginia, 1997).

17. See Linda Gordon, *Pitied But Not Entitled* (Cambridge, Mass.: Harvard University Press, 1994); Gwendolyn Mink, *The Wages of Motherhood* (Ithaca, N.Y.: Cornell University Press, 1995); Gwendolyn Mink, *Welfare's End* (Ithaca, N.Y.: Cornell University Press, 1998); Dietrich Rueschemeyer and Theda Skocpol, eds., *States, Social Knowledge and the Origins of Modern Social Policies* (Princeton, N.J.: Princeton University Press, 1996); Theda Skocpol, *Protecting Soldiers and Mothers* (Cambridge, Mass.: Harvard University Press, 1992); Theda Skocpol, *Social Policy in the United States* (Princeton, N.J.: Princeton University Press, 1995).

18. Marvin Olasky, *Abortion Rites: A Social History of Abortion in America* (Wheaton, Ill.: Crossways, 1992).

19. Olasky, *Abortion Rites,* 134.

20. Olasky, *Abortion Rites,* 208, 215, 242.

21. Olasky, *Abortion Rites,* 248.

22. See Janet Farrell Brodie, *Contraception and Abortion in 19th-Century America* (Ithaca, N.Y.: Cornell University Press, 1994); and Nicola Beisel, *Imperiled Innocents: Anthony Comstock and Family Reproduction in Victorian America* (Princeton, N.J.: Princeton University Press, 1997).

23. Leslie J. Reagan, *When Abortion Was a Crime: Women, Medicine, and Law in the United States, 1867–1973* (Berkeley: University of California Press, 1997), 28.

24. Regina Kunzel, *Fallen Women, Problem Girls: Unmarried Mothers and the Professionalization of Social Work, 1890–1945* (New Haven, Conn.: Yale University Press, 1993), 68–69.

25. For an excerpt of Hammack's critical review of *The Tragedy of American Compassion*, which was published in *Nonprofit and Voluntary Sector Quarterly* (Spring 1996), see his website at www2.hnet.msu.edu/~ethnic/archives/logs/feb96/0011.html (accessed September 20, 2000).

26. "Learn the Basics: Faith-based Welfare Reform," by Paul Liben, appeared in Joseph Holland's online newsletter *TOOLLINE. Holistic Hardware: Tools That Build Lives: A Monthly Electronic Newsletter for Faith-Based Workers, Welfare Reformers, and Poverty-Fighters,* no. 1.2 (December 1, 1999) at www.holistichardware.com/ (accessed September 20, 2000). For her ongoing navigation of these debates and her wise and fiery words in their midst, I thank C. Ditmar Coffield.

27. Liben, "Learn the Basics."

28. For an article on claims of the efficacy of faith-based organizations made without grounds, see Eyal Press, "Lead Us Not into Temptation," *American Prospect* 12, no. 6 (April 9, 2001), at www.prospect.org/print-friendly/print/V12/6/press-e.html (accessed May 6, 2001).

29. All quotations are from Liben, "Learn the Basics."

30. See, for instance, anything by Sally Satel, M.D., who argues that the systems of public provision evolved in welfare states enable addiction.

31. For a critique of "welfare dependency," see Sanford F. Schram, *After Welfare: The Culture of Postindustrial Social Policy* (New York: New York University Press, 2000). The quotation illustrates Olasky's construction of social decline so perfectly that he used very similar words in both *Renewing American Compassion* (78) and *The Tragedy of American Compassion* (5). Constructions of social decay and disorder impart urgency to those who argue for reform: "While we sit around and debate, generations are being lost."

32. The three preceding quotes are all from Liben, "Learn the Basics."

33. Michael Fitzgibbon, "Authority and Social Policy: The Transformation of Charity in Cleveland, 1870–1920" (paper presented at the Policy History conference, Bowling Green State University, Bowling Green, Ohio, June 6, 1997).

34. Marvin Olasky, *Renewing American Compassion* (New York: The Free Press, 1996), 30.

35. Olasky, *Renewing American Compassion,* 26.

36. Olasky, *Tragedy of American Compassion,* xiii.

37. Olasky, *Tragedy of American Compassion,* 67.

38. Olasky, *Tragedy of American Compassion,* xi.

39. Olasky, *Tragedy of American Compassion,* xiv. The primitivizing tone references animalistic behavior in which women become "indiscriminately" pregnant and men "sire" children. While the rhetoric conveys the message that the poor are subhuman, the content humanizes them so as to deflect the criticism that conservatives are inhumane.

40. Olasky, *Renewing American Compassion,* 9.

41. Patricia Hill Collins, "A Comparison of Two Works on Black Family Life," *Signs* 14, no. 1 (summer 1989): 875–84; Leith Mullings, *On Our Own Terms* (New

York: Routledge, 1997); Maxine Baca Zinn, "Family, Race, and Poverty in the Eighties," *Signs* 14, no. 1 (summer 1989): 856–74; Margaret Weir, "From Equal Opportunity to the 'New Social Contract'" in *Racism, the City, and the State*, ed. Malcolm Cross and Michael Keith (New York: Routledge, 1993).

42. Olasky, *Renewing American Compassion*, xi.

43. Olasky, *Renewing American Compassion*, xii.

44. John R. Jacobs, *The Compassionate Conservative: Seeking Responsibility and Human Dignity* (Oakland, Calif.: Institute for Contemporary Studies, 1996), 108.

45. Jacobs, *Compassionate Conservative*, 44, 78.

46. Jacobs, *Compassionate Conservative*, 80, 171, 212–13.

47. Jacobs, *Compassionate Conservative*, 55–56.

48. Quoted in Robert Jervis, *System Effects: Complexity in Political and Social Life* (Princeton, N.J.: Princeton University Press, 1997), 15.

49. The features of postmodernity that are most significant for understanding postmodern progressivism are the neoconservative rollback of social provision; the containment of many of the achievements of the civil rights movement, the women's movement, and movements for sexual and reproductive rights; the experience of fragmentation or "disorientation"; the loss of stability coupled with the advent of flexibility; and economic and social dislocation. See Wendy Brown, *States of Injury: Power and Freedom in Late Modernity* (Princeton, N.J.: Princeton University Press, 1995), 33–37; J. K. Gibson-Graham, *The End of Capitalism (As We Knew It): A Feminist Critique of Political Economy* (Oxford: Blackwell, 1996).

7

"Family Values": Social Conservative Power in Diverse Rhetorics

Valerie Lehr

Feminist ideas play oddly in current discussions of family: the Right (mis)uses them to argue that the selfishness of 1960s liberals led the United States astray in the 1990s, while a vast array of politicians, commentators, and activists draw on elements of feminism to bolster their cases for or against social policies. For the latter, feminist ideas are a source of reinforcement, not a theoretical perspective that informs a comprehensive alternative analysis of family. Thus, it may appear that feminist ideas have penetrated our national consciousness and influence political debate about family issues, but the examples that follow suggest that, despite its potential, feminist theory has had little influence in constructing an alternative to traditional American, and liberal, understandings of the relationship between the individual, the family, and the social. As a result, those who make ostensibly pro-feminist arguments often reinforce key elements of the Right's discourse and rhetoric.

In order to understand the costs of not having an alternative rhetorical construction, I want to explore the ways by which language and ideas critical to the Right inform discourses as disparate as those of gay marriage activists, New Democrats, and advocates for the childless. I begin by discussing why family values matter to the Right and how they are embedded in discourses of blame, followed by an exploration of how ostensibly more liberal voices maintain these values. Finally, I draw upon feminist theory to show that feminism can and must provide a deeper challenge to the Right than that presented in public discourse. The choice to draw on conservative rhetoric may play well politically at times, but the cost—reinforcing power and stereotypes—is high.

RIGHT RHETORIC:
BUILDING A WHITE, MIDDLE-CLASS NATION

In the post–Cold War and pre–September 11th era, conservatives needed a program with the potential to unite and build their constituency. The need to create this political platform coincided with economic restructuring that took a toll on many, especially the working class and poor. As conservatives have little desire to either intervene in the free market or use government programs to enhance economic security, this was an ideal moment for fears concerning those who were "illegitimately" gaining from government in terms of monetary benefits or "special rights" and fears concerning young people as criminals, parents, and victims of day care sexual abuse. "Family values" and a particular definition of "privacy" could provide at least an illusory solution to people's real fears. As Edsall and Edsall argue, the Republican Party placed its hopes for electoral success in the 1980s on the ability to divert attention from the role that global economic change, often enabled by U.S. policies, played in decreasing the standard of living of most Americans. By constructing "special interests" not as business interests, but as those who had gained from the 1960s, Reagan was able to draw on fear to create a push toward family values and away from social change and "selfishness." If the external enemy of the past was gone, they suggest, Americans could easily be left to wonder why they should remain committed to a state that did little to protect them from external threats, while also allowing their material standard of living to decline.[1] Internal enemies, including young people and those who failed to teach them proper values, that is, those families that chose to fulfill the selfish desires of adults, rather than sacrifice for their children, could provide such a rationale.

Maintaining a central role in defining the appropriate family is critical for the Right. Social conservatives see an ongoing battle between government and traditional authorities for control within society. The family, or at least the heterosexual, nuclear family, is the savior that can rescue people from the power of government and allow them to lead "natural," well-ordered lives. Although "family values" may contain many different premises, some of which are suppressed at any given moment, three interrelated ideas are centrally located within this general rubric: there is a single, natural family, and that family is both patriarchal and self-sufficient. Martha Fineman's discussion of the "sexual family" helps us to understand how these three characteristics are important for politicians who want to minimize the role of the state. The "sexual family" is, she notes, the appropriate form of family because it is able to take advantage of the complimentary roles that men and women play to deal with "inevitable dependencies." "Dependency," she notes, "is allocated away from the state to the private grouping. These ideas of natural and privatized dependency reinforce one another on an ideological level. They perversely interact so that the societal tasks assigned to the natural family inevitably assume the role differentiation that exists within the sexually affiliated family."[2] Further, the natural power of the father to provide for protection is parallel to that of the state;[3] if the father's power is illegitimate, so too is the state's power. Declining paternal power is perceived as leading to social and political chaos.[4]

Some attempts have been made to update the gender assumptions built into the sexual family, yet as Fineman argues:

> The family continues to be defined as an entity built on the sexual affiliation of two adults. This heterosexual unit continues to be considered as presumptively appropriate and it has ongoing viability as the core family connection. At worst, heterosexual marriage is viewed as in need of some updating and structural revisions, and we seem caught in an "equality trap" about these revisions.[5]

The equality trap exists because of the assumption that men and women can simply rearrange tasks within the family to create equality. The belief that families should and can, as individual units, work out conflicts is connected to the third point: as entities that reside in the private sphere, families should be self-supporting units, with the power to make decisions for their members. This is particularly true in relation to children, who themselves come to be seen as mature adults when they are ready to form their own families, in other words, when they marry.

Using law and family policy to further the development of "proper" values and behavior is certainly not new to the United States, nor is the idea that people should be judged based on how their families fit the dominant, naturalized model. Nancy Cott's history of marriage in the United States makes it clear that integration into the dominant European American culture has been predicated on adapting to (and being legally allowed to adapt to) the norm of monogamous, heterosexual marriage.[6] Proponents of welfare state policies from the turn of the twentieth century forward argued that these policies should create and support a particular family unit.[7] Such policies constructed a system of economic privilege that provided safety and security only for those deemed "deserving," which came to be a code for "white" as a variety of ethnic groups were Americanized. This ideology continued to be embedded in Great Society policies.[8]

Recognizing how social policy in the United States has simultaneously been premised on and reinforcing of family values *and* central to constructing and maintaining racial and ethnic hierarchy can help us to understand two observations made by Kirk Mann and Sasha Roseneil in their discussion of the power of antisingle mother discourse in Britain. They observe that compared to the United States: (1) the Right discourse opposing single mothers was not as racialized and (2) that although the discourse has been used not just by conservatives, but also, in forms by socialists and liberals, "it has achieved far greater hegemony in the U.S."[9] In fact, I suggest that it was more successful *because* of the ease with which discussions about "inadequate" families are a code for nonwhite people and families in the United States. Appeals to a rhetoric that reinforces the middle-class ideal of family invoke a set of norms, emotions, and values that have consistently been used to oppress.

CIVILIZING MEN

The centrality of marriage to civilization was articulated in early-twentieth-century America, as white Americans used the sexual family as a model to contrast to more "primitive" arrangements.[10] The Right echoes these beliefs, asserting that male sexuality is dangerous unless it is channeled to the marital relationship. Social conservatives argue that feminism is responsible for the family controlling men less effectively by devaluing motherhood and freeing men, thus increasing the burdens that women face.[11] Klatch notes: "The underlying image of men is of creatures with uncontrollable passions and little sense of commitment or loyalty. Only moral *and legal* authority can restrain the savagery of male nature."[12] Social conservatives see the Promise Keepers as men who are trying to create a social movement to help men fight for family identities rather than self-interest. They cannot, therefore, understand critiques of the Promise Keepers by feminists, libertarians, or others.[13] For women who feel threatened with single parenthood (which often results in a lower standard of living or poverty) or a double work day, the appeal of conservative family values is clear, particularly if Christian men's groups, such as Promise Keepers, can help to civilize their husbands.[14] The construction of feminists, not men, as responsible for family breakdown leads many feminists to see "family values" rhetoric as a challenge to feminist gains.[15] Ironically, the devaluing of feminism requires a negative understanding of masculinity, one with wider currency in the United States, as well as other Western countries, than simply among the Right. In fact, the idea that men need marriage is heard as reasonable not just because it shifts blame to feminists, but also because it has been a dominant discourse of masculinity, one that Richard Collier demonstrates is assumed and created by law.[16] The antifeminism of family values rhetoric "works" because of its ability to draw from and reinforce a vision of masculinity as a force that needs to be constrained by women.

This vision of masculinity is central to both William Eskridge's and Andrew Sullivan's highly publicized arguments in favor of gay marriage. Although they believe that conservatives such as George Gilder have misdiagnosed what it takes to tame the antisocial desires of men, they leave little doubt that they believe that men have such desires. Whereas for social conservatives marriage to a woman is necessary, for these proponents of gay marriage, it is simply marriage that tames male desire. Sullivan sets forth this proposition in a way that rhetorically reinforces the ideas of Gilder and other conservatives, even while he tries to normalize gay male desire. Imagine, he suggests, the alternatives: "Surely even conservatives who think women are essential to the successful socialization of men would not deny that the discipline of domesticity, of shared duties and lives, of the give-and-take of cohabitation and love with anyone, even of the same sex, tends to benefit men more than the option of free-wheeling, etiolating bachelorhood."[17] Both Sullivan and Eskridge attempt to persuade middle-class Americans that gay men will be better men if they are securely located in the closest approximation of the sexual family possible.[18]

Alternatively, many argue that gay relationships are often based on different norms than marriage and may need different legal constructions. Those who make this argument do not accept that men need marriage to be safe enough for society, and, therefore, they provide a more full rhetorical alternative to conservative ideas, one that may be connected to feminist and postmodern understandings. Sullivan provides the beginning of grounds for such a counterargument in the epilogue to *Virtually Normal*.[19] But he also denies the implications of his claim that "two men would understand the need for extra-marital outlets better than a man and a woman" in the afterword, asserting that marriage should be monogamous. Rather than pursuing the question of what we can learn about the ethics of relationship, Sullivan reinforces the centrality of marriage and control of male sexuality for civil society.[20]

Those who suggest alternatives to marriage do not receive nearly as much mainstream attention as authors such as Sullivan and Eskridge, and as a result, the radical potential of gay relationships remains outside of mainstream political discussion and rhetoric.[21] As Julie Abraham has argued, the argument for gay marriage rights that has received the most prominence is premised on including gay men within the institution in order to allow them to be more fully both gay and masculine.[22] Eskridge might well deny this, arguing that he explicitly wishes to tie his argument for gay marriage to feminist concerns for equality within marriage.[23] He does not, however, recognize the extent to which inequality in heterosexual relationships comes from structural inequalities, rather than lack of role models. Aside from this, his inability to counter conservative understandings of masculinity and monogamy make the linkage between gay marriage rights and feminism less than successful. Blasius, Seidman, and Weeks[24] each take up the project of rethinking the meaning of ethics, family, and sexuality.

Most work on gay couples, from the interviews of Blumstein and Schwartz[25] to those of Weeks, Heaphy, and Donovan,[26] indicate that many gay couples are not monogamous and do not see monogamy as a goal. Instead, they form strong, enduring relationships in which sex may or may not be central to a coupled relationship. It is the ability to negotiate these relationships and create safe spaces for those involved that has prompted reflection on ethics in relationships where monogamy, if it exists, is an agreement, rather than a social precept. In relation to marriage and relationships, Weeks, Heaphy, and Donovan argue that balance between individual freedom and commitment to others allows gay men and lesbians to build "families of choice."[27] What social conservatives see as a decline of commitment, many gay/lesbian couples see as the freedom to construct new visions of commitments, visions that require an understanding of sexuality different from that embodied in traditional values and that undermine gender binarism by suggesting that unmarried men do not threaten society. Gay relationship recognition will only progress when it is possible to persuade people that individuals can be responsible and not married. This is a significant challenge, particularly because not only conservatives, but also their Democratic opposition, have constructed debates about welfare not as debates about social rights, but as a debate about the failure of welfare recipients to meet their responsibilities, with responsible family again defined as both heterosexual and married.

DEPENDENCE AND THE SEXUAL FAMILY

Welfare reform in the 1990s moves us back to an earlier understanding that welfare is necessary because of individual failings.[28] In this understanding, programs such as Aid to Families with Dependent Children (AFDC) fail to change people and therefore cause poverty to continue. Fighting the "dependence" that results is a mechanism with which to attack women's freedom, but as Teresa Amott notes, the phrase "long-term dependent" has also long "functioned as a code word for black."[29] The legacy of our racial past makes this a particularly persuasive discourse in the United States. Blaming poor (black) women for not being independent, while blaming (white) feminists for trying to become independent seems like an odd combination for the Right to justify.[30] These positions are reconcilable if the centrality of the male breadwinner model to Right discourse is understood: what women on welfare and feminists are guilty of is failing to marry and be dependent on a husband. The costs of this failure are particularly high in relation to the poor because it is also connected to youth crime and pregnancy.[31] The policies that the Right advocates to address such concerns are varied. At the most extreme, though also most consistent, are those that promote "wedfare" not workfare, limit benefits to mothers who have additional children, and require that teen mothers live with their parents in order to get benefits.[32] The goal of wedfare is to create two-parent families, whether by teaching abstinence until marriage, encouraging adoption, or providing higher state benefits to married couples or mothers. Such policies do not just save the state money, but further a vision of appropriate behavior. A less punitive version of such policies promotes "responsible fatherhood," a concept that is as related to monetary support, thus government savings, as to significant involvement by men in families.

The extent to which this language and definition of reality gained the political upper hand is clear from the support that policy changes similar to those in the Republican Party's Contract with America received from many congressional Democrats, as well as Bill Clinton. In its summary of the welfare reform legislation, the *Washington Post* noted, "The federal welfare overhaul signed into law last August gradually upends the notion of cash benefits for single mothers and mandates that states promote stable, two-parent households that can make it on their own."[33] Signing the Personal Responsibility and Work Reconciliation Act (PRWORA) into law, though a compromise for Clinton, was consistent with his goal of fostering two-parent, "independent" households. The Clinton administration, following his Republican predecessors, had already granted waivers to states to allow them to set time limits for welfare, put work requirements in place, and require teenage mothers to live at home.[34] State waivers, Cammisa argues, were generally premised on the idea that the behavior of the poor needed be controlled and that they needed to be forced into dominant social values.[35]

The process that ended welfare as an entitlement is most intriguing because these changes were signed into law by a president whose support came from the constituencies most harmed either directly or indirectly by the law; that is, those who need welfare entitlements and those who do not see heterosexual nuclear families with males as the dominant providers as desirable. The latter are harmed because Clinton based his rationale on the need to restore fathers to families in order to end child poverty. As a recent report prepared by the Policy Institute of the National Gay and Lesbian Task Force so clearly points out, holding fathers liable for child support or trying to minimize welfare by encouraging women to marry men assumes or coerces heterosexuality.[36] Al Gore agrees with Clinton that the sexual family is central for coping with the many problems associated with poverty: "The father can no longer be cropped out of the family photograph."[37]

An interesting glimpse into this rhetoric for New Democrats is present in Hillary Clinton's *It Takes a Village,* published in 1996.[38] The timing of this book—it was published in the same year that Clinton signed the PRWORA and as he was running for reelection—combined with her history as the initiator of "big government" health care reform suggests that it was an attempt by the Clintons to construct themselves as opposed to big government but concerned about children's needs. The book failed to provide leadership on these issues and, instead, reinforced conservative values. The chapter "Every Child Needs a Chance" is an excellent example of these dynamics.[39] The chapter begins (as do most) with personal reflections from the Clintons' own divorced birth families. She suggests that in the cases of her mother and her husband, positive growth was realized because each was surrounded by caring adults. Clinton notes that such caring is a greater problem today because nonparental adults are often less available. She moves on to uncritically and without citation summarize research that finds children in single-parent homes more at risk for a variety of behavioral pathologies and poor social outcomes.[40] After warning that child poverty has increased in part because of divorce and out-of-wedlock births, she reflects on making divorce more difficult and/or preparing people better for marriage and helping them to divorce with greater civility and concern for children.[41]

"Every Child Needs a Chance" ends by conceding that although divorce and single-parent families may correlate with negative outcomes, they do not directly cause them. She cites a long-term study in Hawaii in which resiliency of children from poor and divorced families was affected by "social supports" and the "dependability of adults."[42] She concludes the chapter by discussing the desirability of making adoption easier, praising her husband's support for such measures, and reaffirming the importance of nuclear families for a critical mass of children. Although Clinton does suggest at times that organizations that provide nonparental support for children are important—after all, it does take a village—the overall tone of the book waivers between condemnation of those who do not fit the nuclear family mold and acknowledgment that perhaps this is not the only possible model. In the process, she does not present poverty as a result of changing economic forces or an increasingly stingy welfare state, nor does she present the need for adoption as in part a failure of policy. Instead, adoption is a good alternative when parents make bad choices. Her ambivalence about how families have changed since the 1950s serves more to reinforce the ideal of the sexual family than to ask how our society might better provide the kind of supports that the Hawaii study suggests are important. Further, her support for women now entering the workforce constructs this decision making as largely a choice rather than as a necessity for many women.[43] I believe the shortcomings of Hillary Rodham Clinton's analysis are emblematic of liberals' failure to confront the ramifications of changes in the labor market and women's roles for society. At the same time, the social programs that both Clintons supported have helped to prompt a backlash from another group—the childless. This backlash reinforces another pillar of the Right's vision of family.

PARENTAL POWER

Children and youth play a particularly important role in social conservative discourse. Social conservatives understand "family" as in part a defense against outsiders influencing children; therefore, they have backed the Parental Rights and Responsibilities Amendment (PRRA) in order to secure control of children for parents.[44] This law would ensure that parental rights are not usurped by schools that teach sex education or that promote "secular humanism." The belief that parents should have a primary voice in relation to their children is not unique to social conservatives. Even without PRRA, it is embedded in U.S. law and is part of the discourse of Clinton Democrats. At the same time, it is a right and an obligation that many parents recognize as problematic in a world in which they have less time to spend with their children and peers exert a powerful influence.

The difficulty that many parents have of combining care for children with employment has been joined to fears of young people and for young people. The common assertion that problems such as youth crime, school violence, and teen pregnancy and sexuality result from young people not being taught proper morality and self-control by their parents puts pressure on parents to be "good parents" and to control their children. Public policy that addresses this pressure helps parents so that they can make good, individual decisions for their children by providing flextime at work, parental leave, resources for day care, increasing tax deductions for mothers who do enter the labor force, and so forth. At the same time, parents who cannot gain control with these resources (or who do not receive them at all since most are in the form of tax deductions) are punished for their children's behavior. The Bush desire to open up after-school programs to "faith-based" groups, as well as his voucher plan, would allow parents increased access to social resources for the instruction of their children into religious beliefs. What is common to both the more ideological Bush proposals and the Clinton policies is that they transfer public resources to parents.

Elinor Burkett opposes these programs, arguing in *The Baby Boon: How Family Friendly America Cheats the Childless,* that they harm the childless.[45] Her arguments reveal the ways social conservative Republicans and Democrats are similar (both advocate policies that harm lower-class children while aiding middle- and upper-class parents) *and* suggests that fairness to the childless requires that we take more seriously the idea that children are private goods. For example, she notes the contradiction embedded in social conservative arguments that parents should make decisions for their children, yet everyone else should pay to enact them. In relation to vouchers for school choice, she notes, "Suddenly we are asked to finance school choice, which means that parents will use *our* money to make *their* choice."[46] Instead, she argues that we should "throw 'parental' entitlements into the dustbin of bad ideas, and, if we really care about children and families, use the money that we save by ending subsidies to parents earning sixty thousand dollars a year or more to make sure that every kid in this nation has enough food, a decent education, and a safe place to live."[47]

Although Burkett lays some blame for the redistribution that she discusses on the selfishness of baby boomers, she argues that the most compelling force driving redistribution to the middle class are race- and class-based fears. She cites Bill Clinton's concern that "deferral of child-bearing" is very troubling for our country: "the people in the best position to build strong kids, and bring the kids up in a good way, are deciding not to do so."[48] Such rhetoric is reminiscent of early-twentieth-century rhetoric designed to prevent "race-suicide" and makes clear how the need to restore the nuclear family is often connected to race- and class-based fears. However, despite this critique of the rationale behind current family policies, Burkett's argument remains firmly within a free-market, privatized understanding of family. Her assertion that children belong to their parents returns us to the public-private separation that feminists identify as the central issue in how "family" is conceptualized: the recognition of the "private" as the realm of women's unpaid labor. "How much further are we going to go," she asks, "in turning what have traditionally been considered private functions into ones that are public enough to demand financial support?"[49] Interestingly, Burkett does not take her own argument seriously enough to suggest that marriage, and the many benefits that come with it, be abolished. It is the most costly and time-consuming caring labor that Burkett defines as "private." Since women can now choose to do other work, this traditional caring labor is an individual's choice, with that choice bearing consequences for the individual.

Clearly, social conservatives (and sometimes New Democrats) would like to find ways to encourage women to choose to provide such labor again, or in the case of poor women, find ways to coerce them into providing it. Burkett, though equally disinclined to recognize caring labor as a public good, reaches a very different conclusion: being childless is a positive choice and those who are childless should not be punished. Such a notion of privacy as a primary good is compatible with a conservative defense of individual choice as essential to preserving public morality. Yet, if we accept family as firmly embedded within the private realm, Burkett's alternative is just as plausible as that of social conservatives. Given statistical analysis, she argues, a significant portion of the public is choosing to not have children. Embedding policy in public morality requires not that social conservative values be applied to public policy, but that policymakers actually begin to listen to those who make other choices about resources. Thus, Burkett is a laissez-faire liberal making an alternative conservative argument about family privacy. Burkett is unable to see social interdependence as a rationale for any but the most minimal of supports. We could cope with the legitimate choice that individuals make to not have children by increasing immigration. This, she argues, would assure the solvency of social security without depending on U.S.-born children. Though immigration is, and will continue to be, a critical means for supporting our aging population, the acceptance of transferring resources from immigrants to aging childless people does not strike Burkett as the kind of transfer to which she is so opposed.[50] Although it is convenient to deny the role that young people play in the lives of all adults in order to justify why parents alone should be responsible for their progeny, it is no easier to be independent today than it was at previous points in history; it is simply easier to deny the dependence. Burkett may wish to see the money that would be saved from cutting programs that benefit the middle class used to "provide food, decent education, and a safe place to live," but once the idea that children are private goods and adults should be independent is reinforced, the lack of will to support such programs becomes easier to justify.

The model of the private, sexual family fails to account for how social change affects families and youth. In a complex society with developed communication technologies, youth are more subject to influences that may not fit with the values of their parents. This can either result in a desire for reprivatized families in which parents can exert control or a desire to help young people develop new skills to cope with their choices. Fostering the growth and protection of youth by recognizing them as capable of making important decisions at a younger age than the legal system acknowledges is a serious social issue. At the same time, balancing the social benefits that young people provide to society with the resources that they require is also a serious question for public policy. Both questions can be effectively ignored if public discourse around families focuses on creating financially independent, two-parent families for which privacy is the central and defining good. As Minow notes, even minimal interventions to give children protections currently come under attack because they are embedded in discussions of race, gender, religion, and poverty.[51] When the private, two-parent heterosexual family is defined as responsible for children, Minow's goal of the "honest assessment of children's entitlements" is exceedingly difficult to attain.[52]

CONCLUSION

New Democrats and gay marriage proponents are trying to gain the support of middle-class Americans by proving their allegiance to middle-class values. The difficulty is that they end up reinforcing an overall value system that often works against the changing families that they seek to recognize, thus helping to create the perspective of Burkett. In this way, liberals and those on the left fail to construct a meaningful vision of family in part because they do not take nonliberal feminist theory seriously. Mona Harrington summarizes the central issues:

> There is no mainstream liberal program that measures the economics of caretaking for the whole country, that charts the distribution of caretaking work, that assigns weight to care as a value defining national goals, that takes a stand on the importance of family as a source of care, that speaks to the moral dimension of families as a social unit, or that even begins to recognize the ways in which women's equality is bound up with the organization of families and care.[53]

Similarly, Nancy Fraser sees liberal feminists as confronting these issues by trying to create the conditions whereby women can themselves become breadwinners, thus able to support their own "independent" families. This is an approach, she argues, that is doomed to fail because it does not recognize the value of what has been traditionally "women's work." Further, although she assumes that a best-case version of liberal feminism would include adequate compensation for those who perform caretaking work in the public realm, this is far from the reality that policy such as welfare reform creates. As Dorothy Roberts argues, it instead reinforces a division between "spiritual" work in the home and "menial" work, with poor, black women doing the latter. Roberts reports "that a third of child care centers surveyed in five cities now employ welfare recipients who are satisfying work requirements."[54] Each argues that we must begin by valuing the labor of all caretakers and recognizing that "dependency" rather than being a negative characteristic of some is, in Eva Kittay's words, "the fount of all social organization."[55]

If we understand dependency as inevitable and social, then we are in a position to consider how, as a society, we can use our resources to provide the care for young people that the Hawaii study suggests is necessary. Other social scientific work also indicates that we might usefully ask how, as a society, we might enhance the freedom of adults in ways that do not threaten the development of the young. Judith Stacey's review of a significant number of studies of families suggests that reframing the questions that we ask can produce useful knowledge for addressing this question. Nancy Dowd indicates that there is no good reason to believe that fathers are necessary to raise healthy children and that there is nothing magical about having two parents. "The support role does not require sexual intimacy nor heterosexuality as a precondition for its performance."[56] Dowd's point is that if we understand that people play roles, we can begin to reconceptualize those roles to fit the realities of people's lives in ways that provide adequate support to children. But, as Stacey points out, social discourse about family is dominated by flawed studies showing that children need two, heterosexual parents. "Once dissenting scholarly views on the pathology of single-parent families had been muffled or marginalized," she observes, "only a rhetorical baby-step was needed to move from the social to the moral inferiority of such families."[57]

Moving away from a view of society that begins from a particular kind of family and a particular definition of what it means to be an American who deserves state resources is a complex undertaking. The task is unlikely to be accomplished by mainstream politicians of either party or by activists committed to liberal, individualist ideas. It is also likely to be much harder in a post–September 11th world with revived nationalism and renewed fears of immigrants and those who are "different." I do not believe that this rhetoric can be challenged without the rebuilding of a feminist and gay liberationist-informed political left, one that is cognizant of the economic relationship between economic issues and identity. Such a political perspective would need to start from exploring the ways in which U.S. citizenship and family values have been constructed to exclude those whose demonization serves to bind the rest together while denying the real needs of those who are not economically privileged. Building such a perspective will not be easy, but to deny the fundamental differences that exist between the Right and those who hope to further the causes of women, the poor, or sexual minorities is to agree to play within a framework that the Right controls.

NOTES

1. Thomas Byrne Edsall and Mary D. Edsall, *Chain Reaction: The Impact of Race, Rights, and Taxes on American Politics* (New York: Norton, 1992), 203.
2. Martha Albertson Fineman, *The Neutered Mother, the Sexual Family, and Other Twentieth Century Travesties* (New York: Routledge, 1995), 161.
3. Paul Gilbert, "Family Values and the Nation State," in *Changing Family Values*, ed. Gill Jagger and Caroline Wright (London: Routledge, 1999), 140.
4. Jyl Josephson and Cynthia Burack, "The Political Ideology of the Neo-Traditional Family," *Journal of Political Ideologies* 3, no. 2 (1998): 227.
5. Fineman, *Neutered Mother*, 159.
6. Nancy F. Cott, *Public Vows* (Cambridge, Mass.: Harvard University Press, 2000). As Cott details, Native Americans were encouraged to marry as part of attempts to make them citizens; African Americans were defined as unable to grant consent and not allowed to marry.
7. As Mink discusses in detail, feminists committed to maternalism were important in furthering policies with racist implications. See Gwendolyn Mink, *The Wages of Motherhood: Inequality in the Welfare State* (Ithaca, N.Y.: Cornell University Press, 1995), 149–50.
8. See Jill Quadagno, *The Color of Welfare* (New York: Oxford University Press, 1994) and Nancy Dowd, *In Defense of Single Parent Families* (New York: New York University Press, 1997).
9. Kirk Mann and Sasha Roseneil, "Gender, Agency, and the Underclass," in *Changing Family Values*, ed. Gill Jagger and Caroline Wright (London: Routledge, 1999), 108.
10. Julian Carter, "Normality, Whiteness, and Authorship," in *Sciences and Homosexualities*, ed. Vernon A. Rosario (New York: Routledge, 1997), 155.
11. Rebecca E Klatch, *Women of the New Right* (Philadelphia: Temple University Press, 1987), 137.

12. Klatch, *Women of the New Right*, 138. Further, this evaluation of men is also racialized, with black men perceived as significantly more dangerous and out of control. For a discussion of the impact of this image on black male youth and of how schools contribute to it, see Ann Arnett Ferguson, *Bad Boys* (Ann Arbor: University of Michigan Press, 2001).

13. "Heroic Selfishness," *Family Research Council*, 1997, at www.frc.org/fampol/fp97llf.html (accessed March 1, 2001).

14. Judith Stacey, *In the Name of the Family* (Boston: Beacon, 1996), 23.

15. Josephson and Burack, "Political Ideology"; Gill Jagger and Caroline Wright, eds., introduction, in *Changing Family Values* (London: Routledge, 1999).

16. Richard Collier, *Masculinity, Law, and the Family* (London: Routledge, 1995), 149.

17. Andrew Sullivan, *Virtually Normal* (New York: Vintage, 1996), 109. See also William N. Eskridge Jr., *The Case for Same-Sex Marriage* (New York: Free Press, 1996), 83.

18. Eskridge bolsters his case by pointing out that two-parent families are superior.

19. Sullivan, *Virtually Normal*, 202.

20. See Jeffrey Weeks, *Invented Moralities* (New York: Columbia University Press, 1995); Mark Blasius, *Gay and Lesbian Politics* (Philadelphia: Temple University Press, 1994); Steven Seidman, *Embattled Eros* (New York: Routledge, 1992); and Jeffrey Weeks, Brian Heaphy, and Catherine Donovan, *Same-Sex Intimacies: Families of Choice and Other Life Experiments* (London: Routledge, 2001).

21. One of the earliest statements of this argument was made by Paula Ettelbrick. See Paula L. Ettelbrick, "Since When Is Marriage a Path to Liberation?" *Outlook*, no. 6 (fall 1989). See also Valerie Lehr, *Queer Family Values* (Philadelphia: Temple University Press, 1999); and Michael Warner, *The Trouble with Normal* (New York: Free Press, 1999).

22. Julie Abraham, "Public Relations: Why the Rush to Same-Sex Marriage? And Who Stands to Benefit?" *Women's Review of Books* 17, no. 8 (2000): 12.

23. Eskridge, *Case for Same-Sex Marriage*.

24. Blasius, *Gay and Lesbian Politics*; Seidman, *Embattled Eros*; and Weeks, *Invented Moralities*.

25. Philip Blumstein and Pepper Schwartz, *American Couples* (New York: Morrow, 1983).

26. Weeks et al., *Same-Sex Intimacies*.

27. Weeks et al., *Same-Sex Intimacies*.

28. Anne Marie Cammisa, *From Rhetoric to Reform?* (Boulder, Colo.: Westview, 1998), 37.

29. Teresa Amott, "Black Women and AFDC," in *Women, the State, and Welfare*, ed. Linda Gordon (Madison: University of Wisconsin Press, 1990), 290.

30. Jeremy Rabkin, "Feminism: Where the Spirit of the Sixties Lives On," in *Reassessing the Sixties*, ed. Stephen Macedo (New York: Norton, 1997), 52.

31. See David Blankenhorn, *Fatherless America* (New York: Basic, 1995); and Dowd, *In Defense*, 10.

32. "America Needs Wedfare, Not Workfare," *Family Research Council,* 1995, at www.frc.org/infocus/i95a3wl.html (accessed March 1, 2001).

33. Jon Jeter, "Making Family a Man's World," *Washington Post,* July 8, 1997.

34. Cammisa, *From Rhetoric to Reform?* 107.

35. Cammisa, *From Rhetoric to Reform?* 114.

36. Sean Cahill and Kenneth T. Jones, "Leaving Our Children Behind" (Washington, D.C.: Policy Institute of the National Gay and Lesbian Task Force, December 10, 2001).

37. "Al Gore on Families and Children," *Issues 2000,* 2000, at www.issues2000.org/celeb/algoreFamilies&Children.htm (accessed October 20, 2000).

38. Hillary Rodham Clinton, *It Takes a Village and Other Lessons That Children Teach Us* (New York: Simon and Schuster, 1996).

39. Clinton, *It Takes a Village,* 33–35.

40. Clinton, *It Takes a Village,* 40.

41. Clinton, *It Takes a Village,* 40.

42. Clinton, *It Takes a Village,* 46.

43. Clinton, *It Takes a Village,* 210.

44. "Parental Rights," *Family Research Council,* 1996, at www.frc.org/fampol/fp96hpa.html (accessed March 1, 2001).

45. Elinor Burkett, *The Baby Boon: How Family-Friendly America Cheats the Childless* (New York: Free Press, 2000).

46. Burkett, *Baby Boon,* 12.

47. Burkett, *Baby Boon,* 214.

48. Burkett, *Baby Boon,* 144.

49. Burkett, *Baby Boon,* 82.

50. Encouraging the best and brightest from other countries to come to the United States to replace the middle class does not seem to strike her as an ethical problem.

51. Martha Minow, "Whatever Happened to Children's Rights?" in *Reassessing the Sixties,* ed. Stephen Macedo (New York: Norton, 1997), 115.

52. Minow, "Whatever Happened to Children's Rights?" 115.

53. Mona Harrington, *Care and Equality* (New York: Routledge, 2000), 7.

54. Dorothy Roberts, "Welfare's Ban on Poor Motherhood," in *Whose Welfare?* ed. Gwendolyn Mink (Ithaca, N.Y.: Cornell University Press, 1999), 162.

55. Eva Feder Kittay, "Welfare, Dependency, and a Public Ethic of Care," in *Whose Welfare?* ed. Gwendolyn Mink (Ithaca, N.Y.: Cornell University Press, 1999), 198.

56. Dowd, *In Defense,* 32.

57. Stacey, *In the Name of the Family,* 60.

8

Not Really a "New Attitude": Dr. Laura on Gender and Morality

Victoria Davion

In this chapter, I discuss the role of concepts such as "natural" and "biological" in the views of Dr. Laura Schlessinger, the well-known talk radio host and author. For those not acquainted with "Dr. Laura," she is the host of a popular internationally syndicated radio talk show and the author of several *New York Times* best-sellers, including *Ten Stupid Things Women Do to Mess Up Their Lives, Ten Stupid Things Men Do to Mess Up Their Lives, Ten Stupid Things Parents Do to Mess Up Their Kids,* and *Ten Stupid Things Couples Do to Mess Up Their Relationships.*[1] In the advice she gives callers on her talk show, and consistently throughout her books, Dr. Laura champions "traditional" values, arguing in favor of strict gender divisions within marriage, stay-at-home moms, raising children religiously, and arguing against working moms, "feminists" (although her characterizations of them are alien to me), "shacking up," homosexual parenting, and any attempt at gender blending. Dr. Laura's position on the moral state of contemporary American society is clear: "Next to the chaotic, amoral, ultraliberal, current social *norms* that currently dictate our behaviors, hyperindividuality is the worst problem we people have in relating to one another."[2] Dr. Laura claims that her advice is the product of an old-fashioned value system respecting "natural" and "biological" differences between the sexes. In other words, her message is not a new one, but an old one that contemporary American society has lost respect for. Her goal is to see that view reinstituted as it respects "healthy" gender differences between men and women and is the best environment for the raising of children.

My project is to use a feminist lens to illuminate Dr. Laura's picture of the role of biology in so-called gender-based differences between the sexes. I argue that when examined from a feminist perspective, views like Dr. Laura's are actually quite antimale. This is important because while many who hold such views believe feminists are man hating, I argue the reverse. Feminist calls for men to change common yet problematic behaviors are far more respectful of men than the Dr. Laura approach, although most who hold such "traditional" views would deny this. Before continuing, I want to restate that Dr. Laura's position is nothing new; the fact that it is old-fashioned is something she is proud of and continually points out in her books. So, what I call the "traditional gender view" should be very familiar to readers of this chapter. I argue that the traditional gender view is completely entrenched in most people's thinking about gender, even if they believe in such ideas as working moms and gender equality in the workplace, and even if they believe that fathers should have equal responsibility in raising children. This view operates on many different levels, and I believe most people hold some version of it, though to differing degrees. Contrary to what Dr. Laura says, this view appears to be incredibly durable, and its durability should be of interest to feminists. I shall first explain the traditional gender view and then critique it from a feminist perspective, showing why I believe it is both dangerous and antimale.

According to the traditional gender view, biological differences between men and women explain differences in behaviors:

> There are clearly bimorphic anatomical and physiological differences between male and female, there's not much argument about that. The fight begins when we introduce bimorphic tendencies to behavior. Well friends, we aren't plants and we aren't minerals; we are animals, and with that comes certain biological imperatives or pressures. The amazing thing about humanity is that we can override biology with a mere decision to do so, e.g., a man staying home as the primary child caretaker, or a man mating with one woman when sexual variety might mean something special to the gene pool. I have come to believe that societal pressures to conform exist not to create something which isn't there, but rather to emphasize something that is built into the animal with respect to masculine and feminine.[3]

While many might disagree with the idea that biological drives dictate such things as staying home or going to work, the belief that there is at least some biological basis for so-called gender-based behavioral differences between the sexes is fairly common. It is the cornerstone of the traditional gender view.

Dr. Laura's fairly typical version of this view is this: "While biologists don't see much noninstinctive behavior in nonhuman animals which they can label as noble or altruistic, they do see a pattern of male aggression ensuring protection of turf, nest, mate, family, and group—a biological division of labor with the females protecting and nurturing their young."

> I was originally trained as a biologist, and I am convinced that the animal part of our nature is the engine of our drives; our ability to reason, to embrace morality, to go beyond the biological navigates the direction of those drives—which is why we can go haywire! Being "animal" is easy, being an "ascendent human" requires manual override of some of our more animal (food consumption, random mating) as well as our less worthy human attributes (laziness, self-centeredness,and so on).[4]

As we shall see, this idea of human morality and reason being able to harness purely biological drives is a key aspect to the traditional gender view. A final central component of the view is the idea that men and women necessarily see sex differently due to differences in "natural" drives. Dr. Laura argues that there is some truth to the old saying that men give love for sex while women give sex for love. Hence, men have a "natural" drive toward polygamy while women have a "natural" drive toward monogamy:

> Most scientists attribute this raging, impersonal male libido to men's nearly infinite potential rate of procreation. A female requires nine months to gestate, followed by a couple of years of breast-feeding and weaning, followed by a dozen and a half years of more nurturing till college and out of the nest. The male's single "biological" imperative is depositing sperm in as many available uteri as possible to increase and extend his gene pool possibilities into the future generations.[5]

Hence:

> The old saying that "men give love to get sex and women give sex to get love" actually has some foundation in the "biology." On the woman's side first: Giving "sex" to a man inspires the "hope" that this availability will keep him near; that when he produces children he'll feel "connected" enough to protect and provide while she nurtures. On the male's side: He talks of love to gain the opportunity to play Johnny Appleseed with his DNA.[6]

These innate differences play out in different ways, which is why it is very important that children be raised by "traditional" families. In the case of men:

> I deeply believe that your ability to be this "human male" (man) absolutely requires femininity—not in yourself, however (so don't get all in a lather

about that "female side" that is supposed to be lurking somewhere in your psychic innards), but instead in your partner. Your expedition from male to "human male" is taught by other men, but tempered and civilized by the significant women in your life; your mother and your wife. For example, it is more likely that your father taught you to "take it (or dole it out) like a man," whereas your mother would more likely care-take your hurt feelings and suggest a more compassionate view of whoever is your nemesis. Neither approach is right or wrong, but both are necessary.[7]

These "natural," "biological" differences lead straight to a gender-complementarity approach that is the final cornerstone of the traditional gender view:

> Therein lies the potential for balance and harmony: men and women, two polarities, each tempered by the unique qualities of the other, a potentially wonderful balance of outer and inner directedness. It only works where there is respect, admiration, and appreciation for what the "opposite" gender has to offer. There is little existing societal respect for masculinity.[8]

According to Dr. Laura, antimale attitudes and lack of respect for anything considered "masculine" are part of the decline of the "traditional family," needed to produce healthy human beings. The respect for masculinity needed to complete necessary gender complementarity is missing. This causes problems for individual men and women, and for society generally. She claims there is a growing "hostility to anything masculine and there is victimization mentality about anything feminine."[9] Dr. Laura blames feminists for this breakdown, and she is clearly very worried about it as there are wildly negative (insulting and misrepresentative) discussions of feminism in all of her books. It is unclear why she believes that feminists have had such a major impact, but that she does believe this is clear: "However, our cumulative awareness of both gender's ability to perpetrate "evil" or stupidity has been ignored, hidden, and lied about in the growing anti-male climate, to which even somewhat decent inappropriately compassionate men, in self-defense to the constant feminist rancor of self-proclaimed oppression and victimization, subscribe."[10]

The result is the creation of a society in which "even the mere mention of 'male' or 'masculine' *nature* is met with a cry for universal rehabilitation."[11] And "The bottom line is that *male* and *masculine* have become synonymous with all that is wrong and evil with society, and femininity is touted as *the* answer."[12]

Here we see the basic tenets of the traditional gender view. It relies on the following: inherent biological differences which lead directly to different behaviors and preferences (although there may be significant disagreements as to exactly what they are); the need for heterosexual unions and a general acceptance of the idea of gender complementarity (each gender has qualities that complement the other) as needed for both the health of adult men and women and healthy rearing of girls and boys. Dr. Laura's version of this view includes the idea that it is "natural" for women to stay at home raising children and men to be the financial providers. Our current "crisis," in Dr. Laura's view, can be attributed to the breakdown of these traditional ideas, apparently facilitated by feminists.

Dr. Laura claims that she is highly pro-men, unlike the general climate in our society. In fact, she says the following in the introduction to *Ten Stupid Things Women Do to Mess Up Their Lives:* "By the way, I'm aware that women psychologists are generally mistrusted by men as male-bashers. If any of you guys are sneaking a peek at this book, you can relax. If anything I'm woman bashing! And get ready, women, because I'm taking off the gloves and telling you the truth. You can take it. You need to hear it."[13]

I agree that Dr. Laura is a woman basher. Her book on men constantly talks about the struggle men have to deal with in order to harness their drive toward polygamy and remain in a faithful relationship. She is highly sympathetic about the difficulty of overriding what she sees as "the single biological imperative" for men, planting their sperm in as many uteri as possible. However, the most forceful "instinct" or "biological drive" Dr. Laura mentions for women is a "maternal instinct," which she sees as basically conducive to monogamy (remember that women "naturally" seek monogamy and provide sex in order to obtain it). Her tone and manner in discussing women is much less sympathetic and more scolding. She blames women for "stupid choices" and objects to blaming such "choices" on oppression, other societal forces, or biology. Hence, she provides a framework in which it is more "natural" and understandable if men mess up in their struggle against the "single biological imperative."

Dr. Laura's woman bashing goes beyond simply blaming individual women for "stupid choices" without providing any analysis of why such choices are in her words "typical." In addition, Dr. Laura blames women for what she sees as the breakdown of the social order and degeneration of the traditional gender view. Hence, it isn't just feminists who are responsible, it is women in general. Dr. Laura is concerned enough to make this point that she tells the same story in two of her books. It appears first in the introduction to her *Women* book, which was published in 1994:

> On the second motivation for this book: my father, who once remarked at
> dinner that men couldn't get away with anything rotten, political, or personal,

unless women let them. He listed every conceivable transgression—petty robbery, abuse, war, governmental corruption, you name it. According to his argument, the ultimate power of women over men was their sexual acceptance and/or approval.

. . . I continued to ponder the possibility that there might be some truth to my father's theory. A woman, I reasoned, is not responsible for a man's choices. She is however, responsible for her own—which too often entail tolerating some obnoxious male behaviors in order to avoid, for example, loneliness, self-assertiveness, and self-sufficiency.

If from the first meeting with an ill-mannered lout, a woman expressed her disdain clearly and confidently, the guy would either shape up or expect to get shipped out. If, instead, she focuses on her dependency and desperate need for male acceptance while forgetting about his dependency and craving for approval and continues to be sexually receptive, she'll be giving him the signal that she condones the behavior.[14]

This is restated again in the *Couples* book in 2001:

I know what you are thinking . . . that I am blaming women alone for the current social mess. I do put more emphasis on women, because I see them as the ones with the ultimate power. What women won't allow, men can't and won't do. I learned this from my now deceased father. The notion inspired my first book *Ten Stupid Things Women Do to Mess Up Their Lives*. He and I argued about responsibility, and he made the point that the upward or downward trend of the morals and morale of a culture was dependent on what women did and permitted. He believed that men, rejected by women, would not continue the behavior that got them rejected in the first place. From womb (mother) to vagina (sex), he said men are judged and approved of by women. Men behave badly when women accept it—simple as that.[15]

So there you have it. Women are to blame for *all* bad behaviors by individual men in their lives, as well as the general conditions within the culture in which they live. This certainly *sounds* like women bashing to me. It blames women for all types of violence against women, including rape, domestic violence, and verbal abuse. All women need to do to prevent these things is to withhold sex from men who are behaving "poorly." And that is it! Dr. Laura offers no other commentary on her key point. She offers no additional discussion of race, class, or ethnicity. The situation is the same for everyone.

In my view, this is a thinly disguised presentation of what well-known feminist theorist John Stoltenberg has called "rapist ethics." According to Stoltenberg, contemporary American society has traditionally subscribed to an "unofficial" yet deeply entrenched moral code (rapist ethics), in which although men rape, women are held responsible. Women "provoke" men into rape, and if women behaved better, rape would not occur. According to Stoltenberg, most would deny holding a gender-based ethic: "Nearly all people believe deeply and unshakably that there are some things that are wrong for a woman to do while right for a man and that other things are wrong for a man to do while right for a woman. . . . It is a creed whose articles never require articulation, because its believers rarely encounter anyone who does not already believe it, silently and by heart."[16] This is part of the "boys will be boys" mentality that excuses much violent and disrespectful male behavior.

The traditional gender view as presented by Dr. Laura encourages "rapist ethics." It is natural for men to want to have sex with as many women as possible; in fact, it is their only "biological imperative." Given this, it is women's responsibility to "control" situations so that rape does not occur. If she fails in this (dresses too provocatively, goes out alone at night, or lets her date into her house), then *she* is responsible for what happens. This explains the odd historical tradition of blaming women for their rapes. According to Stoltenberg, this ethic is justified precisely by the idea that men are motivated by a powerful "biological" sex drive they cannot be expected to control. Stoltenberg believes this is actually a myth that we teach young boys, and in teaching that it is "normal" or "natural" for them to want sex all the time, we create a situation in which men become obsessed with sex in order to prove their manhood. I return to this point later.

Dr. Laura believes that in spite of the "one biological imperative," men can learn to be monogamous. To explain this, she invokes the categories of male and man. The male part is the animal part that responds only to biological impulses and is driven by animal instinct. This must be balanced with the "human" part to produce "civilized man." In explaining this to men, she states: "This is an area where biology, though true, significant, and powerfully driven must duel with morality. When what 'is natural' is deemed 'good,' the fabric of lives begins to unravel."[17] However, this will be a struggle, particularly for men, because "men's sexual biology is compelling . . . a profound struggle with respect to making the 'natural' more 'human.'"[18]

This brings us to an interesting twist in the Dr. Laura logic. While men's biology is in conflict with moral duties such as monogamy and commitment to one family, women's biology is presented as consistent with the higher moral imperatives required of humans:

Human males have always had a typically restless attitude about new adventure, exploit, challenge, battle, etc., human females with their more highly developed emotional empathy gravitate toward relationships, understanding, and feelings. Given this inherent difference in drive and perspective, it becomes clearer why women have been the civilizing factor for men and society as they strive for family, monogamy, stability, order, and peace.[19]

So, despite what can be taken as Dr. Laura's women-bashing attitudes, she seems to believe that women are more "naturally moral" (read: better, as it is better to be moral) than men. Our biological drives aim us at the human good, while the biological drives of men aim them at lower "animal" behavior. This explains why Dr. Laura holds that it is women's responsibility to civilize (read: train) men by giving or withholding sex. Dr. Laura states this over and over again: "Women historically set the limits of appropriate, permissible, and moral behavior. It was expected that a man might 'offer' or 'try' some things which came close to the line, but that he ultimately knew that the line would be set and enforced by the woman."[20]

I can remember a conversation with my grandfather that was similar to the one Dr. Laura relates with her father, in which women are said to hold the ultimate "power" over men and are therefore responsible for the general moral climate. The major difference was that my grandfather clearly stated that this meant women are *better* than men. Women possess the truly "human" qualities of kindness and compassion, while men are basically animals to be held in check by women. Despite herself, Dr. Laura practically says this, although in her "official view" gender differences are neither better nor worse, just different. Hence, while Dr. Laura claims, "It has become increasingly clear that men and women do not think alike, but too many academic and psychological research types are so determined to prove feminine equality or superiority, they can't seem to be honest and nonjudgmental about gender *differences*."[21] Yet, Dr. Laura's discussion clearly implies female superiority, and at times, she comes close to, if not actually, admitting it:

> As you can see, being a man has a lot to do with reconciling classical masculine ideals with so-called feminine (actually, deeply human), qualities that deal with the truth of one's human nature with respect to feelings. Because, without an awareness and acceptance of feelings, a male doesn't become a man, he becomes a male cartoon—the animation required for humanness is *feelings*.[22]

Suddenly, being attuned to one's feelings is something that is *said* to be more feminine but really is simply human. However, Dr. Laura herself consistently states that women are more in tune with feelings and that this is a feminine quality. In fact, it is clearly stated in one of the quotes about differences between males and females previously presented in this chapter, which says that due to a more developed emotional capacity, women tend to gravitate toward feelings. And she says it again in the following: "What is 'natural' for females (spirituality, feelings, nurturing, verbalizing, interpersonal bonding) has been devalued." Given the number of times that Dr. Laura associates feelings with femininity, it seems to be part of her view. And, while she clearly asserts that men do not need to be feminine (a feminine partner completes the whole), the quote about femininity and feelings stated earlier clearly implies the reverse. Hence, Dr. Laura can't seem to avoid the obvious implication of her own view, although she denies it, and contradicts herself to try to avoid it. Women are naturally morally superior. One can hardly get more antimale than that.

Dr. Laura is another antifeminist who claims that feminists hate men. I submit that a careful reading of Dr. Laura's work shows it is she who is antimale. Her views justify the excuse-based rapist ethic that John Stoltenberg has illuminated and critiqued. They provide excuses for sexual violence, rape, and infidelity based on what is supposed to be male biology. That Dr. Laura is willing to accept problematic male behavior as "natural" is obvious:

> Most mothers teach their sons to call their penis a pee-pee partly as a reminder of what and where and how they are supposed to use it so they won't wet their pants anymore; partly because most people can't handle the correct names for things; and—not so incidentally—because they're putting off the notion of their sons becoming the sex-crazed young men they themselves had to fight off as young girls.[23]

Notice how the implication is that it is "natural" (read: inevitable) that boys will become people who attack young girls. And, in discussing women that men should beware of, she warns, "Beware of the woman who thinks even marital sex is rape unless she is profoundly in the mood."[24] As if waiting is simply too much to ask!

While both Dr. Laura and John Stoltenberg agree that there are "typical" male behaviors that are problematic (to say the least), this is where their agreement ends. Stoltenberg and other feminists argue that the source of many "gender-based" behavioral differences is not biology, but certain myths about biology,[25] the central one being that men act under the "single biological imperative" so eloquently articulated by Dr. Laura: putting their sperm in as many uteri as possible. According to Stoltenberg, the idea that men and women necessarily have drives and feelings based on biological drives is a myth dangerous not only for women, but for men as well. Because men do not "naturally" feel the way "real men" are supposed to feel (constantly thinking about sex, for example), many overcompensate so that they can feel like "real men" and be viewed as "normal." They learn to feel what they are supposed to feel. However, for many men, anxiety about not being "man enough" lurks beneath the surface, causing them to constantly try to prove manhood:

> Behaving within the ethical limits of what is wrong or right for sexual identities is critical anxiety about being male enough or female enough indistinguishable from bodily sensations regarded as erotic. For the male—what he wants to make happen in a sexual encounter with a partner—when, and for how long, is rarely unrelated to pivotal considerations about what it is to be the man there.[26]

Stoltenberg believes *men* can and should change typical problematic, violent, abusive behaviors. In his view, society teaches boys this behavior and it can be untaught. He argues that there is something highly problematic about some men's tendency not to care whether the woman they are with wants sex or not, but this can be changed, while Dr. Laura warns men to "beware" of women who are upset when men try to have sex with them and they (women) don't want to. Stoltenberg writes to men, holding them responsible for bad and violent behavior against women. Dr. Laura holds women responsible for men's bad behavior, urging women to "train" men out of it like animals. Stoltenberg believes the problems are social; Dr. Laura seems at times to blame biology and, at other times, society. As a philosopher, I am not taking a position on whether biology or society or a combination dictates "gender-based" behaviors, or even whether these are really intelligible dichotomies. However, I believe that the traditional gender view sets up a system for excusing men and at the same time is not very respectful of them. Feminists who want to hold men responsible for their bad behavior treat men more like "humans" and less like "animals" than Dr. Laura does.

John Stoltenberg urges us to give up on the myth about natural "biological" drives undergirding both rapist ethics and the traditional gender view. It is a dangerous lie preventing recognition of people's uniqueness and promoting and excusing highly problematic behaviors in men, including rape. Although he discusses how views promote male supremacy, his analysis would be greatly strengthened if he included how the attribution of overly aggressive "sex drives" can and has been used in the promotion of racism. For example, the idea that white women are unsafe around African American men due to their high sex drives, while in reality it was white men who systematically raped African American women during slavery. Dr. Laura takes the opposite view: we are in trouble today because we no longer respect key biological differences. The "big lie" that she worries about is the idea that such differences *don't* exist. In asking who benefits from the big lie, she asks:

> Is it those who wish to justify their challenges and choices? The agenda of homosexual activists has moved past the demand for sexual tolerance and respect demanding acceptance of homosexuality as healthy, normal, and equivalent in every way to heterosexuality. Necessary to advancing this agenda is undermining the significance of the traditional definition of family as husband, wife, and children.[27]

And:

> Are the beneficiaries of the "big lie" to be found among the feminists? The lesbian feminist activists at Barnard College in New York were successful in "cleansing" the recruitment brochure sent to parents of marriage statistics for Barnard graduates. The statistics had to be removed to calm the nerves of lesbians who claimed it was insulting for the college to attempt to assure parents that Barnard graduates *do* get married.[28]

Interestingly, both Stoltenberg and Dr. Laura blame problematic male behavior on "big lies." Dr. Laura blames women for this behavior, along with the lie that there aren't crucial biological gender differences that must be accepted and respected. Stoltenberg argues that the lie is precisely the idea that there are biologically based behavioral differences between the sexes. Hence, their positions are almost polar opposites. As a moral philosopher, I am not in a position to offer a view on the relationship between biology and behavior. However, I am in a position to comment on the logic of each position.

I have always been attracted by Stoltenberg's analysis because it makes sense of the otherwise absurd logic that holds women responsible for male violence against them. I believe that Stoltenberg does an excellent job of teasing out this logic. And I believe he is right that its foundation rests upon accepting the idea that men often have "uncontrollable biological urges." Stoltenberg believes that any biological explanations explaining differences in attitudes and behaviors between the sexes is a dangerous, ideological myth. In fact, he even believes that the idea of a biologically based "metaphysical" distinction between the sexes is itself problematic. However, one does not have to go as far as Stoltenberg does in order to grasp the significance and problematic nature of rapist ethics. For, even if there are biological drives (whatever this turns out to mean), there are always environmental factors. Any respectable scientist will tell you that it would be highly difficult to link biology to specific behaviors, such as rape or being a stay-at-home dad! Hence, the idea that men are "naturally" aggressive and women are "naturally" nurturing would be extremely difficult to prove. In fact, feminist epistemologists and philosophers of science have wondered what *could* count as "objectively" proving it at all.[29] Rapist ethics excuse men from controlling their drives (biological, socially constructed, or both). Stoltenberg calls for an end of such excuses. And, unless men's so-called biological urges are uncontrollable, they need to be held responsible for controlling them. Certainly, if they exist, many decent, kind men do control their biological urges; otherwise, we would have even greater problems than we do now.

The idea that men should be held responsible for their actions does not sound like a radical view at all. However, this is exactly what views such as Dr. Laura's, which is wildly popular, deny. *Men* are not held responsible for their behavior, or the "moral climate" of the cultures in which they live, even if they hold a high majority of the positions with real political power. *Women* are responsible for controlling men because men cannot be expected to control themselves. This is simply a "biological given." Frankly, it saddens me that this old story still survives. I find it highly insulting to men and dangerous to both men and women. Those concerned with issues of real sexual equality (my definition of feminists) must pay very close attention to why such views remain popular. True equality is not between the "trainer" and the "trained," the "civilizer" and the "civilized." In my view, a precondition for the idea that men and women are morally equal is that both sexes are equally capable of being respectful and basically moral. Views like Dr. Laura's deny men this basic equality and the moral responsibility that comes along with it. Hence, these views are deeply and tragically antimale.

NOTES

The phrase "New Attitude" in this chapter's title is drawn from the popular song "New Attitude" (by Patti LaBelle, 1984), adopted by Dr. Laura as her radio show theme.

1. Laura Schlessinger, *Ten Stupid Things Women Do to Mess Up Their Lives* (New York: HarperCollins, 1994); Schlessinger, *Ten Stupid Things Men Do to Mess Up Their Lives* (New York: HarperCollins, 1997); Schlessinger, *Ten Stupid Things Parents Do to Mess Up Their Kids* (New York: HarperCollins, 2000); Schlessinger, *Ten Stupid Things Couples Do to Mess up Their Relationships* (New York: HarperCollins, 2001).

2. Schlessinger, *Stupid Things Men Do,* 6.
3. Schlessinger, *Stupid Things Men Do,* xviii.
4. Schlessinger, *Stupid Things Men Do,* 3.
5. Schlessinger, *Stupid Things Men Do,* 124.
6. Schlessinger, *Stupid Things Men Do,* 127.
7. Schlessinger, *Stupid Things Men Do,* 60.
8. Schlessinger, *Stupid Things Men Do,* 35.
9. Schlessinger, *Stupid Things Couples Do,* 3.
10. Schlessinger, *Stupid Things Men Do,* 271.
11. Schlessinger, *Stupid Things Men Do,* 271.
12. Schlessinger, *Stupid Things Men Do,* 273.
13. Schlessinger, *Stupid Things Women Do,* xx.
14. Schlessinger, *Stupid Things Women Do,* xix.
15. Schlessinger, *Stupid Things Couples Do,* 8.
16. John Stoltenberg, *Refusing to Be a Man: Essays on Sex and Justice* (New York: Meridian, 1990), 12–13.
17. Schlessinger, *Stupid Things Men Do,* 125.
18. Schlessinger, *Stupid Things Men Do,* 129.
19. Schlessinger, *Stupid Things Men Do,* 34.
20. Schlessinger, *Stupid Things Men Do,* 69.
21. Schlessinger, *Stupid Things Men Do,* 33.
22. Schlessinger, *Stupid Things Men Do,* 282.
23. Schlessinger, *Stupid Things Men Do,* 121.
24. Schlessinger, *Stupid Things Men Do,* 169.
25. Marilyn Frye, *The Politics of Reality: Essays in Feminist Theory Freedom* (Trumansburg, N.Y.: Crossing Press, 1983); Sandra Lee Bartkey, *Femininity and Domination* (New York: Routledge, 1990); Judith Butler, *Gender Trouble: Feminism and the Subversion of Identity* (New York: Harper and Row, 1990); Stoltenberg, *Refusing to Be a Man.*
26. Stoltenberg, *Refusing to Be a Man,* 14.
27. Schlessinger, *Stupid Things Parents Do,* 16.
28. Schlessinger, *Stupid Things Parents Do,* 17.
29. Sandra Harding, *The Science Question in Feminism* (Ithaca, N.Y.: Cornell University Press, 1986); Lorraine Code, *What Can She Know? Feminist Theory and the Construction of Knowledge* (Ithaca, N.Y.: Cornell University Press, 1991); Bat-Ami Bar On, "Marginality and Epistemic Privilege," in *Feminist Epistemologies,* ed. Linda Alcoff and Elizabeth Potter (London: Routledge, 1993).

9

Neopatriarchy and the Antihomosexual Agenda

R. Claire Snyder

In the late 1990s, decisions by the Supreme Courts of Hawaii and Vermont raised the possibility that the civil right to marriage might soon be accorded to all citizens, not just to heterosexuals.[1] These decisions both bolstered the burgeoning lesbian/gay civil rights movement and triggered a nationwide mobilization of conservative forces in "defense" of heterosexual-only marriage.[2] In their attempt to prevent the logical extension of liberal principles to lesbian and gay citizens, right-wing activists have made common cause with a number of other reactionary movements that want to undo the progress of feminism and reestablish the patriarchal nuclear family as the dominant family form. This chapter examines the interconnected arguments advanced by a number of conservative constituencies committed to the politics of neopatriarchy, including the religious particularism of the Christian Right, the homophobic antifeminism of Concerned Women for America, the "family values" of James Dobson, the fatherhood movement spearheaded by David Blankenhorn, and the conservative democratic theory of William Galston. While the details of these arguments differ, all have a similar form and use the same authorities, and all are both homophobic and antifeminist. Thus, all undermine the principles of liberal democracy, despite rhetorical assertions to the contrary.

LESBIAN/GAY CIVIL RIGHTS AND THE LOGIC OF LIBERALISM

Legal equality constitutes one of the most important founding principles of liberal democracy in the United States. While the equal rights of the Declaration of Independence were largely aspirational at the time they were written, over the course of the twentieth century, American society became increasingly imbued with a liberal public philosophy that values individual choice, "rights as trumps," legal equality, and a "neutral state" that leaves individuals free to pursue their own vision of the good life in civil society and the private sphere without interference from the government.[3]

The revolutionary principle of legal equality has been successfully used to justify progressive change. African Americans utilized this principle during the civil rights movement in their struggle to end segregation. While violently opposed by the Right at the time, the principle of color-blind law has been largely accepted by contemporary conservatives. The struggle for gender-blind law has also been largely successful. Although feminists lost the battle for the Equal Rights Amendment (ERA) during the 1970s, since that time the principle of legal equality for women has been implemented through the Courts,[4] which are charged with following the logic of liberalism as they apply the principles of the Constitution to new areas. While progress has not been inevitable or without setbacks, overall the level of legal equality within American society has advanced over time.

Despite the compelling logic of philosophical liberalism, the American Right actively opposed the extension of legal equality in every instance. The Old Right was explicitly racist and violently fought to stop the extension of civil rights to African Americans. By 1965, however, Gallup polls "showed that 52 percent of Americans identified civil rights as the 'most important problem' confronting the nation, and an astonishing 75 percent of respondents favored federal voting rights legislation."[5] With explicit racism on the decline, in 1965 right-wing leaders began developing a more marketable message, "mainstreaming the ideological positions of the Old Right and developing winnable policies" that "highlighted a protest theme" against a wide range of cultural changes inaugurated by the new social movements of the 1960s.[6] This "New Right" successfully created a coalition between cultural conservatives, including Christian fundamentalists, and antigovernment, fiscal conservatives (aka neoliberals).

Feminism constituted precisely the enemy the New Right needed to consolidate its base. Antifeminism "provided a link with fundamentalist churches," focused "the reaction against the changes in child rearing, sexual behavior, divorce, and the use of drugs that had taken place in the 1960s and 1970s," and "mobilized a group, traditional homemakers, that had lost status over the two previous decades and was feeling the psychological effects of the loss."[7] The conservative mobilization against feminism solidified the New Right during the 1970s and played a "very important" role in its success: the election of Ronald Reagan in 1980 and the rightward shift of American politics.[8]

The women's movement and the lesbian/gay civil rights movement were linked theoretically and through common struggle, and the Right used this connection to its advantage. For example, Phyllis Schlafly's Eagle Forum argued, "Militant homosexuals from all over America have made the ERA issue a hot priority. Why? To be able finally to get homosexual marriage licenses, to adopt children and raise them to emulate their homosexual 'parents,' and to obtain pension and medical benefits for odd-couple 'spouses.' . . . Vote *NO on 6!* The Pro-Gay E.R.A."[9] In its rise to power, the New Right successfully manipulated homophobia to increase opposition to gender equality and explicitly condemned all attempts to accord lesbians and gay men the equal protection of the law.

While the Christian Right continues to pose a serious threat to civil rights and has achieved unprecedented levels of power since 1980, the logic of liberalism in American society is hard to deny. Many Americans see the right of lesbians and gay men to marry as a civil rights issue plain and simple. Fifty-eight percent of first-year college students now "think gay and lesbian couples should have the right to 'equal marital status,' i.e., civil marriage"—including "half" who identify as "middle-of-the-road" or "conservative"[10]—and the Courts are beginning to recognize this right as well. Nevertheless, a coalition of religious, secular, and academic activists and organizations continue to oppose, and organize around their opposition to, the rights of gays and lesbians to marry or form civil unions.

RELIGIOUS PARTICULARISM AND THE ANTIHOMOSEXUAL AGENDA

The Christian Right opposes legal equality for lesbians and gay men when it comes to marriage because it defines marriage as a sacred religious institution, and its particular version of Christianity views homosexuality as a sin. According to the Family Research Council (FRC), marriage is "the *work of heaven and every major religion* and culture throughout world history."[11] Concerned Women for America (CWA) proclaims, "We believe that marriage is *a covenant established by God* wherein one man and one woman, united for life, are licensed by the state for the purpose of founding and maintaining a family."[12] Focus on the Family (FOF) opposes even "civil unions" because they "would essentially legalize homosexual marriage and therefore undermine the *sanctity* of marriage."[13] Indeed, because of this religious worldview, all three groups have made opposition to same-sex marriage a centerpiece of their political agendas.[14]

The Christian Right's vision of heterosexual marriage directly relates to its understanding of gender differences, which it bases on its particular interpretation of the Bible. More specifically, this reading focuses on the *second* creation story in Genesis, in which God created Eve out of Adam's rib to be his helper and declared that the man and his wife would become "one flesh" (Gen. 18:21–24).[15] The belief in natural heterosexuality is bolstered by a reading of the Sodom and Gomorrah story (Gen. 18:16–19:29) that interprets the city's destruction as God's punishment for homosexuality, as well as the sentence in Leviticus that proclaims "do not lie with a male as one lies with a woman; it is an abhorrence" (Lev. 18:22). Right-wing Christians also emphasize New Testament verses stating that woman is the "weaker vessel" (1 Pet. 3:7), that man is "joined to his wife, and the two become one flesh" (Eph. 5:31–32), and that the "husband is the head of the wife" (1 Cor. 11:4; Eph. 5:23). The meanings of all these passages have been debated at length by religious scholars, and no consensus exists as to their meanings. Nevertheless, for conservative Christians, God's will is as clear as it is specific: man and woman are naturally different, designed by God for heterosexual marriage and the establishment of the patriarchal family.

As far as their own religious rites are concerned, Christian Right churches certainly have the religious liberty to define marriage any way they see fit. However, when the faithful of the Christian Right ask the U.S. government and the governments of the states to restrict the right to civil marriage because of their particular interpretation of revealed religion, they violate the separation of church and state mandated by the First Amendment. Not all religions share the Christian Right's definition of marriage. For example, Reform Judaism not only favors civil marriage for gays and lesbians but also allows for religious unions, and many Muslims practice polygamy.[16] In fact, even within Christianity, no clear consensus exists on the question of same-sex marriage. Nevertheless, despite the diversity of beliefs within America's religiously pluralistic society, the Christian Right group Alliance for Marriage has introduced a Federal Marriage Amendment that declares, "Marriage in the United States shall consist only of the union of a man and a woman."[17] Clearly this amendment asks the federal government to establish one particular religious definition of marriage as the law of the land, thus violating the separation of church and state.[18]

THAT 1970s ARGUMENT: THE ANXIETY OF RIGHT-WING WOMEN

The Christian Right group Concerned Women for America, which claims to be the largest women's group in the country, consistently asserts that the struggle of lesbians and gay men for the right to marry is not an attempt to participate in the institution of marriage but rather an attempt to "undermine marriage" and destroy the family.[19] In strictly logical terms, this makes no sense. Aren't lesbians and gays actually *reinforcing* the legitimacy of marriage as an institution through their struggle for the right to marry? Indeed, many within the lesbian, gay, bisexual, and transgender (LGBT) community have criticized this struggle for doing precisely that and not much more.[20] While same-sex marriage would not undermine the institution of marriage in general, it would undermine the *traditional patriarchal heterosexual vision of marriage* in particular, which is precisely what the Christian Right desperately wants to reestablish.

Concerned Women for America wants heterosexual marriage to maintain its privileged status in American society and to continue to function as the justification for special rights. This line of argumentation plays on a number of anxieties expressed by the first generation of New Right women who mobilized in opposition to the ERA and abortion rights during the 1970s. Status was a key concern for those women. "At the beginning of the contemporary women's movement, in 1968, women of all classes found themselves in something like the same boat." Most were homemakers and/or low-level employees. However, over the course of the next two decades, "homemakers suffered a tremendous loss in social prestige" as "high-status women" began choosing careers over homemaking. Consequently, conservative homemakers—who, after all, had done the *right thing* for their time—now found themselves facing "status degradation," and they resented it.[21] Twenty-five years later, the special status of heterosexual marriage is being threatened by lesbians and gays, and many right-wing women again feel diminished.

Opposed to government-sponsored family support, Christian Right women favor laws that force individual men to take responsibility for the children they father and for the mothers who bear those children. The 1970s generation feared that the changes inaugurated by feminism—the ERA, reproductive freedom, no-fault divorce, and the loosening of sexual mores—would make it easier for men to get out of their familial commitments. As opposed to liberal feminist women who wanted the right to compete equally with men, many antifeminist women did not have the educational level or job skills that would allow them to pursue satisfying careers if forced to work outside the home.[22] They feared that the ERA would eliminate the traditional legal requirement for husbands to support their wives financially.[23] Phyllis Schlafly told homemakers that the ERA would say, "Boys, supporting your wives isn't your responsibility anymore."[24] At the same time, the rise of "no-fault" divorce laws during this period further threatened the economic security of traditional "housewives."[25] As Schlafly put it, "Even though love may go out the window, the obligation should remain. ERA would eliminate that obligation." To this day, Christian Right women condemn no-fault divorce, which "allows one person to decide when a relationship can be severed," often catapulting women into poverty.[26] While higher wages for women, safe and affordable child care, and universal health insurance constitute a progressive solution to the problems caused by the fragility of marriage and callousness of deadbeat dads, right-wing women demand the return of a traditional patriarchal vision of marriage, ignoring the reality of social change.[27]

In the 1970s, conservative women worried that if sex became widely available outside of marriage, they would have difficulty keeping their husbands interested in them. Kristin Luker's interviews with the first generation of "pro-life" women revealed the following insight:

> If women plan to find their primary role in marriage and the family, then they face a need to create a "moral cartel" when it comes to sex. . . . If many women are willing to sleep with men outside of marriage, then the regular sexual activity that comes with marriage is much less valuable an incentive to marry. . . . [For] traditional women, their primary resource for marriage is the promise of a stable home, with everything it implies: children, regular sex, a "haven in a heartless world."[28]

For the first generation of Christian Right women, the sexual liberation of many feminist women threatened to destabilize the marital bargain that many traditional women relied upon.[29] Given the option, their husbands might abandon them for more exciting women.

Do today's Christian Right women fear that if given the choice their husbands might choose other men? Perhaps. After all, antigay activist Dr. Paul Cameron tells them that "the evidence is that men do a better job on men, and women on women, if all you are looking for is orgasm." If you want "the most satisfying orgasm you can get," he explains, "then homosexuality seems too powerful to resist. . . . It's pure sexuality. It's almost like pure heroin. It's such a rush." In opposition, "marital sex tends toward the boring" and generally "doesn't deliver the kind of sheer sexual pleasure that homosexual sex does."[30] Although the American Psychological Association expelled Cameron for ethics violations in 1983, he still serves as an oft-quoted right-wing "expert" on homosexuality.[31] In light of his comments, it would be understandable if Christian Right women feel anxious about their ability to keep their husbands interested in heterosexual marriage.

Fundamentally different, men and women come together to reproduce and remain coupled in order to rear their children. Because homosexuality severs the connection between sex and reproduction, CWA sees homosexual relationships as necessarily fleeting, as driven by sexual gratification alone. For example, Beverly LaHaye insists, "Homosexual relationships are not only the antithesis to family, but also threaten its very core. It is *the compulsive desire for sexual gratification without lasting commitment*, the high rate of promiscuity, and the self-defined morality among homosexuals that sap the vitality of the family structure, making it something less than it was, is, and should be."[32] Clearly the desire of many gay and lesbian couples to marry and to raise children belies this argument. Nevertheless, Christian Right groups such as the CWA purposely depict the struggle for lesbian/gay civil rights in a reductive and patently distorted way in order to manipulate the anxieties of traditional women, secure their own special interests, and advance their larger political agenda.

NEOPATRIARCHY AND THE FATHERHOOD MOVEMENT

Joining the opposition to same-sex marriage are advocates of the fatherhood movement who seek to restore traditional gender roles and reestablish the patriarchal family as the dominant family form in America. Because no evidence exists that same-sex couples are less functional than heterosexual ones, or that their children are more likely to suffer negative effects, allowing same-sex couples to marry and have children would clearly undermine the myth that the patriarchal heterosexual family is the superior family form.[33] Consequently, the fatherhood activists repeatedly assert that children need both a masculine father and a feminine mother in order to develop properly.

The fatherhood movement blames feminism and single mothers for the social problems caused by men and teenaged boys. While the packaging of their arguments varies slightly, advocates of this school of thought generally make a similar claim: refusing to respect natural gender differences, feminists have pathologized masculinity and futilely attempted to change the behavior of men and boys. They have undermined the rightful authority of men as the head of the household, attempted to change the natural division of labor that exists between mothers and fathers, and propagated the idea that a woman can fulfill the role traditionally played by a man, thus rendering fathers superfluous to family life. Consequently, men have lost interest in fulfilling their traditional family responsibilities, and boys have no one to teach them how to become responsible men. Detached from the civilizing influence of the traditional patriarchal family, males increasingly cause a wide array of social problems, and everybody suffers.[34]

Focus on the Family president James Dobson makes this argument from a Christian Right perspective. In *Bringing Up Boys,* he argues that traditional gender roles are natural and cannot be changed. He points to the continued power of men in society as evidence of their natural, "biochemical and anatomical," dominance.[35] Dobson strongly opposes attempts to change the gender socialization of children and explicitly links this "unisex" idea to "the powerful gay and lesbian agenda," whose propagandists are teaching a revolutionary view of sexuality called "gender feminism," which insists that sex assignment is irrelevant.[36] While Dobson sees this as dangerous for both sexes, it is particularly harmful for boys: "Protect the masculinity of your boys, who will be under increasing political pressure in years to come."[37]

Dobson believes that a breakdown of traditional gender roles within the family fosters homosexuality in children. The prevention of homosexuality among boys requires the involvement of a properly masculine heterosexual father, especially during the early years. Dobson relies on the work of Dr. Joseph Nicolosi, a leading proponent of the Christian Right's "ex-gay" movement,[38] who urges parents to monitor their children for signs of "prehomosexuality," so professionals can step in before it is too late. While "feminine behavior in boyhood" is clearly a sign, so is "nonmasculinity," defined as not fitting in with male peers.[39] "The father," Nicolosi asserts, "plays an essential role in a boy's normal development as a man. The truth is, Dad is more important than Mom." In order to ensure heterosexuality, the father "needs to mirror and affirm his son's maleness. He can play rough-and-tumble games with his son, in ways that are decidedly different from the games he would play with a little girl. He can help his son learn to throw and catch a ball. . . . He can even take his son with him into the shower, where the boy cannot help but notice that Dad has a penis, just like his, only bigger."[40]

Based solely on the work of Nicolosi, Dobson concludes, "If you as a parent have an effeminate boy or a masculinized girl, I urge you to get a copy [of Nicolosi's book] and then seek immediate professional help." Beware, however, of "secular" mental health professionals who will most certainly "take the wrong approach—telling your child that he is homosexual and needs to accept that fact." Instead, Dobson recommends a referral from either Exodus International, the leading organization of the ex-gay ministries, or the National Association for Research and Therapy of Homosexuality, "formed to oppose the 1973 decision by the American Psychological Association to no longer classify homosexuality as an emotional or mental disorder."[41]

Dobson's emphasis on the important role played by fathers bolsters the arguments of the fatherhood movement, which emerged during the 1990s. One of the first organizations to spearhead this movement was the Promise Keepers (PK), founded by Bill McCartney[42] in 1990 as a "Christ-centered ministry dedicated to uniting men through vital relationships to become godly influences in their world."[43] This organization wants to restore fathers to their rightful place at the head of the patriarchal family.[44]

Institute for American Values president David Blankenhorn advances a similar agenda using secular arguments. His book *Fatherless America* (1995) and the follow-up volume *The Fatherhood Movement* (1999)—coedited with Wade Horn (George W. Bush's secretary of Health and Human Services) and Mitchell Pearlstein—blames the "declining child well-being in our society," not on growing levels of poverty, deteriorating public services, lack of safe and affordable child care, the lower income of women, child abuse, racism, or misogyny, but rather on fatherlessness.[45] Fatherlessness, he tells us, is "the engine driving our most urgent social problems, from crime to adolescent pregnancy to child sexual abuse to domestic violence against women."[46] While some conservatives argue that "the best anti-poverty program for children is a stable, intact family," Blankenhorn demands more: "a married father on the premises."[47]

Like those on the Christian Right, Blankenhorn insists that children need not just two involved parents but more specifically *a male father and a female mother enacting traditional gender roles.* Citing two anthropologists, Blankenhorn claims, "Gendered parental roles derive precisely from children's needs." During childhood, "the needs of the child compel mothers and fathers to specialize in their labor and to adopt gender-based parental roles." Consequently, men and women should stick with traditional roles, Blankenhorn insists, even if this conflicts with their "narcissistic claims" to personal autonomy.[48]

Like Dobson, Blankenhorn condemns attempts to equalize the roles of mothers and fathers in child rearing, and derides what he calls the new "like-a-mother father."[49] While Blankenhorn barely mentions lesbians and gay men in his analysis, his argument clearly justifies an opposition to same-sex marriage. Obviously, his insistence that proper childhood development requires heterosexual parents who enact traditional gender roles implies that, in his view, homosexual couples cannot raise healthy children. In addition, however, Blankenhorn specifically advocates laws to prohibit unmarried women from accessing sperm banks.[50] Perhaps he shares the fear of the CWA that gender equality would mean that "lesbian women would be considered no different from men," especially once they get access to male seed.[51] If that were to happen, where would that leave men?

"SEEDBEDS OF VIRTUE": WHAT
LESSONS DOES THE PATRIARCHAL FAMILY TEACH?

Building directly on the body of literature outlined previously, a growing number of right-wing activists, respectable scholars, and well-known political theorists have begun connecting the neopatriarchal movement to the survival and revitalization of American democracy. This approach claims, in short, that liberal democracy requires virtuous citizens, and virtue is best learned at home in a traditional family with two married parents. The Institute for American Values sponsored a conference on this topic that resulted in the publication of *Seedbeds of Virtue: Sources of Competence, Character, and Citizenship in American Society*[52] that Blankenhorn edited with Mary Ann Glendon, who so strongly opposes same-sex unions that she worked with Robert Bork "to draft an Amendment to the U.S. Constitution to protect the holy sacrament of marriage from those who would legalize same-sex 'marriage.'"[53]

While many conservative thinkers support the "seedbeds of virtue" approach to justifying the patriarchal heterosexual family—many in exactly the same terms as the fatherhood movement—I concentrate on the arguments advanced by democratic political theorist William Galston, who served as deputy assistant to the president for domestic policy under Bill Clinton, a *Democratic* president. While Galston's defense of the family does not explicitly specify the patriarchal heterosexual family form in particular, one can only infer that he endorses that vision for several reasons. First, he makes arguments similar to those of the neopatriarchalists *without any caveats*. Second, he explicitly praises Mary Ann Glendon and Jean Bethke Elshtain for having "already said nearly every thing that needs saying on [the subject of the family]."[54] While Glendon works politically in opposition to same-sex marriage, Elshtain's scholarship specifically proposes "a normative vision of the family—mothers, fathers, and children" and claims that this particular family form "is not only *not* at odds with democratic civil society but is in fact, now more than ever, a prerequisite for that society to function."[55] Third, Galston himself signs *A Call to Civil Society: Why Democracy Needs Moral Truths*, which says the number one priority for American democracy should be "to increase the likelihood that more children will grow up with their two married parents."[56]

In addition, the lack of explicit references to homosexuality should not be interpreted as a lack of homophobia. As Jean Hardisty has discovered, since the mid-1980s, Christian Right organizations have tended to "highlight the religious principles undergirding their anti-homosexual politics only when they are targeting other Christians. When organizing in the wider political arena, they frame their anti-gay organizing as a struggle for secular ends, such as 'defense of the family.'"[57] Thus, you get James Dobson in Christian Right circles, David Blankenhorn in secular circles, and William Galston in academic circles. Despite variations on the theme, one thing remains constant: the normative vision presented by these conservatives gives lesbians and gay men absolutely no place in family life and, by extension, no place in democratic society.

Working from a firm foundation in the history of political thought, Galston argues that liberal democracy requires individuals who have the virtues necessary for life in a free society. The claim is simple: "that the operation of liberal institutions is affected in important ways by the character of citizens (and leaders), and that at some point, the attenuation of individual virtue will create pathologies with which liberal political contrivances, however technically perfect their design, simply cannot cope."[58] Cataloguing the wide array of virtues necessary for liberal democracy, Galston only implies that the traditional family best teaches these virtues to youngsters; he never argues it explicitly.

An examination of how the particular virtues cited by Galston relate to the traditional family produces three different arguments. First, many of the virtues Galston emphasizes, while originally acquired in a family, do not require a patriarchal heterosexual family form in particular. For example, such important virtues as civility, the work ethic, delayed gratification, adaptability, discernment, and "the ability to work within constraints on action imposed by social diversity and constitutional institutions" could certainly be instilled in children by any functional family, including one headed by same-sex parents. Galston makes no argument for the superiority of heterosexuals in fostering these characteristics in children, and such an argument is not supported by empirical evidence.[59]

Second, the traditional patriarchal family could actually undermine a number of important virtues extolled by Galston. For example, he argues that a liberal society is characterized by two key features—individualism and diversity.[60] While children certainly need to learn independence, *how does the traditional patriarchal family, in which wives are dependent upon their husbands' leadership and economic support, teach the virtue of independence to future female citizens?* Galston must be focusing on boys only. Additionally, Galston cites "loyalty" as a central virtue for liberal democracy, defining it as "the developed capacity to understand, to accept, and to act on the core principles of one's society." This "is particularly important in liberal communities," he argues, because they "tend to be organized around abstract principles rather than shared ethnicity, nationality, or history."[61] But if one of the fundamental principles of liberal democracy is legal equality for all citizens, again we must ask: *what lessons does a child learn about equality growing up in a patriarchal nuclear family in which men lead and women submit?*[62] While the traditional family may provide certain benefits to children, it is unclear how it teaches them the universal principle of equality for all citizens, when this family form models gender inequality.

Third, a number of the democratic virtues Galston emphasizes could be undermined by the normative vision of the Christian Right. For example, Galston emphasizes "the willingness to *listen seriously to a range of views*" and the "willingness to set forth one's own views intelligibly and candidly as the basis of *a politics of persuasion rather than manipulation or coercion.*"[63] This directly relates to the virtue of *tolerance*. While Galston stresses that tolerance does not mean a belief that all lifestyles are "equally good," it does mean that "the pursuit of the better course should be (and in some cases can only be) the consequence of *education or persuasion rather than coercion.*"[64] While open-mindedness, tolerance, and noncoercion certainly constitute important virtues for any democratic society, they are not hallmarks of the Christian Right, especially when it comes to its antihomosexual agenda.

CONCLUSION

The fight against the extension of civil rights to lesbians and gay men forms a central component of the larger battle against women's equality. While the rhetoric deployed by conservatives resonates with many of our most cherished cultural narratives and personal fantasies, their overarching agenda actually undermines our most precious political values, including the separation of church and state, legal equality, and personal liberty. While liberal democracy has its limitations, its virtue is that it maximizes the freedom of all by allowing individuals to organize their personal lives as they see fit. While a liberal state may respond to the will of its citizens by providing a default set of legal entanglements that make it easier for individuals to establish families (i.e., civil marriage), it may not legitimately deny equal protection of the laws to particular groups of citizens, no matter how unpopular they are. The conservative arguments against same-sex marriage, whether religious, secular, or academic, are all similarly structured and based on an idealized, inegalitarian heterosexual family with rigid gender roles. Justified by references to the well-being of children, these arguments are unsustainable when subjected to close scrutiny.

NOTES

1. See *Baehr v. Lewin* 852 P.2d 44 (Haw. 1993) and *Stan Baker, et al. v. State of Vermont, et al.* 744 A.2d 86 (Vt. 1999).

2. See Urvashi Vaid, *Virtual Equality: The Mainstreaming of Gay and Lesbian Liberation* (New York: Anchor, 1995).

3. Michael J. Sandel, *Democracy's Discontent: America in Search of a Public Philosophy*, rev. ed. (Cambridge, Mass.: Belknap Press of Harvard University Press, 1998).

4. Jane Mansbridge, *Why We Lost the ERA* (Chicago: Chicago University Press, 1986), 91.

5. Maurice Isserman and Michael Kazin, *America Divided: The Civil War of the 1960s* (Oxford: Oxford University Press, 2000), 138.

6. Jean Hardisty, *Mobilizing Resentment: Conservative Resurgence from the John Birch Society to the Promise Keepers* (Boston: Beacon, 1999), 38.

7. Mansbridge, *Why We Lost the ERA*, 5–6.

8. Hardisty, *Mobilizing Resentment*, 72.

9. Mansbridge, *Why We Lost the ERA*, 137.

10. Paul Varnell, "College Freshmen Support Gay Marriage," *Chicago Free Press*, January 30, 2002, at www.indegayforum.org/articles/varnell85.html (accessed April 17, 2002).

11. Fund-raising ad in favor of Defense of Marriage Act (DOMA), paid for by the Family Research Council (FRC), included in FRC information packet, emphasis added.

12. Concerned Women for America (CWA), "Lawfully Wedded?" *Family Voice* (April 1996), at www.cwfa.org/library/family/1996-04_fv_marriage-gay.shtml (accessed November 14, 2001), emphasis added.

13. Focus on the Family, "Keep Fighting Gay Marriage!" *Citizen Link* (January 15, 2002), at www.family.org/cforum/feature/A0019218.html (accessed April 6, 2002), emphasis added.

14. Hardisty, *Mobilizing Resentment*, 98.

15. *TANAKH: A New Translation of the Holy Scriptures, According to the Traditional Hebrew Text* (Philadelphia: Jewish Publication Society, 1985).

16. Gustav Niebuhr, "Reform Rabbis Back Blessing Gay Unions," *New York Times*, March 30, 2000, p. 1A.

17. David Crary, "Coalition Wants Marriage Amendment," *Associated Press*, July 10, 2001.

18. See Didi Herman, *The Antigay Agenda: Orthodox Vision and the Christian Right* (Chicago: Chicago University Press, 1997), 168.

19. CWA, "History: 1978–2001," at www.cwfa.org/about/his (accessed April 2, 2002).

20. See Michael Warner, *The Trouble with Normal: Sex, Politics, and the Ethics of Queer Life* (New York: Free Press, 1999); and Valerie Lehr, *Queer Family Values: Debunking the Myth of the Nuclear Family* (Philadelphia: Temple University Press, 1999).

21. Mansbridge, *Why We Lost the ERA*, 105–7.

22. Mansbridge, *Why We Lost the ERA*, 105–7.

23. Mansbridge, *Why We Lost the ERA*, 108.

24. Quoted in Mansbridge, *Why We Lost the ERA*, 109.

25. Mansbridge, *Why We Lost the ERA*, 108.

26. Trudy Hutchens, "Marriage: The State of the Union," 1996, at www.cwfa.org/library/family/1996-10_fv_marriage.s (accessed April 2, 2002), 4.

27. See Stephanie Coontz, *The Way We Never Were: American Families and the Nostalgia Trap*, 2d ed. (New York: Basic, 2000).

28. Kristin Luker, *Abortion and the Politics of Motherhood* (Berkeley: University of California Press, 1984).

29. See also David Popenoe, "Challenging the Culture of Fatherlessness," in *The Fatherhood Movement: A Call to Action*, ed. Wade F. Horn, David Blankenhorn, and Mitchell B. Pearlstein (Lanham, Md.: Lexington, 1999), 21.

30. Quoted in Robert Dreyfuss, "The Holy War on Gays," *Rolling Stone*, March 18, 1999, 41.

31. Hardisty, *Mobilizing Resentment*, 102.

32. Beverly LaHaye, *The Hidden Homosexual Agenda* (Washington, D.C.: Concerned Women for America, 1991), 8.

33. See Judith Stacey and Timothy J. Biblarz, "(How) Does the Sexual Orientation of Parents Matter?" *American Sociological Review* 66, no. 2 (April 2001): 159–83.

34. For examples of this argument, see Lionel Tiger, *The Decline of Males: The First Look at an Unexpected New World for Men and Women* (New York: St. Martin's Griffin, 2000); Christina Hoff Sommers, *The War against Boys: How Misguided Feminism Is Harming Our Young Men* (New York: Simon & Schuster, 2000); and James Dobson, *Bringing Up Boys: Practical Advice and Encouragement for Those Shaping the Next Generation of Men* (Wheaton, Ill.: Tyndale House, 2000).

35. Dobson, *Bringing Up Boys*, 23.

36. Dobson, *Bringing Up Boys*, 16–17.

37. Dobson, *Bringing Up Boys*, 17.

38. Hardisty, *Mobilizing Resentment*, 117.

39. Dobson, *Bringing Up Boys*, 119.

40. Dobson, *Bringing Up Boys*, 122.

41. Dobson, *Bringing Up Boys*, 123. Quotations from Hardisty, *Mobilizing Resentment*, 117.

42. McCartney is explicitly antihomosexual. See Hardisty, *Mobilizing Resentment*, 115.

43. *Seven Promises of a Promise Keeper* (Nashville, Tenn.: Word Publishing, 1999), 235.

44. Cited in Linda Kintz, *Between Jesus and the Market: The Emotions That Matter in Right-Wing America* (Durham, N.C.: Duke University Press, 1997), 129.

45. David Blankenhorn, *Fatherless America: Confronting Our Most Urgent Social Problem* (New York: Basic, 1995); Horn, Blankenhorn, and Pearlstein, *Fatherhood Movement*.

46. Blankenhorn, *Fatherless America,* 1.

47. Blankenhorn, *Fatherless America,* 43.

48. Blankenhorn, *Fatherless America,* 101.

49. Blankenhorn, *Fatherless America,* 99.

50. Blankenhorn, *Fatherless America,* 223.

51. Concerned Women for America, "The 'Second Wave's Last Hurrah." (Washington, D.C.: Concerned Women for America, November 3, 1999) at www.cwfa.org/library/family/1999-11-03_era.shtml (accessed April 3, 2002).

52. Mary Ann Glendon and David Blankenhorn, eds., *Seedbeds of Virtue: Sources of Competence, Character, and Citizenship in American Society* (Lanham, Md.: Madison Books, 1995).

53. Fund-raising letter authored by Pete Knight in 2002.

54. William Galston, "The Reinstitutionalization of Marriage: Political Theory and Public Policy," in *Promises to Keep: Decline and Renewal of Marriage in America,* ed. David Popenoe, Jean Bethke Elshtain, and David Blankenhorn (Lanham, Md.: Rowman & Littlefield, 1996), 271.

55. Jean Bethke Elshtain, "Family and Civic Life," in *Rebuilding the Nest: A New Commitment to the American Family,* ed. David Blankenhorn, Steven Bayme, and Jean Bethke Elshtain (Milwaukee, Wisc.: Family Service America, 1990), 122. See Jill Locke, "Hiding for Whom? Obscurity, Dignity, and the Politics of Truth," *Theory & Event* 3 (1999): 3.

56. Council on Civil Society, *A Call to Civil Society: Why Democracy Needs Moral Truths* (New York: Institute for American Values, 1998), 18.

57. Hardisty, *Mobilizing Resentment,* 114.

58. William Galston, "Liberal Virtues and the Formation of Civic Character," in *Seedbeds of Virtue: Sources of Competence, Character, and Citizenship in American Society,* ed. Mary Ann Glendon and David Blankenhorn (Lanham, Md.: Madison Books, 1995), 38.

59. Stacey and Biblarz, "(How) Does the Sexual Orientation of Parents Matter?"

60. William Galston, "Liberal Virtues," 43, emphasis added.

61. Galston, "Liberal Virtues," 43.

62. Susan Moller Okin, *Justice, Gender, and the Family* (New York: Basic, 1989).

63. Galston, "Liberal Virtues," 48, emphasis added.

64. Galston, "Liberal Virtues," 44, emphasis added.

10

The Missing Children: Safe Schools for Some

Jyl J. Josephson

RESPONSES TO COLUMBINE

Although concern with school violence and the means to address it predates the Columbine incident by at least a decade, the intensity of discussion, and the efforts by schools of all types to respond to school violence, was heightened by the events at Columbine High School and the subsequent flood of media attention. Commentators across the political spectrum tended to see a reflection of their own analysis of contemporary social ills in the incident.[1] Social conservatives saw the shooters as products of moral decay in schools and in society. The mistaken account of the female student who was reportedly killed because she said she believed in God seemed plausible to many religious conservatives precisely because the shooters were seen as products of secularism and moral decay.[2]

One factor that was discussed in the educational literature following the Columbine incident was the issue of school climate. Based on the accounts of many students, it became very clear that Eric Harris and Dylan Klebold were subjected to a great deal of verbal harassment by their peers. One of the athletes felt no compunction about reporting his participation in this harassment to *Time Magazine:* "Sure we teased them . . . they're a bunch of homos. . . . If you want to get rid of someone, usually you tease 'em. So the whole school would call them homos."[3] While the existing evidence indicates that Harris and Klebold were straight, it is clear that they were subjected to constant antigay harassment.

A wide range of remedies to the problem of school violence, from prayer, to scrutiny of students who fit certain profiles, to restrictions on violent media, to zero-tolerance policies, to the use of metal detectors and security guards, have been proposed.⁴ These remedies, however, miss two important factors in incidents such as Columbine: each incident involved a white, middle-class, male student or students, and many of these students had been subjected to harassment, including antigay harassment. Since the incidents themselves are relatively rare, one might think that the problem occurs in only a few schools. But in fact there is significant evidence that students in many schools are subjected to harassment, verbal and otherwise. And the problem is not so much the threat of "another Columbine" as the reality that for many students, their school environments are places where they experience daily homophobic harassment.

The problem evidenced by Columbine is not the same as the problem faced by students who are actually sexual minorities. But both are indicative of a larger problem in American schools: the extent to which the failure to intervene in homophobic bullying and harassment leads to school climates that are harmful to many students. When schools fail to systematically and intentionally communicate to students that such harassment is inappropriate and unacceptable, both the students who are harassed, and the students who are permitted to engage in harassment, get the wrong message. Harassers learn that it is permissible and acceptable to engage in behaviors that harm others, and those who are harassed learn that schools are dangerous and harmful places and that adults will not protect them.

Yet, social conservatives have attacked efforts to make schools safer for lesbian, gay, bisexual, and transgender (LGBT) youth, characterizing these efforts as promoting homosexuality. Thus, groups such as the Family Research Council, Concerned Women for America, and the American Family Association (AFA) urge their supporters to oppose any programs that teach faculty or other school staff about how to stop antigay harassment, about tolerance, or about addressing the needs of LGBT youth. Despite the fact that these same conservatives decry violent incidents in schools, they have opposed efforts to make schools safer for all students by creating environments that are safer for students who are or are perceived to be gay, lesbian, bisexual, or transgender. Conservative objections are generally based on abstract fears of moral harm to children, while they ignore the reality of actual harms to children based on homophobic harassment. This chapter critiques the selective conservative concern regarding school violence.

THE PROBLEM OF SAFETY AND THE DEVELOPMENT OF SAFE SCHOOLS PROGRAMS

There is persistent evidence that sexual minority youth do not feel safe in schools in the United States and that public schools have failed in many instances to provide minimal physical safety for youth who are perceived by their peers as nonheterosexual. Data collected by public schools, by gay rights organizations, and by scholars have shown that youth who self-identify as gay, lesbian, or bisexual are more likely to report many different kinds of harassment in school than are students who self-identify as heterosexual.[5] Human Rights Watch conducted a nationwide study of this problem and found, among other things, that harassment is often precipitated by both sex and gender: male students who are perceived as behaving in feminine ways, and female students who behave in masculine ways (including by objecting to sexual harassment by male students) are more likely to be harassed.[6]

Studies of the harassment, verbal and physical, of sexual minority youth in schools indicate that school officials often do not intervene in harassment and that, as a consequence, the harassment escalates.[7] Some students have successfully sued school districts in the United States and elsewhere, but given the nature of litigation and the standard of evidence required, students who are vindicated through legal victories are generally adults before they receive this vindication and have already been harmed in their pursuit of education.[8] Indeed, all of the students who have received settlements or legal decisions in their favor experienced sustained and extensive physical as well as verbal harassment. In each case, school officials were regularly informed of the harassment and failed to intervene or provide adequate assistance to prevent it from recurring. Thus, litigation after the fact is not the most effective solution to the problem of homophobic harassment. It would be much more desirable for schools to create inclusive and safe climates for all students.

Fortunately, many school districts, and some state departments of education, have not waited for litigation to address the problem of homophobic harassment in schools. The state of Massachusetts is usually seen as pioneering in the area of making schools safer for LGBT students. In 1989, the Department of Health and Human Services released a report on youth suicide that raised a good deal of concern in the gay and lesbian community, since it reported that youth who identified as gay, lesbian, or bisexual accounted for about 30 percent of completed suicides among teens. As a result of this report, gubernatorial candidate William Weld promised, and upon election created, the Governor's Commission on Gay and Lesbian Youth.[9] After hearings held around the state at which many youth testified as to discriminatory treatment in schools, the state created the Safe Schools Program, which provided training for teachers and other school staff, resources, and funds for such activities in schools as the formation of Gay/Straight Alliance clubs. This program is the model for other programs that have been created across the country. The state of Washington began with a statewide study of the problem of harassment in schools and is now implementing safe schools strategies statewide.[10] While most such programs have been implemented by state or (more often) local schools, some states have taken the step of adding sexual orientation to state education laws that prohibit discrimination against students and staff. In 1999, the California legislature adopted a law that specifically prohibits antigay harassment in schools and has since adopted procedures to implement this provision.[11] The effort in California has precipitated significant responses from social conservatives.

Of course, these programs have come about in part due to the advocacy work done by gay rights and other civil rights organizations. The Gay, Lesbian, and Straight Education Network (GLSEN); Parents, Families and Friends of Lesbians and Gays (PFLAG); the American Civil Liberties Union (ACLU); and Lambda Legal Defense and Education Fund have all developed resources for use by local and state advocacy groups for implementation of safe schools programs. The purposes of these programs are to make schools safe places for all students, to create educational environments that are open to everyone, and to reduce the drop-out rate and other risk factors for self-identified sexual minority youth.

The problem of school safety for sexual minority youth also has not gone unnoticed by national education organizations such as the National Education Association (NEA). For example, in a speech given at the annual conference of GLSEN in October 2000, NEA president Bob Chase spoke of the necessity of protecting sexual minority students from harassment and including these issues in the curriculum.[12] Chase notes at the beginning of his speech that the Family Research Council had organized an e-mail campaign to discourage him from speaking at the GLSEN conference. Other national organizations, such as the Association for Supervision and Curriculum Development, the American Federation of Teachers, and the American School Counselor Association, have also addressed these issues in their conferences and publications. Thus, educators and educational administrators themselves have begun to recognize the importance of addressing these issues in schools.

CONSERVATIVE RESPONSES TO SAFE SCHOOLS PROJECTS

Not surprisingly, such measures have met with significant resistance by social conservatives and conservative Christian organizations. Certainly, programs such as the one developed by Massachusetts are engaged with issues that are central to the social conservative political agenda: education, sexuality, gender roles, perceived threats to religious beliefs, and the proper instruction of children with respect to morality and values. Given that these programs are being carried out in *public* schools, the antigovernment rhetoric that is often part of social conservative concerns regarding religious beliefs also comes into play. After all, ever since the *Engel v. Vitale* school prayer decision in 1962, religious conservatives have seen a need to restore religious values in public schools.

A number of social conservative organizations have developed resources to encourage and assist parents and other conservative activists to oppose the development and implementation of safe schools projects. Focus on the Family offers a set of resources for antigay activists to use to prevent the implementation of safe schools programs and of other measures to make schools safer places for LGBT students and their allies. A checklist prepared by Linda Harvey, who is active in the "Love Won Out" movement among conservative Christians (an effort to "convert" gays and lesbians to heterosexuality), lists a set of twelve activities that "protect and promote homosexuality and sexual promiscuity." Harvey identifies practices on her list including safe schools antiharassment programs, the establishment of gay–straight alliances, the adoption of nondiscrimination policies, and safe sex and AIDS education programs that teach that all students (not just gay students) are at risk of contracting AIDS. Also included is the placement of literature about LGBT issues in school libraries.[13] This list is indicative of the responses of many conservative organizations to safe schools projects. These organizations see safe schools projects as part of the "gay agenda." For example, the Family Research Council's Peter Sprigg argues: "A fifth element of the homosexual agenda is the effort to get homosexual propaganda included in the curriculum of public schools. The intent of these efforts is obvious— to ensure that the next generation will grow up with an unquestioning acceptance of all the myths that the homosexual activists want young people to believe."[14]

The American Family Association has a similar viewpoint. In response to the resources developed by gay-friendly organizations such as the film *It's Elementary*, the AFA has recently produced a film entitled *It's Not Gay*. The film is intended for use with students and is described as containing both the testimony of "former homosexuals" as well as "medical and mental health experts" who show that "the prevalent view of homosexuality being presented to students is not the whole story." The description goes on to indicate that the film will be useful for "anyone who wants to present a fair and balanced approach to this challenging subject."[15] The AFA intends for the film to be used as a tool for those opposing safe schools projects, with the argument that only by showing this

film in addition to any film produced by gay-friendly groups will educa
tors be presenting information that is "fair and balanced."

Concerned Women for America (CWA) has focused some of its work in
the area of education on what it sees as the promotion of homosexuality
in schools. In her column in the September 2001 issue of *Family Voice,* for
example, CWA chairman Beverly LaHaye writes about the California initiative, characterizing this law and its implementation as a "radical" and "elit-
ist" attempt to indoctrinate students with "political or social beliefs" and as
a violation of the duty of schools to "educate children in academics." Interestingly, this column is one of the few conservative sources that acknowledges that young people might identify as gay, lesbian, bisexual, or transgender. However, LaHaye does so to note the correct response to such
students: "The acts of homosexuality are dangerous, and students who are
trapped in that lifestyle are susceptible to high rates of suicide, dropping out
of school, and serious health risks. These students need the truth, not a program or a poster or the lies of a gender-tolerance police guard."[16]

By "the truth," LaHaye means conservative Christian teachings about
homosexuality and, presumably, treatment through an ex-gay ministry
program. CWA provides many materials on its website regarding safe
schools programs. It was also instrumental in organizing a rally against
the NEA at its national meeting in 2001, at which a resolution on safe
schools programs and curricula was scheduled to be addressed. NEA
chose to postpone consideration of the resolution, a decision for which
CWA took credit.[17]

In addition to national groups, state and local affiliates and more local
groups of social conservatives have taken up the cause of opposing safe
schools programs. The Pacific Justice Institute (PJI) is a conservative legal advocacy organization that describes itself as "specializing in the defense of religious freedom, parental rights, and other civil liberties." In
January 2000, when the California legislation that included sexual orientation and gender identity as protected categories in the state education
code took effect, the PJI pronounced that California was the location
where all conservative nightmares were coming true, and it promised to
fight implementation of the law in the courts.[18] PJI, along with several
other California-based social conservative organizations, initiated what
they termed a "Parental Opt Out Program," so that parents who wished
to could "ensure that their children are not exposed to such controversial
and potentially harmful social instruction."[19] Of course, school districts
historically permit parents to request that their children not participate in
certain activities, and the legislation contained provisions which specifically indicated this parental option. By disseminating this form, and ad-

vocating for parents who make such requests, these groups hoped to "save children from dangerous new laws promoting perverse sexual behavior."[20] Indeed, going beyond opting out of a specific program, Dr. James Dobson of Focus on the Family urges Christian parents to remove their children from California public schools, and a number of other conservatives echo this sentiment, urging parents to home school their children or send them to private Christian schools.[21]

One of the most well-known incidents of conservative opposition to efforts to make schools safer for sexual minority youth occurred when a group of students at East High in Salt Lake City, Utah, tried to form a gay–straight alliance club in 1995. Because of previous cases interpreting the Equal Access Act, which prohibits schools from discriminating on the basis of viewpoint against extracurricular after-school activities, the Salt Lake City school board chose to eliminate all extracurricular clubs rather than permit the gay–straight alliance club to form. After subsequent litigation, the school board has restored extracurricular activities and a similar club has been permitted to meet.[22]

In Massachusetts, a coalition of parents organized against the Safe Schools Program. Jeff Perrotti and Kim Westheimer, two Massachusetts Department of Education staff who each served as director of the Safe Schools Program, note that there was some conservative opposition to the project from the beginning. However, it was not until the decision was made to incorporate sexuality education into some aspects of the program that conservatives were able to succeed in curtailing funding and support for the Safe Schools Program. Initially, administrators had chosen to separate sexuality education from the program and to focus on the effort to make schools physically safe for LGBT students. As they worked with students, however, they came to feel that an important aspect of safety for LGBT students was the inclusion of HIV/AIDS prevention education. As a result, one workshop at the March 2000 Safe Schools Program conference was on gay and lesbian sex and sexuality. In attendance at the workshop were high school students, teachers, and parents. Illegally, without the knowledge of participants, including the minors who were present, parents from the Parents Rights Coalition, the group that formed to oppose the Safe Schools Program, taped the workshop. They edited the tape to sensationalize what occurred and released it to the news media. One radio talk show host played the tape constantly for a week. According to Perrotti and Westheimer, the mainstream media did not pick up the story until the Massachusetts Department of Education issued a press release that condemned the workshop and fired the two employees who had led it.[23]

The conservative press discussion of this series of events is quite different. According to a story on the CWA website, "A number of conservatives uncovered and recorded the truth behind homosexual behavior that stunned the nation."[24] The article describes the purpose of the conference as follows: "GLSEN trains teachers and students and develops programs to fight those who oppose homosexual behavior."[25] And the article notes that the parents who tape-recorded the event had "educated New England on the terrors of homosexual curriculum" but now "face heavy legal costs for a trial in a liberal state that donates $1.5 million tax dollars annually to gay and lesbian youth organizations." And, although this article praises the firing of the staff who led the workshop, it also criticizes David Driscoll, head of the state Department of Education, for continuing the Safe Schools Program and describes the use of "safe schools" to describe the program as "rhetoric to create a victim status for those practicing homosexuality." The story about the incident printed in the conservative *Weekly Standard* criticizes the efforts of both GLSEN and public officials to prevent the distribution of the tape, only briefly noting that the tape was made in violation of state wiretap laws. This story also raises the concern that Massachusetts may be leading a national trend: "As goes Massachusetts, in time, so may go the rest of America . . . as the powerful GLSEN organization, with sponsorship money from American Airlines, Dockers Khakis, and Kodak, presses its radical agenda under the innocent-sounding guise of 'safety,' 'human rights,' and 'suicide prevention.'" One of the parents interviewed for the story noted that "the point of this activist drive . . . is to desensitize children to gay sex at a very young age and counteract moral instruction to the contrary given by their parents and religious leaders." This same parent characterized GLSEN and other safe schools advocates as "bullies."[26]

In July 2002, Citizens for Community Values (CCV), a Cincinnati-based group, sent letters to all public schools in the state of Ohio indicating that any public schools who permit GLSEN or PFLAG access to the school might be subject to legal liability for "endangering the physical health" of children and violating the First Amendment. As I write this chapter, CCV is conducting an "audit" of Ohio schools, asking all schools for their policies regarding hate speech, diversity, discrimination, and sexual orientation. They have issued a press release indicating that they would provide free legal assistance to "parents and students hurt by the 'gay agenda' in schools," along with a "report" that purports to analyze the legal liability schools might incur if they provide safe schools programs. The majority of the report contains "assessments" of the dangers of homosexual behavior, along with arguments that any antiharassment code that includes sexual orientation is a violation of the First Amendment.[27]

THE STRUCTURE OF CONSERVATIVE
ANTI-SAFE SCHOOL ANALYSIS

One important trope of antigay activism is the idea that gay and lesbian people pose a threat to children, and it is not surprising that this concern shows up in the conservative discourse regarding issues of sexual orientation and schools.[28] As Didi Herman notes, in the early 1990s the Christian Right began to respond more directly to the gay rights movement. She traces the coverage of these issues in *Christianity Today;* the first article that discusses safe schools programs was published in 1993. This article critiques the use of the idea of tolerance to argue for safe schools programs, seeing these projects as aimed at the effort by gay rights activists "to encourage acceptance of homosexuality among public-school students."[29]

Among the conservative groups that oppose the safe schools movement, I find no analysis of actual incidents of violent attacks against gay students, and the most common strategy is to deny that such events occur. These groups see even tolerance programs and programs to promote diversity that include discussion of sexual orientation as promoting sexual promiscuity and silencing people with traditional religious beliefs. Those who advocate for safe schools programs, and the educators who support them, are depicted by social conservatives as extremely powerful; indeed, as bullies who promote homosexuality and ignore the objections of parents to creating school climates that are safe for sexual minority students and their allies.

One of the reasons that the conservative effort in Massachusetts was successful was because the Safe Schools Program Conference actually involved a discussion of sexuality. Opponents of safe schools programs generally depict such programs as being about sex and about introducing homosexual sex into school classrooms. Advocates of such programs argue that such depictions are based on the misperception that any discussion of sexual orientation is necessarily a discussion of sex. As Herman points out, one of the common features of what she terms the "old" antigay discourse is the depiction of sexual minorities as perverted, "disease-ridden and a threat to children."[30] Certainly, conservative sources generally depict sexual orientation in this way: the image of sexual minorities as purveyors of a disease-ridden, immoral, and sexually perverted "lifestyle" is pervasive in these sources.

Herman also identifies a newer discourse among antigay social conservatives: a more pragmatic discourse aimed at countering the rights-based arguments of sexual minority advocacy groups. This newer discourse—which argues that sexual minorities are not oppressed minorities in the same way that other groups such as racial and ethnic minorities have been, and are thus not in need of civil rights protections—is less evident in the antisafe schools rhetoric. Yet, this latter claim is also implicit in the effort to deny the existence of discrimination against students based on perceived or actual sexual orientation or gender identity. Interestingly, some of the strategies used to counter safe schools programs are based on arguments for a right to conservative religious views, such as the "opt out" provisions for the California safe schools initiative or CCV's strategy in Ohio. Social conservatives depict themselves as defending the rights of parents and of children to an education free from any but negative mentions of homosexuality. The rhetoric of social conservatives frequently refers to the innocent young children who will be harmed by safe schools programs. Thus, the Right depicts itself as the defender of children against "homosexuals."

There is a mismatch between efforts by safe schools advocates to document the concrete threat to students and the relatively abstract, fear-based response of social conservatives. The arguments of social conservatives are generally not based on incidents that have taken place in actual schools. Rather, they are a reflection of fears of moral harms or threats to beliefs about the sinfulness of homosexuality that are assumed to result from safe schools programs. Social conservatives characterize any type of workshop on school safety issues or on the value of tolerance and of diversity as an effort to promote "homosexual behavior."

One conservative source that does acknowledge that bullying (though not homophobic bullying) in schools is a problem is an article on bullying for *Focus on the Family*.[31] Frank Peretti, who was himself bullied as an adolescent, connects the bullying experienced by Dylan Klebold and Eric Harris at Columbine High School to lasting problems suffered by victims of bullying. However, Peretti presents the solution to these problems as a matter of individual action. Peretti cites his own experience, and the teacher who intervened to help him. But the solution to the fact that he was bullied in gym class was to remove him from the class, not to confront the behaviors of his peers that made his life in gym class so miserable. However, persistent evidence on the extent to which bullying unchecked leads to further and more violent behaviors indicates that such individualized solutions are inadequate. If we truly want to address the problem of school safety, schools need to respond systematically to these problems. Safe schools programs are designed precisely to help schools address problems of homophobic harassment in a systematic and proactive way.

THE MISSING CHILDREN

The children who are missing from right-wing discourse, of course, are the youth who are negatively affected by homophobia: the concrete, real youth the safe schools programs are trying to help. This includes youth who identify as gay, lesbian, bisexual, or transgender, other youth who are perceived to be sexual minorities, and youth who are subjected to homophobic harassment or who are harassed because their parents are gay, lesbian, bisexual, or transgender. Given the pervasiveness of homophobic attitudes among students, particularly in middle schools and high schools, this problem has negative effects on a significant proportion of young people.[32] Indeed, the youth who are affected by harassment are not only youth who self-identify as sexual minority youth. In a 1999 study of youth in Seattle high schools, half of youth who self-identified as gay or lesbian had been harassed or attacked at school because someone thought they were gay or lesbian, while only 4 percent of students who identified as heterosexual reported such harassment. Since the total numbers of students who identified as heterosexual were so much larger—7,459 compared to 65 who identified as gay or lesbian—the actual number of self-identified straight students who reported harassment was much higher: nearly 300, compared with 32 of 65 self-identified gay or lesbian students. Thirty-nine percent, or 104, of the 266 students who identified as bisexual were also subject to such harassment. Thus, antigay harassment is a problem for many youth, whether or not they self-identify as gay, lesbian, or bisexual.[33] This same study also showed the negative effects of harassment for students, whether the basis for that harassment was race, gender, or sexual orientation. Students who had been harassed were more likely than their peers to feel unsafe and miss school because of it, to have considered or attempted suicide, and to feel more pessimistic about their future.

Conservative organizations deny the data on gay youth suicide rates. They criticize the initial study which helped lead to the Massachusetts program, published by the federal Department of Health and Human Services, as being methodologically flawed and inaccurate, and they deny that the risk of suicide might be higher for teens who identify as sexual minorities than for teens who identify as heterosexual. They criticize safe schools programs as suicide prevention measures, since according to social conservatives they are based on the false assumption that young people are "'naturally' homosexual."[34] Further, they deny that violence against sexual minority students is a problem. Linda Harvey, for example, notes correctly that violence in schools is declining, and then goes on to ridicule the idea that sexual minority students are subjected to harassment and to dismiss the idea that homophobic name-calling is harmful.[35] Harvey argues that safe schools programs are really intended to target any speech that is critical of homosexuality and that Christians are being unfairly stereotyped by these safe schools programs. In her analysis, the real threat is to Christians and to those who "disagree with homosexuality"; they are being discriminated against by schools. Thus, the problem of harassment and violence against sexual minorities is deflected and transformed into an argument that safe schools programs threaten Christianity and Christian values. The socially conservative Christian becomes the victim. The structure of this argument is quite similar to the social conservative argument against hate crime laws; social conservatives argue that hate crimes are not a problem, that sexual minorities are not frequent targets of hate crimes, and that laws to address hate crimes are violations of equal protection and are efforts to regulate speech.[36]

In none of the literature did I find any reference to actual instances of homophobic harassment in schools, or any mention of the empirical studies that document this harassment. These instances are well documented, and indeed there have been numerous successful lawsuits on the issue. Yet, the arguments made by social conservatives do have real negative consequences for actual children. One recent example took place near Ames, Iowa, at Gilbert High School. Jerryn Johnston, an openly gay student, was repeatedly harassed in his school, his car was vandalized, and his tires were slashed, and other students tore down posters he had put up for the National Day of Silence, a student-organized event to recognize the problem of homophobia. He and his mother requested that sexual orientation be added to the school nondiscrimination code, but the school board declined to do so although it did clarify some aspects of the harassment policy. A number of conservative parents argued that adding sexual orientation to the harassment and nondiscrimination policy "would silence those who believe homosexuality is immoral." One parent told Mr. Johnston at the hearing that everyone gets bullied, and he should just "deal with it." Although teachers initiated a reward fund for information leading to an arrest in the car vandalism, no perpetrators have been arrested.[37]

CONCLUSION

The football player at Columbine, the students who harassed Jerryn Johnston, and the perpetrators of violence against students who later successfully sued their schools all got the same message from the adults in their school: it's okay to engage in homophobic harassment and violence. Yet, instead of being concerned about this violence and the children who are negatively affected by it, social conservatives are concerned about the potential that their views will not take precedence over other views regarding homosexuality. When conservative opposition to safe schools projects succeeds in derailing safe schools work by intimidating school officials into failing to address these issues, not only are LGBT students harmed, but so is education for all students. If schools are to be safe places for all children to learn, schools must end homophobic harassment of students, whether they are gay, bisexual, or straight.

NOTES

I wish to thank Cynthia Burack, Paula Ressler, Frank Beck, James Nelson, and David Foster for helpful ideas and suggestions on this chapter.

1. B. A. Robinson, "Why Did the Columbine Shooting Happen? Beliefs from Secular Sources," Ontario Consultants for Religious Tolerance, 1999–2001, at www.religioustolerance.org/sch_viol.htm (accessed March 25, 2002).

2. Robinson, "Columbine Shooting," 1.

3. Nancy R. Gibbs and Timothy Roche, "The Columbine Tapes," *Time* 154, no. 125 (December 20, 1999): 40–51.

4. Elliot Aronson, *No One Left to Hate: Teaching Compassion after Columbine* (New York: W. H. Freeman, 2000).

5. There are numerous studies. A useful summary can be found in appendix A, *Assembly Bill 537 Advisory Task Force Report* (Sacramento: California Department of Education, 2001).

6. Michael Bochenek and A. Widney Brown, *Hatred in the Hallways: Violence and Discrimination against Lesbian, Gay, Bisexual, and Transgender Students in U.S. Schools* (New York: Human Rights Watch, 2001), 49–56.

7. Stephen L. Wessler, "Sticks and Stones," *Educational Leadership* 58, no. 4 (December 2000/January 2001): 28–33.

8. The first federal case in which damages were awarded involved a student named Jamie Nabozny; the case was *Nabozny v. Podlesny* 92 F.3d 446 (7th Cir. 1996). More recent cases include those discussed in Gerry Weiss, "Youth to Get Landmark Settlement on Anti-Gay Harassment Case," *Erie Times News,* January 17, 2002; and in Nathan Greenfield, "School Failed to Stop Gay Bullying," *Times Education Supplement,* April 19, 2002, no. 4477, p. 20.

9. Jeff Perrotti and Kim Westheimer, *When the Drama Club Is Not Enough: Lessons from the Safe Schools Program for Gay and Lesbian Youth* (Boston: Beacon, 2001), 2.

186   *Jyl J. Josephson*

10. Safe Schools Coalition, "They Don't Even Know Me! Understanding Anti-Gay Harassment and Violence in Schools" (Seattle: Safe Schools Coalition of Washington State, January 1999), at www.safeschoolscoaltion.org/theydontevenknowme.pdf (accessed July 2, 2002). See also the website of the coalition at www.safeschoolscoalition.org.

11. Vanessa Eisemann, "Protecting the Kids in the Hall: Using Title IX to Stop Student-on-Student Anti-Gay Harassment," *Berkeley Women's Law Journal* 15, no. 58 (2000): 125–60.

12. Bob Chase, speech from 2000 GLSEN Conference, October 7, 2000, at www.glsen.org/templates/resources/record.html?section=14&record=255 (accessed January 22, 2001).

13. Linda Harvey, "A Checklist to Assess Your School's Risk for Encouraging Homosexuality," Citizen Link: A Web Site of Focus on the Family, 2001, at www.family.org/cforum/tempforum/A0015282.html (accessed March 25, 2002).

14. Peter S. Sprigg, "Defending the Family: Why We Resist Gay Activism," address delivered October 13, 2001, Madison, Wisconsin, at www.frc.org/get/pd0111.cfm?CFID=922322&CFTOKEN=43478426 (accessed June 30, 2002).

15. AFA Resources, *It's Not Gay* description, AFA website, at www.afa.net/videos/ing.asp (accessed July 2, 2002).

16. Beverly LaHaye, "Chairman's Desk," *Family Voice,* September/October 2001, at www.cwfa.org/library/_familyvoice/2001-09/04-05.shtml (accessed June 30, 2002).

17. Pamela Pearson Wong, "Activists Rally against NEA: Education Lobby Proposes Pro-Homosexual Resolution" (Washington, D.C.: Concerned Women for America, July 2, 2001), at www.cwfa.org/library/education/2001-07-02_nearally.shtml (accessed June 30, 2002).

18. Pacific Justice Institute, "California: Where the Worst Is Happening" (Citrus Heights, Calif.: Pacific Justice Institute, November 16, 2000), at www.pacificjustice.org/articles_9.html (accessed November 6, 2001).

19. Pacific Justice Institute, "'Homosexuality in Schools' Bill to Become Law in Four Days" (Citrus Heights, Calif.: Pacific Justice Institute, December 29, 2000), at www.pacificjustice.org/pr122800.htm (accessed November 6, 2001).

20. Julie Foster, "Coalition Helps Kids Avoid 'Homosexual Curriculum,'" *WorldNetDaily,* January 17, 2001, at www.worldnetdaily.com/news/article.asp?ARTICLE ID=21361 (accessed October 20, 2001).

21. Warren Smith, "Is It Time to Abandon Public Schools?" guest commentary, *Agape Press Christian News Service,* June 7, 2002, at headlines.agapepress.org/archive/6/72002ws.asp (accessed July 2, 2002).

22. Ruthann Robson, "Our Children: Kids of Queer Parents and Kids Who Are Queer: Looking at Sexual Minority Rights from a Different Perspective," *Albany Law Review* 64 (2001): 915–47.

23. Perrotti and Westheimer, *When the Drama Club Is Not Enough,* 140–41.

24. Suzanne McDuffie, "Parents Battle Homosexual Activism in Schools"

(Washington, D.C.: Concerned Women for America, July 31, 2000), at www.cwfa.org/library/education/2000-07-31_hs.shtml (accessed June 30, 2002).

25. McDuffie, "Parents Battle."

26. Rod Dreher, "Banned in Boston: Better Not Complain about the Gay Agenda in Massachusetts Schools," *Weekly Standard*, July 3–10, 2000, 16.

27. These materials are available on the CCV website at www.ccv.org (accessed July 11, 2002).

28. Didi Herman, *The Antigay Agenda: Orthodox Vision and the Christian Right* (Chicago: University of Chicago Press, 1997).

29. Herman, *Anti-Gay Agenda,* 57; quotation is from Dale Buss, "Homosexual Rights Go to School," *Christianity Today* 37, no. 6 (1993): 70–72.

30. Herman, *Anti-Gay Agenda,* 123.

31. Tom Neven, "The Wounded Spirit," *Focus on the Family Magazine,* 2001, at www.family.org/fofmag/pf/a0017468.html (accessed July 3, 2002).

32. Laurie Mandel and Charol Shakeshaft, "Heterosexism in Middle Schools," in *Masculinities at School,* ed. Nancy Lesko (Thousand Oaks, Calif.: Sage, 2000), 75–103.

33. Seattle Teen Health Survey, "Health of Harassed Youth" (Seattle: Safe Schools Coalition of Washington State, 2001), at www.safeschoolscoalition.org (accessed January 20, 2002).

34. Scott Lively, "Q&A: Using 'Suicide' to Promote False Identities to Kids" (Washington D.C.: Concerned Women for America, May 18, 2001), at www.cultureandfamily.org/report/2001-05-18/questions (accessed July 3, 2002).

35. Linda P. Harvey, "'Safe Schools'—The Trojan Horse of the 'Gay' Education Movement?" *Culture and Family Report,* May 16, 2002, at cultureandfamily.org/report/2002-05-16/n-harvey.shtml (accessed July 3, 2002).

36. Robert Knight, "The Hate Crimes Agenda: An Attack on Faith," *Family Voice,* July/August 2001, at cwfa.org/library/_familyvoice/2001-07/22-26.shtml (accessed July 3, 2002).

37. Ben Godar, "Some Gilbert Parents Oppose Adding Sexual Orientation to Harassment Policy," *Ames Tribune,* March 27, 2002, 000.

11

Leaving Children Behind: Criminalizing Youth in American Schools

Valerie C. Johnson

THE CONSERVATIVE AGENDA IN PUBLIC EDUCATION

In 1994, the U.S. Congress passed the Gun-Free Schools Act (GFSA). The GFSA requires all states receiving federal funds to enact laws requiring local educational agencies to expel for a period of not less than one year students found to have brought weapons to school. By 1995, forty-seven states and the District of Columbia had passed state laws or enacted policies that established zero-tolerance policies for weapons. By the end of the 1998–1999 school year, fifty-six jurisdictions (states and territories) had complied. In implementing zero-tolerance policies, however, administrators broadened the original intent of the legislation to include drugs, alcohol, tobacco, and physical conflicts in order to "send a message" to potential violators.[1]

The impact of zero-tolerance policies on school violence has been questionable at best. Thus far, the most that can be said is that these policies do little more than assuage public fear about school violence—fear that is in most instances out of step with reality. Zero-tolerance policies are leaving children behind by expelling them for violations that had previously been considered minor. In doing so, school administrators have criminalized youth by subjecting them to law enforcement, increasing their likelihood for future contact with the juvenile justice system.

As zero-tolerance policies have proliferated, so too have juvenile incarceration rates. Neither, however, has anything to do with increasing crime rates, but rather is the result of a social conservative policy shift that focuses on "getting tough" on crime. The impact of social conservative measures is manifested in a comparison between crime and incarceration rates. Although crime rates have fallen nationally since 1992, prison populations have more than tripled since the early 1980s. Overall juvenile crime rates declined by 30 percent between 1993 and 1998; nonetheless, there has been a rise in juvenile incarceration, particularly among African American youth.

A large proportion of the growth in U.S. incarceration, both adult and juvenile, has its roots in the War on Drugs, inaugurated by the Reagan administration in 1982. The arsenal in the War on Drugs has been lengthy sentencing policies designed to ensure maximum penalties (i.e., mandatory minimums, three-strikes policies, and truth in sentencing). "Largely as a result of these laws, the chances of receiving a prison term after being arrested for a drug offense rose dramatically, by 447 percent between 1980 and 1992."[2] Similar to zero-tolerance policies in schools, these laws remove discretion from the sentencing judge. Factors pertaining to the individual that would normally be a routine part of the sentencing or expulsion process are removed, ruling out a problem-solving approach. The application of such conservative "get tough" policies in America's schools has spelled disaster for many youth by treating them as incorrigible offenders. As I show later, these policies have had a particularly harsh effect on African American and other minority youth.

This chapter details the origins of zero-tolerance policies in schools; summarizes the 1999 Decatur, Illinois, expulsions, which heightened public awareness of school-based zero-tolerance policies; and draws a connection between zero-tolerance policies and juvenile incarceration. This chapter also questions the efficacy of draconian discipline policies and addresses their impact on the educational and developmental processes of youth who, in many instances, are already at risk for dropping out of school or having encounters with the law.

THE BACKGROUND OF ZERO TOLERANCE IN U.S. SCHOOLS

As indicated, the origins of zero-tolerance school-based discipline policies can be found in the drug enforcement policies of the Reagan administration. As a demonstration of the lack of discretion inherent in zero-tolerance policies, in 1988 Attorney General Edwin Meese "authorized customs officials to seize boats, automobiles, and passports of anyone crossing the border with even trace amounts of drugs and to charge those individuals in federal court."[3] Although significant public outcry led to the U.S. Customs Service suspension of zero-tolerance policies in drug enforcement, the policies were quickly picked up by school districts across the nation, leading to wide support and to passage of the Gun-Free Schools Act (GFSA).

PERCEPTIONS VERSUS REALITY IN SCHOOL VIOLENCE

American youth have a one in two million chance of being killed in school.[4] Between 1993 and 1998, there was a 56 percent decline in juvenile homicide arrests and a 30 percent decline in the juvenile crime rate overall.[5] During the 1996–1997 school year, a national survey of principals and school disciplinarians reported tardiness (40 percent), absenteeism (25 percent), and physical conflicts between students (21 percent) among the most frequently cited school-related problems. Major infractions such as drug use (9 percent), gangs (5 percent), student possession of weapons (2 percent), and physical abuse of teachers (2 percent) were reported less frequently.[6] These figures were virtually unchanged in comparison to findings from those reported in a similar 1990–1991 survey. In the 1990–1991 survey, for example, student possession of weapons was reported as a frequent problem by 3 percent of respondents.[7] Nonetheless, American parents are increasingly fearful of school-related violence. Largely fueled by sensationalized media reports of school shootings in West Paducah, Kentucky; Jonesboro, Arkansas; and Pearl, Mississippi, 71 percent of respondents in a 1998 poll believed that a school shooting was likely to happen in their community.[8]

Policymakers have responded to increasing fear by instituting unreasonable and harsh disciplinary measures whose justification have little basis in reality. In the process, youth across the nation have been increasingly subjected to expulsion and suspension for relatively minor offenses that had been previously handled by school administrators. Stories abound of student expulsions for possession of plastic knives, innocuous key chains, or toys that are characterized as weapons or acts deemed hostile by increasingly fearful teachers and school administrators.

RECENT TRENDS IN SCHOOL-RELATED VIOLENCE

As is the case for juvenile crime, in recent years there has been a decline in school-related offenses. Between 1993 and 1998, student reports of physical fights on and off school grounds decreased by 14 percent (see table 11.1). During the same time period, student reports of being injured in a physical fight declined by 20 percent, while students who reported carrying a gun to school declined by 25 percent.

Table 11.1 Student Self-Reporting of Fights and Gun Possession in Schools

Incidents	1993 (%)	1997 (%)	Change (%)
Physical fights on and off school grounds	42.5	36.6	−14
Physical fights on school grounds	16.2	14.8	−9
Injuries in a physical fight on or off school grounds	4.4	3.5	−20
Carrying a weapon	26.1	18.0	−30
Carrying a gun to school	7.9	5.9	−25

Source: Nancy D. Brener, Thomas R. Simon, Etienne G. Krug, and Richard Lowry, "Recent Trends in Violence Related Behaviors among High School Students in the United States," *Journal of the American Medical Association* 2112, no. 5 (1999).

Recent research tracking school-related violence indicates that 115 times as many youth are murdered away from school than in school.[9] Researchers have also concluded that more heavily secured school buildings face greater incidents of victimization and disorder (fights, thefts) than schools that are less secure, and they add to the overall climate of fear.[10] Thus, the trend toward greater use of metal detectors, locker searches, and security guards is not only, in many cases, unreasonable, but is largely ineffective in stemming violence and disorder. This is also true for zero-tolerance policies.[11]

The U.S. Department of Education defines a *zero-tolerance policy* as a policy that mandates "predetermined consequences or punishments for specific offenses." Stories abound of school district administrators who, in their zeal to foster school safety, enact policies that limit sound reasoning and discretion.[12] In many instances, youth who are suspended or expelled have no option for alternative education. Currently, twenty-six states "require by law, that school districts make alternative education opportunities available to students suspended or expelled. In eighteen states, it is within the discretion of school districts to provide alternative education."[13] Referrals to alternative schools, however, are predicated upon available openings, which in turn are dependent upon the amount of resources that states commit to alternative schools. In some states, it is clear that the educational development of expelled youth is not a priority.

Another devastating consequence of zero-tolerance policies is its effect on the criminalization of youth. "It is often the case that students are subjected to criminal charges or juvenile delinquency charges for conduct that poses no serious danger to the safety of others. In forty-one states, schools are required to report students to law enforcement agencies for various conduct committed in school."[14] In some cases conduct that was once considered a sign of immaturity or ordinary childhood behavior is now criminalized. This was the case for the six African American students who were expelled from Decatur Public Schools. After facing a two-year expulsion for their participation in a fight at a football game, they were subsequently subjected to criminal prosecution for the incident.

Zero-tolerance policies are particularly pernicious for African American students because they are more likely to exist in predominantly African American and Latino schools. "During the 1996–97 school year, these districts were more likely to have policies addressing violence (85 percent), firearms (97 percent), other weapons (94 percent), and drugs (92 percent), than white school districts (71 percent, 92 percent, 88 percent, 83 percent, respectively)."[15]

The 1999 Decatur, Illinois, expulsion case was simply the tip of the iceberg, as numerous youth across the nation encounter school districts that are increasingly intolerant of even the most minor infractions. In the Decatur case, as well as in others, school officials operating under zero-tolerance policies have subordinated the educational development of youth to an irrational fear of potential violence. The rise in school suspensions and expulsions is a testament to these trends.

ZERO TOLERANCE IN DECATUR, ILLINOIS

Between October 1 and 4, 1999, six African American male students were expelled from the Decatur, Illinois, public schools for two years for their alleged participation in a fistfight at a football game on September 17, 1999.[16] On October 2, 1999, the day after three of the youth had been expelled, Rainbow/PUSH Coalition (R/PC) Decatur chapter vice president Keith Anderson arrived at the National R/PC headquarters in Chicago, seeking assistance with the case. Chief among Anderson's concerns was a quote that appeared in the local Decatur newspaper by a board of education member, claiming that the expulsion decision was in line with the board's zero-tolerance policy toward violence.[17]

As far as Anderson knew, the district had not publicized such a policy in its manual of Student Discipline Policy and Procedures. Upon discussing the merits of the case with Reverend Jesse L. Jackson Sr., it was decided that I should travel to Decatur to meet with local school officials in my role as the R/PC National Education Spokesperson.[18] At first glance, the issue appeared to be an isolated case of injustice. Over the course of several months, however, it became exceedingly clear that the case of the Decatur six was symptomatic of the larger national trend in the use of zero-tolerance policies as a strategy to reduce school violence.

The involvement of Jackson and the R/PC in the Decatur, Illinois, expulsion case raised the issue to national prominence. Proponents of the expulsions viewed Jackson's involvement in the case as dalliance in the local affairs of the Decatur school board and its ability to counter school violence. Opponents, on the other hand, raised questions regarding the equity and efficacy of school discipline policies. Although contentious, the debate has grave implications on the policies and practices of local school boards, and particularly the plight of African American students who are disproportionately impacted by school discipline policies.

In line with the national and Illinois legislative trend, the Decatur, Illinois, Board of Education unanimously adopted and passed a joint resolution, in early August 1999, which declared a no-tolerance position on school violence. The resolution in part read: "Be it resolved that the Board of Education for the following School Districts support and join Macon County . . . the law enforcement and mental health agencies in declaring a no tolerance position on school violence, and encourages all citizens to make a commitment to violence free schools."

The confluence of these factors set off a chain of events that ultimately led to the crisis in Decatur. Absent a growing national concern about school safety or subsequent legislation, the fistfight that occurred on September 17, 1999, in Decatur would have likely been punishable by a ten-day suspension at most. Certainly, the Decatur expulsions went far beyond the intent of the GFSA, which sought a minimum one-year expulsion for gun possession on school property.

Although the fight involved no weapons and resulted in no sustained injuries, the school board contended that it constituted an extreme act of violence and charged the boys with "Gang-Like Activities" and two counts of "Physical Violence with Staff or Students." On October 7, 1999, joined by concerned ministers and community leaders, I met with Decatur Board of Education president Ms. Jackie Goetter and other Decatur Public Schools officials to set forth objections to the expulsions.

Several concerns were presented at the meeting. The first was that the district's zero-tolerance resolution was arbitrarily applied. Having examined the district's school discipline code, which sets forth disciplinary violations and penalties, I found no mention of any zero-tolerance resolution. We therefore felt that it was an undue burden that the youth were subject to penalties resulting from an infraction that had not been clearly set forth and disseminated in the district's school discipline code.

Second, although the youth had varying levels of participation in the fight, ranging from victim to perpetrator, and all had different school records, all received the same punishment. This suggested that the board viewed the youth as a group rather than as individuals and points to one reason why zero-tolerance policies are so objectionable. Rather than considering mitigating circumstances, zero-tolerance policies are absolute—regardless of the context or consequences, minimal involvement results in the same punishment as maximum involvement.

In the football game fistfight, even the victim faced a two-year expulsion. Although he was subsequently given the opportunity to withdraw, his withdrawal carried the same weight as an expulsion because he, too, was not allowed to enroll in any public or private school in Decatur. Further, if the student later sought reinstatement, he would once again be subject to an expulsion hearing before the board. When later asked why even the victim of the fight was subject to expulsion, school board attorney Jeffrey Taylor indicated that the victim had also thrown some punches. In response to Jackson's query as to whether the punches might have been defensive in nature, Taylor indicated that they were disturbing nonetheless.

There was also evidence that at least one of the expelled youth had not actually thrown any punches in the fight, but like other youth had run toward the fight. According to district representatives, the student was expelled because he had reportedly pushed past a principal when he was asked to stop for questioning—hence, resulting in charges of "Physical Violence with Staff or Students."

Third, and equally disturbing, the punishment of a two-year expulsion from school did not fit the infraction. A record search turned up no prior example of an expulsion solely on the basis of a fistfight. Other two-year expulsions in Decatur were the result of weapon or drug violations, bomb threats, or a case in which there had been sustained injuries resulting from a fight in which karate was used.

Fourth, the youth were denied due process in their expulsion hearings. Although two student eyewitnesses to the youths' involvement were allowed to enter written statements into the record, they were not present at the hearings and therefore were not subject to examination. Equally problematic, witnesses who were present at the hearing to testify against the six youth testified to second-hand information reportedly handed down through an investigation of the fight.

Further, although the youth were all minors, the youth's parents were discouraged from participating in the decision-making process. The parents viewed the notices of the expulsion hearings as an accomplished fact. The notice to parents indicated that while they were welcome to come to the hearings, they were not required to attend. The notice also indicated that the school administration recommended a two-year expulsion. In the parents' view, this suggested that there was nothing that they could do and that the board had predetermined their children's guilt.

Upon setting forth the aforementioned objections and viewing a videotape of the fight, I finally appealed to district officials on the basis of morality and ethics. My central argument was that there was no educational or societal value in expelling the youth for two years. In a later meeting between Jackson and district officials, Superintendent of Schools Dr. Kenneth Arndt confirmed the basis of this concern when he explained that approximately 80 percent of youth who had been expelled for extended periods did not return to finish their education, but instead typically dropped out and become involved in more serious offenses.

After a very public campaign, the youth were ultimately allowed to enroll in alternative schools—an option that had not been offered prior to R/PC intervention. Upon arriving to enroll the youth in school, however, Jackson and R/PC representatives were met with protesters who opposed the youths' enrollment in alternative schools. We were not informed that there was a long waiting list of youth who had been expelled and who were awaiting placement. Thus, although there was a system of alternative schools in place, the state had not appropriated sufficient funds to accommodate all youth who needed placement. Without adequate space, many youth were forced to postpone their education. In this instance, despite protests, Illinois governor George Ryan's order allowed the youth to enroll.

One of the most distressing factors related to the Decatur expulsions surfaced months afterward when the elementary and secondary education committee of the Illinois state legislature voted against introducing legislation that would apply discipline policies uniformly throughout the state. After my impassioned appeal to legislators at a hearing on the legislation, opponents argued that school districts should maintain local control over their affairs. Conservatives advanced similar arguments during the civil rights movement in opposition to federal mandates. This conservative trend continues to run through the education policy arena, impacting school discipline policies and school funding.

Current policies allow a broad range of disciplinary options depending on the district in which the infraction occurred. Similarly, school funding relies heavily on the amount of property taxes that a district is able to collect, thereby guaranteeing funding inequalities between districts. In many ways, it is likely that funding disparities may lead to a lack of uniformity in disciplinary measures. High-funded districts are more likely than low-funded districts to provide counseling services and options that circumvent long-term expulsions. It is thus no surprise that predominantly minority districts, which are typically low-funded, have higher rates of expulsions and suspensions.

Although a few of the Decatur youth had a history of education-related problems, counseling was never an option for them. Fortunately, however, as a result of external pressure from the R/PC and the governor, the two youth who were seniors were allowed to complete their requirements in an alternative school and subsequently graduate on time. Although R/PC attorneys lost their legal case on behalf of the boys, Jackson and R/PC representatives ultimately won a quiet victory. At the time of this writing, three of the youth are currently enrolled in local colleges. Without intervention, there is no doubt that the youth would have likely been counted among the numerous youth who are locked out of educational opportunities as a result of zero-tolerance policies. Their numbers are represented in the growth of expulsions and suspensions nationwide.

RACIAL DISPARITIES AND EFFECTS OF THE
INCREASE OF EXPULSIONS AND SUSPENSIONS

In May 2000, the U.S. Department of Education reported that suspensions rose from 1.7 million in 1974 to 3.1 million in 1997. The department also reported that African Americans are suspended at roughly 2.3 times the rate of whites nationally.[19] Although African American students comprise 17 percent of the national school-aged population, they represented 32 percent of the total suspensions in 1997. Comparatively, white students make up 64 percent of the total student population and 51 percent of the total suspensions nationwide. African American males are particularly impacted. A U.S. Department of Education report indicates that almost 25 percent of all African American males are suspended at least once over a four-year period.[20] There is perhaps no irony in the fact that these figures mirror the rate of African American male involvement in the criminal justice system.

RACIAL DISPARITY IN SCHOOL DISCIPLINE

Research conducted by the Applied Research Center on twelve school districts across the nation bears out the magnitude of the disparity (see table 11.2). Key findings from the Applied Research Center report on racial discrimination in public schools include the following:[21]

- African American, Latino, and Native American students are suspended or expelled in numbers vastly disproportionate to those of their white peers. This was true in every school district surveyed. Furthermore, zero-tolerance policies exacerbate this trend.

- Students of color are more likely to drop out or be pushed out of school and are less likely to graduate than white students.
- Students of color have less access to advanced classes and gifted programs.
- The racial makeup of faculty rarely matches that of the student body. Most school districts do not require antiracist or multicultural training for teachers and administrators.

When Jackson and the R/PC intervened in the Decatur expulsions, they found a similar trend. Although African American youth comprised

Table 11.2   School Expulsions and Suspensions in Select Cities in the United States, by Race (1997–1998 and 1998–1999)

School District	Race	Student Enrollment (%)	Students Suspended and Expelled (%)
Austin, TX	Black	18	36
1997–1998	White	37	18
Boston, MA	Black	55	70
1998–1999	White	13	9
Chicago, IL	Black	53	63
1997–1998	White	10	9
Denver, CO	Black	21	42
1998–1999	White	24	15
Durham, NC	Black	58	68
1998–1999	White	36	15
Los Angeles, CA	Black	14	30
1997–1998	White	11	8
Phoenix, AZ	Black	4	21
1998–1999	White	74	18
Providence, RI	Black	23	39
1997–1998	White	21	13
Columbia, SC	Black	78	90
1998–1999	White	20	9
San Francisco, CA	Black	16	52
1998–1999	White	12	10

Source: Applied Research Center at www.arc.org (accessed July 10, 2002).

Table 11.3   School Discipline in the Decatur Public Schools (1998–1999)

	Enrollment	Suspensions	Expulsions
Total	11,339	1,730	7
White	59.9%	38.7%	29%
African American	38.6%	60.0%	71%
Other	1.5%	1.3%	0%

Source: Decatur Public Schools.

39 percent of the district's student population during the 1998–1999 school year, they represented 60 percent of the suspensions and 71 percent of the expulsions. Between the 1994–1995 school year and the end of the fall term of the 1999–2000 school year, African American youth represented 83 percent of the district's expulsions. These trends are consistent across Illinois and are particularly acute in the central part of the state. While African American youth represented 21 percent of the total student population in Illinois, during the 1997–1998 school year, they represented 43 percent of the state's 2,744 expulsions. Whether the subject is school discipline in Decatur or across the nation, the result is the same—minority youth bear the brunt of school punishment (see table 11.3).

Zero-tolerance policies have also had a disproportionate impact on students with special needs. Although the Individuals with Disabilities Act (IDEA) affords special protection for children with disabilities, in many circumstances school officials ignore the law, and parents and students are unaware of their rights or are unable to enforce them.[22]

DEBATE ON THE CAUSES OF
DISPROPORTIONATE DISCIPLINARY ACTION

Two arguments that are perennially advanced to explain disproportionate rates of school discipline among African American students are (1) that minority students engage in greater rates of disruptive behavior and (2) that disproportionate rates are associated with socioeconomic status. Russell Skiba addressed these issues in his study of race and school discipline and concluded that disproportionate rates of suspension among African Americans were not the result of socioeconomic status, but instead the result of disparities in office referrals at the classroom level. Skiba found that African American students were "referred to the office for infractions that are both less serious and more subjective in their interpretation than white students."

According to Skiba, "White students were significantly more likely than black students to be referred to the office for smoking, leaving without permission, vandalism, and obscene language. Black students were more likely to be referred for disrespect, excessive noise, threat, and loitering."[23] Thus, African American youth are punished for less-serious infractions and for those that are more subject to bias.

Skiba's study raises grave implications about the manner in which teachers, particularly white teachers, interpret African American students' behavior. His findings are consistent with studies that suggest that the overreferral of African American students may be the result of fear, acquiescence to stereotypes, and a lack of familiarity and ease with the communications styles of African American youth.[24] In *Bad Boys: Public Schools in the Making of Black Masculinity,* Ann Arnett Ferguson argues that school practices and teacher expectations contribute to the making of delinquent African American boys. According to Ferguson, "Two cultural images stigmatize Black males in the United States today. One represents him as a criminal, and the other depicts him as an endangered species."[25] Clearly, teachers and administrators are not immune to common stereotypes that depict African American males as prisonbound. Unfortunately, however, in too many instances, these stereotypes become self-fulfilling prophecies.

THE IMPACT OF HARSH AND EXCESSIVE SCHOOL DISCIPLINE

Whatever the causes of these biases, it is clear that African American students feel and respond to differences in ways that may exacerbate tensions and lead to dropping out.[26] At best, zero tolerance and other harsh disciplinary policies lead to short- and long-term exclusion from educational instruction. At worst, they lead to alienation from educational processes, which in turn leads to dropping out of school and involvement in risky behavior. When children are shut out of school, they are left without adequate resources or qualifications to engage in lawful employment. This in turn presents dire consequences to families and communities.

Studies confirm a strong correlation between suspension and dropping out. In some instances, suspended youth are three times more likely to drop out than their peers are.[27] Out-of-school adolescents are also more likely to smoke, use drugs and alcohol, and engage in sexual intercourse.[28]

JUVENILE CRIME AND INCARCERATION

As a result of higher participation in antisocial behavior, out-of-school adolescents are more likely to become involved in behavior that results in contact with the law. It stands to reason that youth who are out of school are more likely to loiter or hang out in the street—behavior that makes them targets for law enforcement officials. The point of entry into the criminal justice system, then, for many youth, is absence from school. Zero-tolerance policies exacerbate this trend because they increase the rate of school suspensions and expulsions.

RACIAL DISPARITIES IN THE JUVENILE JUSTICE SYSTEM

As indicated, juvenile crime rates declined by 30 percent between 1993 and 1998. Nonetheless, there has been a rise in juvenile incarceration. Most devastating, all fifty states now have laws that allow juveniles to be tried as adults.[29] The movement toward youth involvement in adult court is similar to "get-tough" schemes in the education system.

And, as is the case for school discipline policies, the rise in juvenile incarceration has disproportionately impacted minority youth. Studies have shown that minority juveniles processed for delinquency offenses receive "more severe (i.e., more formal and/or more restrictive) dispositions than their white counterparts at several stages of juvenile processing." A Florida study found that "when juvenile offenders were alike in terms of age, gender, seriousness of the offense which promoted the current referral, and seriousness of their prior record, the probability of receiving the harshest disposition available at each of several processing stages was higher for minority youth than for white youth."[30] Patricia Williams notes that among the white public, perceptions of behaviors that would be seen as harmless if the youth involved were white are seen very differently if the youth involved are African American, Asian American, or Latino.[31]

In states across the nation, African American youth are disproportionately arrested and incarcerated. In Illinois, African American youth represent 19 percent of the youth population statewide but comprise 58 percent of the total number of juveniles incarcerated in the state. In Georgia, African American youth comprise 34 percent of the youth population and 83 percent of the total number of juveniles incarcerated in adult prisons. In Ohio, the results are the same. Minorities are 14.3 percent of the juvenile population in Ohio, but 30 percent of juveniles arrested and 43 percent of the juveniles placed in secure corrections.[32] In Texas, minorities make up 50 percent of the youth population statewide, but account for 65 percent of the juveniles held in secure detention, 80 percent of the juveniles placed in secure corrections, and 100 percent of the juveniles held in adult prisons.[33] In California, the state with the largest number of juvenile commitments, minorities comprise 53.4 percent of the youth population and 59 percent of all juveniles arrested, almost 64 percent of the juveniles held in secure detention, and 70 percent of the juveniles placed in secure corrections.[34]

On the national level, data are consistent with state-by-state findings. Although minority youth are 30 percent of the youth population nationwide, they represent 60 percent of all youth confined in local detention and state correctional systems. African American youth represent the largest group confined in juvenile facilities. The admission rates to public facilities are twice the rate for Latino youth than for their white counterparts with similar prior admissions. For African American youth, the admission rate is seven times greater. "Even when referred for the same offense, African American youth are more likely than white youth to be formally charged in juvenile court." [35] As an example, "just over 50 percent of drug cases involving white youth" and other non–African American youth "result in formal processing." In contrast, 75 percent of drug cases involving African American youth result in formal processing.[36]

In 1998, African American youth were overrepresented as a proportion of arrests in twenty-six of twenty-nine offense categories documented by the FBI. In the detention process, African American youth made up 31 percent of court referrals but 44 percent of the detained population. White youth, on the other hand, represented 66 percent of court referrals and 53 percent of the detained population.[37]

Similar to arguments advanced regarding disparities in school discipline policies, some argue that disparities in juvenile arrest and incarceration are due to greater rates of criminal behavior among minority youth. Numerous studies, however, contradict this claim. A Justice Policy Institute study found that minority youth were 2.8 times more likely to be arrested for felony violent crimes (murder, rape, robbery, and aggravated assault) than their white cohorts. African American youth were six times more likely. This data is consistent with Skiba's findings that disproportionate rates of suspension and expulsion among African American youth are the result of bias in office referrals—actions taken at the beginning of the process.

Even more compelling, however, once processed through the system, African American youth who are arrested for felony violent offenses are twelve times more likely than whites to be transferred to adult court in Los Angeles County.[38] While it has been argued that biases in the arrest rate of African American youth may be associated with higher incidences of criminal behavior, this data makes a compelling case for racial profiling and discrimination. According to the Justice Institute report, racial disparities accelerate as youth move into the adult system. Once minority youth are remanded over to the adult system, they are then seven times more likely than their white cohorts to be sent to prison by adult courts. "Something happens after arrest to increase a minority youth's odds of imprisonment from 2.8 times that of a white youth (based on violence arrest) to 7 times more (based on adult court sentencing)."[39] Thus, while nonwhite youth in Los Angeles County are 2.8 times more likely to be arrested for violent offenses, they are seven times more likely to face adult imprisonment for similar offenses.

On the national level, again, the results are the same. As is the case in state-by-state findings, nationally, disparities accelerate as youth move into the adult system. Minority youth represent 75 percent of youth incarcerated in adult prisons. In 1997, the proportion of African American juveniles admitted into adult prisons involving a drug offense was three times greater than for their white counterparts. Therefore, on all levels of the justice system, African American youth face differential treatment. Given this reality, social conservative "get tough on crime" policies have been disproportionately harmful to African American youth.

CONCLUSION

Differential treatment of African American and other minority youth in the education and criminal justice systems is well documented. The data presented in this chapter argue that biases exist in both systems. In the process, we are losing too many of our youth and ill preparing them to meet the challenges of the new millennium. To be sure, there is a slippery slope from harsh discipline policies to the juvenile justice system. When one considers the social conservative shift toward more punitive policy measures, it becomes apparent that rising expulsion and juvenile incarceration rates, particularly among minority youth, are less the result of rising violations, but are rather the result of policies that seek punishment first when dealing with minority youth.

We must venture to reclaim our youth. An extraordinary problem requires extraordinary solutions and a significant commitment on the part of adults throughout the system. We must refrain from sitting idly by while our youth are excluded from educational opportunities and remanded over to an increasingly unyielding criminal justice system. While both problems impact African American and minority youth disproportionately, we must recognize that all youth are suffering under the weight of our unrealized fears, and that the welfare of the collective is predicated upon the welfare of the individual. If we are to advance as a nation, we must ensure that all youth are given adequate opportunities to reach adulthood as self-sufficient and productive members of society—that no child is left behind. We will either flourish together or perish together. The choice is ours to make.

NOTES

1. Russ Skiba and Reece Peterson, "The Dark Side of Zero Tolerance: Can Punishment Lead to Safe Schools?" *Phi Delta Kappan* 80, no. 5 (January 1999): 372–76.
2. "Drug Policy and the Criminal Justice System" (Sentencing Project, Washington, D.C., 2001).
3. Skiba, "Darker Side of Zero Tolerance."
4. Kim Brooks, Vincent Schiraldi, and Jason Ziedenberg, "School House Hype: Two Years Later" (Washington, D.C.: Justice Policy Institute, 2000), at www.justicepolicy.org/schoolho/ (accessed July 10, 2002).
5. FBI Uniform Crime Reports, 1993–1998.
6. U.S. Department of Education, National Center for Education Statistics, "Violence and Discipline Problems in U.S. Public Schools: 1996–97," NCES 98-030, Washington, D.C., 1998.
7. Skiba, "Darker Side of Zero Tolerance."
8. Nancy Belden, John M. Russonello, and Kate Stewart, "Americans Consider Juvenile Crime, Justice and Race: Executive Summary" (unpublished report, Building Blocks for Youth, Washington, D.C., 1998).
9. Howard N. Snyder and Melissa Sickmund, "Juvenile Offenders and Victims: 1999 National Report" (Washington, D.C.: Office of Juvenile Justice and Delinquency Prevention, 1999).
10. Matthew Mayer and Peter Leone, "A Structural Analysis of School Violence and Disruption: Implications for Creating Safer Schools," *Education and Treatment of Children* 22, no. 3 (August 1999): 333–56.
11. See "Opportunities Suspended: The Devastating Consequences of Zero Tolerance and School Discipline" (Advancement Project and the Civil Rights Project, Harvard University, June 2000).
12. "Opportunities Suspended," iv.
13. "Opportunities Suspended," vi.
14. "Opportunities Suspended."
15. "Opportunities Suspended."
16. Although seven Decatur public school students were originally implicated, one student was allowed to withdraw, pending expulsion. He was, however, included in all negotiations to return the youth to school.

17. Brad Mudd, "Rainbow/PUSH Spokesman Says Punishment Too Severe; Fight Being Investigated," *Decatur Herald & Review,* October 5, 1999, p. 1A.

18. The following account of the Decatur case is based on my experiences as the national education spokesperson for Reverend Jesse L. Jackson Sr. and the Rainbow/PUSH Coalition. In this role, I had in the past met with numerous school administrators in districts in which apparent injustice had occurred. Unlike these instances, however, the Decatur case proved resistant to initial negotiations.

19. Cited in Kim Brooks et al., "School House Hype," 12.

20. U.S. Department of Education, "The Condition of Education" (U.S. Department of Education, Washington, D.C., 1997).

21. Rebecca Gordon, Libero Della Piana, and Terry Keleher, "Facing the Consequences: An Examination of Racial Discrimination in U.S. Public Schools" (Oakland, Calif.: Applied Research Center, 2000).

22. The Advancement Project and the Civil Rights Project, Harvard University, "Opportunities Suspended: The Devastating Consequences of Zero Tolerance and School Discipline," report from a National Conference on Zero Tolerance, June 15–16, 2000, (Cambridge, Mass.: Civil Rights Project), at www.civilrights project.harvard.edu/research/discipline/call_opport.php (accessed July 10, 2002).

23. Russell Skiba, Robert S. Michael, Abra C. Nardo, and Reece L. Peterson, "The Color of Discipline: Sources of Racial and Gender Disproportionality in School Punishment," Policy Research Report #SRS1 (Bloomington: Indiana Education Policy Center, Indiana University, June 2000).

24. Brenda Townsend, "Disproportionate Discipline of African American Children and Youth: Culturally Responsive Strategies for Reducing School Suspensions and Expulsions," *Exceptional Children* 66, no. 3 (Spring 2000): 381–91.

25. Ann Arnett Ferguson, *Bad Boys: Public Schools in the Making of Black Masculinity* (Ann Arbor: University of Michigan Press, 2000).

26. D. T. Bullara, "Classroom Management Strategies to Reduce Racially-Biased Treatment of Students," *Journal of Education and Psychological Consultation* 4 (1993): 357–68.

27. Skiba and Peterson, "Dark Side of Zero Tolerance"; Ruth B. Ekstrom, Margaret E. Goertz, and Judith M. Pollack, "Who Drops Out of School and Why? Findings from a National Study," *Teachers College Record* 87, no. 3 (Spring 1986): 356–73.

28. Centers for Disease Control and Prevention, "Health Risk Behaviors among Adolescents Who Do and Do Not Attend School: United States, 1992," *Mob Mortality Weekly Report* 43, no. 8 (March 4, 1994): 129–32.

29. Office of Juvenile Justice and Delinquency Prevention, "Juvenile Offenders and Victims: 1999 National Report" (United States Department of Justice, Washington, D.C., 1999).

30. Donna Bishop and Charles Frazier, "A Study of Race and Juvenile Processing in Florida: A Report Submitted to the Florida Supreme Court Racial and Ethnic Bias Study Commission" (1990), cited in Mike Males and Dan Macallair,

"The Color of Justice: An Analysis of Juvenile Adult Court Transfers in California" (Washington, D.C.: Building Blocks for Youth, February 2, 2000), at www.building blocksforyouth.org/colorofjustice/ (accessed July 10, 2002).

31. Patricia Williams, "Obstacle Illusions: The Cult of Racial Appearance," in *Police Brutality: An Anthology,* ed. Jill Nelson (New York: W. W. Norton, 2001), 149–56.

32. Donna Hamparian and Michael Leiber, "Disproportionate Confinement of Minority Juveniles in Secure Facilities: 1996 National Report" (Champaign, Ill.: Community Research Associates, 1997), 9, cited in Mike Males and Dan Macallair, "Color of Justice."

33. Hamparian and Leiber, "Disproportionate Confinement," 9.

34. Hamparian and Leiber, "Disproportionate Confinement," 9.

35. Eileen Poe-Yamagata and Michael A. Jones, "And Justice for Some" (Washington, D.C.: A Building Blocks for Youth Report, 2000).

36. Poe-Yamagata and Jones, "Justice for Some," 1.

37. Poe-Yamagata and Jones, "Justice for Some," 26.

38. Mike Males and Dan Macallair, "Color of Justice."

39. Males and Macallair, "Color of Justice."

12

From Welfare to Wedlock: Marriage Promotion and Poor Mothers' Inequality

Gwendolyn Mink

For the past several years, marriage has figured prominently in debates about welfare. The idea of government as dating service or matchmaker doesn't seem to resonate widely with the public, yet the idea that welfare policy should encourage or pressure poor single mothers into marriages nevertheless has bewitched policymakers of all political stripes.[1] During the 107th Congress (2001–2003), marriage promotion provisions figure prominently in welfare reauthorization proposals touted by Senators Hillary Clinton and Joe Lieberman as well as by President George Bush and the marriage moguls in his party and administration.

The seeming irresistibility of the call to marry poor mothers off of welfare is patent evidence of the precariousness of both feminism and democracy. Evidence of a dangerous assault on the rights of unmarried mothers who need welfare, efforts to use income policy to promote marriage directly contradict the intimate decisional rights that extended late-twentieth-century democratization into the personal sphere.

It was *Loving v. Virginia,* the famous antimiscegenation case decided in 1967, that definitively established the significance of intimate associational liberty to our equality as citizens. Asserting the national citizenship rights of individuals against race-based state laws restricting marital freedom, the Court in *Loving* shifted the axis of marital decision making from government to adult individuals—at least for heterosexuals. Before *Loving,* laws governing access to legally valid marriage, relationships within marriage, as well as the status of marital bonds accomplished government's cultural, moral, eugenic, racial, and patriarchal regulation of the citizenry. With *Loving,* however, government's power to police and to stratify the adult citizenry by conferring marital status on some intimate partnerships while withholding it from others declined, though only for heterosexuals.

Although *Loving* most importantly established the right to marry a partner of one's (heterosexual) choosing regardless of race, the decision also incorporated the right *not to marry* as a core element of the fundamental right at stake in the case.[2] Soon after *Loving,* the Court applied heightened constitutional protection to the right to be *not*-married when it held that the right to dissolve a marriage could not be conditioned on the ability to pay court costs and related fees[3] and when it ruled that the right to receive welfare benefits could not be limited to families in which parents were "ceremonially married."[4] Both cases involved welfare recipients, so both decisions explicitly extended fundamental intimate associational rights across the divides of class and poverty.

Loving was first and foremost a decision against racial regulation of intimacy, demography, and citizenship. But especially in noticing that the right to marry includes the right not to, *Loving* and its progeny carried special significance for women. Intimate associational liberty implies a collateral right to maintain an independent household even if outside patriarchal, marital norms. It establishes a right to exit from perhaps unhappy, perhaps violent, marital relationships. And it disentangles reproductive choices from the marital circumstances in which they are made. We may mostly think of reproductive liberty in terms of the right not to bear children; and we may mostly think of marital freedom in terms of the right to get married. But *Loving* and related decisions that democratized personhood established also that we can bear children and not be married and—because each right is fundamental—we can do both at the same time.

Yet, despite judicial signals that the choice to not marry or to unmarry were among the intimate associational liberties at the core of democratic personhood, government continues to treat marriage as a necessary condition of worthy adult citizenship. Indeed, in 1996, Congress enacted two new laws deploying marriage to stratify citizenship. One of the new laws, the Defense of Marriage Act, stringently limits the rights and benefits of intimate association by defining marriage as a union between "one man and one woman." The other law, the Personal Responsibility and Work Opportunity Reconciliation Act (PRWORA), injures or disables poor single mothers' basic civil rights because they are not married. One law withholds from lesbians and gay men the right to become marital citizens; the other punishes poor single mothers for not choosing marital citizenship.

I want to explore, here, how the federal government wields its power over certain women who are not married and what that means for equality. Feminist and other advances in the late twentieth century have enabled many women to defer, avoid, or exit from marriages, sometimes without suffering opprobrium. For women with children, however, such choices exact heavy costs: single mothers pay for their intimate decisions with their material security and with their rights. Government argues "child well-being" to justify its interventions into the associational autonomy of single mothers—especially if they are poor. Wielding the choice to bear children against the choice to not marry, government delivers some of the most severe blows to women's equality. One need only examine welfare policy, which aims to end unmarried mothers' marital status rather than their poverty, to see how.

MARRIAGE PROMOTION UNDER THE 1996 WELFARE LAW

Let me turn now to the Temporary Assistance to Needy Families (TANF) program, which the Personal Responsibility Act created when it "reformed" welfare in 1996. In its famous "findings," the TANF provision of the PRWORA blames countless social ills on black single mothers; in its statement of purpose, TANF policy pledges to promote marriage, reduce out-of-wedlock births, and to "encourage the formation and maintenance of two-parent families."[5]

Toward these ends, TANF subjects single mothers to work rules that deprive them of the right and the flexibility to make parenting decisions about the care needs of their children. It subjects them to paternity disclosure rules that vitiate their sexual and reproductive privacy. It subjects them to family formation rules, which confer social and financial fatherhood on biological fathers (and instantiate their legal rights) regardless of a mother's say. In these ways and more, TANF punishes single motherhood, endangering the physical, emotional, and material security of poor mothers and their children, jeopardizing poor mothers' custody of their own children, and negating their right to form intimate associations on their own terms.

Governmental interference in intimate life—especially in the formation of families through marriage—has almost always forwarded dominant societal and governmental goals for racial and gender order. That's what antimiscegenation laws were all about. That's what coverture was all about. That's what countless immigration and naturalization laws were all about, laws that restricted the entry of wives and women, or that stripped U.S. women of citizenship if they married noncitizen men.

TANF recapitulates the racialized, undemocratic, patriarchal tradition in its pronouncements and punishments regarding childbearing and child rearing by single mothers. Marriage serves several functions in TANF: it privatizes poverty, it reaffirms patriarchy, and it spotlights women of color as moral failures.

Noting the color of welfare and the color of nonmarital mothers who are poor, TANF proponents attribute the need for welfare to the moral or cultural deficits of racialized individuals rather than to racialized opportunities and economic conditions.[6] For example, the *2000 Green Book,* published by the House Ways and Means Committee, proclaimed in retrospect: TANF stakes itself to "the perspicacity of Moynihan's vision" that "black Americans [are] held back economically and socially in large part because their family structure [is] deteriorating."[7] According to this argument, single-mother poverty arises from single mothers' failure to choose marriage; in turn, the failure to marry is a measure of single mothers' impoverished citizenship.

Under the 1996 welfare law, TANF's most extensive efforts to push mothers into heterosexual families headed by fathers arise from its child support and paternity establishment requirements affecting mothers. These provisions do not go so far as to compel marriage or residential co-parenting, but they do require mothers to maintain association with biological fathers (so that they can inform on them!) even if mothers do not want biological fathers involved with their children. Under the paternity establishment provision, a mother must disclose the identity of her child's biological father or must permit the government to examine her sex life so that it can discover the DNA paternal match for her child. Under the child support enforcement provision, a mother must help government locate her child's biological father so that the government can collect reimbursement from him for the mother's TANF benefit. A mandatory minimum sanction against families in which mothers do not cooperate in establishing paternity or collecting child support enforces government's determination that a biological reproductive nexus constitutes a social family.

Numerous other TANF provisions and guidelines promote marriage either directly or by discouraging women from bearing children if they are not married. For example, executive branch guidelines for TANF implementation reward states for promoting marriage. Both the Clinton and Bush administrations have awarded TANF "high-performance bonuses" to states that most increase the percentage of children living in married-parent families. Moreover, Department of Health and Human Services guidelines specifically tell states that, given the purposes of TANF, they can develop pro-marriage policies with TANF funds.[8] As a result, several states have used TANF funds to disseminate the pro-marriage message, to provide marriage classes, or to reward actual marriage in the structure of TANF benefits (as does West Virginia through $100 monthly bonuses for TANF families in which parents are married).

Another provision of the 1996 welfare law gave incentives to states to reduce "illegitimacy." The "illegitimacy bonus" provided extra money to states that achieve the greatest reductions in nonmarital births without increasing their abortion rates.[9] The bonus gave states a green light to interfere in unmarried women's intimate family decisions, including reproductive decisions—such as by offering bonuses to unmarried pregnant women who agree to relinquish their babies at childbirth; by pressuring unmarried pregnant recipients to marry; or by encouraging or rewarding long-term contraception by unmarried women who are poor.

Abstinence-only education is yet another prong of the federal effort to prevent childbearing by unmarried women. This provision of the 1996 welfare law pays states to teach "groups which are most likely to bear children out-of-wedlock" that "sexual activity outside the context of marriage is likely to have harmful psychological and physical effects" and that one should "attain . . . self-sufficiency before engaging in sexual activity."[10]

These and other TANF provisions compromise poor mothers' rights, more so if they never have been married. The rights compromised include intimate association, reproductive and sexual privacy rights, not to mention the right to parent one's own children. These rights abuses are not the haphazard detritus of welfare policy. Rather, they are the arsenal of marriage promotion among poor women with children. To all mothers who might want to choose nonmarriage, and to mothers who are barred from marriage because their partners are women, TANF's rights abuses send an unmistakable warning to find a man and stand by him. To mothers who are unmarried and poor—disproportionately mothers of color—TANF's rights abuses teach that the only path out of poverty is through marriage or marriage-like financial association with biological fathers. In these ways, welfare policy makes unmarried mothers' economic insecurity an opportunity for public intervention in private choice and an excuse for impoverishing unmarried mothers' citizenship.

TIGHTENING THE KNOT

The 1996 welfare law was plenty heavy-handed in promoting marriage and punishing mothers' independence, but interest currently abounds among policymakers to make that heavy hand even stronger. Although TANF has been in effect for only five years, the need to reauthorize its federal funding has created an occasion to stiffen the marriage lever in welfare policy. Many other issues are on the table as well, ranging from how much to spend on welfare to whether to allow adult recipients to go to school to how much work should be required. Views on these matters vary across the political spectrum. Less varied are views about TANF's role in engineering marital family formation. Among conservatives, moderates, and even among liberals can be found proposals to augment TANF's capacity to promote marriage and fatherhood, as well as to prevent sex and reproduction outside of marriage.

One goal of the family formation agenda is to make fathers pay for families. As Senator Evan Bayh put it in the Democratic Leadership Council's *Blueprint* magazine, "We . . . have to make specific demands of American men. . . . Do not bring children into the world until you are prepared to support them."[11] Another goal, as Will Marshall, president of the DLC's Progressive Policy Institute stated it in *Blueprint,* is to promote marriage as a way of choking off independent or nonmarital childbearing, which he calls the "'feeder system' for both welfare and child poverty."[12] Still a third goal of the family formation agenda is to return poor mothers and their children to the patriarchal family by withholding economic security unless they do so.

The most extreme calls to turn welfare into a marital family formation policy come, not surprisingly, from the Republican right wing. Robert Rector of the Heritage Foundation, for example, has urged policymakers to set aside $1 billion in TANF funds annually for marriage promotion activities, to offer incentives and rewards to parents who marry, and to create an affirmative action program in public housing for married couples.[13] Another leading proponent of fatherhood and marriage is Wade Horn, the Bush administration's assistant secretary of Health and Human Services for welfare, who supports such proposals as rewarding women "at risk of bearing a child out of wedlock" with annual payments of $1,000 for five years if they bear their first child within marriage and stay married.[14]

President Bush's proposal for TANF reauthorization, not surprisingly, advances the family formation agenda. One of the statutory goals of the 1996 welfare law is to encourage the formation and maintenance of two-parent families. The Bush plan would amend and extend that goal "to encourage the formation and maintenance of healthy two-parent married families and responsible fatherhood." It goes on to redirect the $100 million "illegitimacy bonus" to fund research and demonstration projects "primarily directed at building strong families, reducing out-of-wedlock pregnancies and promoting healthy marriages." It also redirects $100 million in "high-performance bonus" funds to support state-level pro-marriage activities. It further requires states to end "discrimination" against two-parent married families enrolled in TANF—for example, by applying the same work rules to single mothers that apply jointly to parents in married families. Finally, the Bush proposal requires states to submit marriage promotion plans as a condition of receiving a TANF block grant. These state plans would have to provide explicit descriptions of state marriage promotion activities. They also would have to establish annual numerical goals for marriage so that the federal government can measure the success of state efforts.[15]

In addition, Bush administration proposals related to TANF call for $20 million in grants to faith-based and community groups to "encourage and help fathers to support their families and avoid welfare, improve fathers' ability to manage family business affairs, and encourage and support healthy marriages and married fatherhood."[16] The Bush budget for 2002, meanwhile, earmarked $135 million for abstinence-only education—a 33 percent increase over current spending—to forward the goal of two-parent family formation by preventing nonmarital pregnancy and childbearing.[17]

The Bush marriage proposals were included in H.R. 4737, the Republican TANF reauthorization bill, that passed the House of Representatives in May 2002. Although the vote on the bill followed party lines, more or less, support for making marital family formation a component of welfare policy abounds in both parties. Bipartisan efforts to link poverty reduction to marriage have been working their way through Congress since 1998. Beginning with the first "Fathers Count Act" in 1998, proposals have encouraged residential fatherhood, often without considering the custodial mother's wishes, and they have promoted marriage. None of the family formation bills has yet become law, but they have been quite popular, passing the House of Representatives by thundering bipartisan majorities in 1999 and 2000.[18]

These bipartisan majorities span the political spectrum. In the 106th Congress, for example, Jesse Jackson Jr. (D-IL)—a leading progressive in the House of Representatives—introduced a fatherhood bill that emphasized marriage, while Benjamin Cardin (D-MD) joined with Nancy Johnson (R-CT) to sponsor legislation linking marriage to responsible fatherhood.[19] In the 107th Congress, Julia Carson (D-IN) introduced H.R.1300, modeled on the Jackson bill, which calls for programs that

> promote marriage through such activities as counseling, mentoring, disseminating information about the benefits of marriage . . . [and] that sustain marriages through marriage preparation programs, pre-marital counseling, marital inventories, skills-based marriage education, financial planning

seminars, and divorce education and reduction programs, including mediation and counseling.[20]

Democratic sympathy for the family formation agenda shows up in several of the Democratic TANF reauthorization bills. In the Senate, Senators Evan Bayh (D-IN) and Tom Carper (D-DE) would reform TANF to promote marriage and "responsible fatherhood" through programs similar to those described in the Jackson and Carson bills, through pro-marriage media and education campaigns, and through related initiatives designed to convince parents to stay married.[21] Other indications of Democratic interest in promoting marital family formation include provisions in Senator Jay Rockefeller's TANF bill that encourage "the formation and maintenance of 2-parent families and healthy marriages and reduc[e] nonmarital births."[22]

In the House of Representatives, a TANF bill sponsored by Congressman Cardin (D-MD), the ranking Democrat on the welfare subcommittee of the House Ways and Means Committee, would redirect the "illegitimacy bonus" into a "family formation fund" much as does the Bush proposal. Although the Cardin bill did not mention marriage per se, like the Bush proposal it would support research and demonstration projects "(i) promoting the formation of 2-parent families; (ii) reducing teenage pregnancies; and (iii) increasing the ability of non-custodial parents to financially support and be involved with their children." The Democratic substitute, offered as an amendment to the Republican TANF bill on the floor of the House in the spring of 2002, repeated Cardin's call for a "family formation fund" that would promote two-parent family life. Given the limited, heterosexual definition of family imposed on federal law by the Defense of Marriage Act, the Democrats' legislative embrace of "2-parent families" in welfare policy lends a Democratic imprimatur to heterosexist and patriarchal intervention into poor mothers' lives.

MARRIAGE PROMOTION AND WOMEN'S EQUALITY

The family formation agenda should not be confused with an agenda to support families. In fact, family formation provisions in both the Bush and the Bayh–Carper TANF reauthorization proposals go hand in hand with harsh new work requirements, while all of the proposals mentioned here continue to neglect the educational and wage opportunities that precondition economic security. Pure and simple, what the family formation agenda is about is engineering the structure of poor mothers' families. It's about Big Brother dictating what families should look like and about punishing families that don't look "right" by privatizing their poverty. This threatens personal, cultural, and associational freedoms, not to mention the economic well-being of families that deviate from the prescriptive norm.

The rights won by women since the 1960s are at risk here. George Bush wants to "improve fathers' ability to manage family business affairs." Will Marshall and Daniel Lichter want to prevent unmarried women from having babies. Evan Bayh wants to teach men "not to bring children into the world" until they can pay for them. One way or another, perpetrators of marriage promotion designate marital fathers the kingpins of legitimate family life.

Think for a minute what this will do to women's reproductive rights. These rights—especially the right to make choices about abortion—are grounded in the constitutional notion that *women*—not husbands, not boyfriends, not male sexual encounters, not sperm donors, but *women*—get to decide whether or not to bear a child. But according to Senator Bayh, *men* "bring children into the world." Dressed in the appealing language of "responsible fatherhood," Bayh's call for men to refrain from childbearing "until [they] are prepared to support" children gives biological fathers standing as childbearing decision makers and thereby imperils a right that is foundational to women's equal and independent personhood.

Among fundamentalist patriarchalists, the argument that welfare policy should be about family formation is racially charged and gender-ideological; it turns on what conservatives call their "family values." The conservative family formation agenda is predictable: it was central to their attack on welfare in the 1980s and 1990s, and it was constitutive of their plans for TANF. Among moderates and liberals, most of whom embrace gender and racial equality as their goals, the argument is more instrumental and accordingly more insidious. Often, it is linked to the observation that families with residential, marital fathers tend to be better off than families without them. As Daniel Lichter reported in the January issue of the DLC's *Blueprint,* "Only 6 percent of married couples with children are poor, compared with 36 percent of female-headed families."[23]

The income disparity between married and mother-only families is not surprising, because married-parent families often have two incomes and because a father's income is generally larger than a mother's. Rarely does the marriage lobby compare the incomes of single-mother to single-*father* families. In 2000, gender-based income disparities among single-parent families consigned the majority of nonmarital female-headed families to economic distress and more than a third of them to abject poverty. Nonmarital male-headed families enjoyed far greater economic security, with fewer than 25 percent earning less than $20,000 annually and only 16 percent earning less than $15,000. Further, whereas a third of nonmarital male-headed families earned more than $50,000, only 15 percent of nonmarital female-headed families did so.[24] Avoiding these facts permits the conclusion that it is family structure rather than inequality that makes and keeps single-mother families poor.

Contemporary welfare reform instantiates marriage as the sine qua non of worthy citizenship. Except as a warning, welfare reform has little bearing upon the rights or lives of childless adults or of unmarried parents who are not poor. But to be a poor and unmarried mother in the United States today is to be unworthy of full citizenship—to be deprived of the rights that have guaranteed equal personhood since *Loving*.

We each do not stand on equal footing as participants and actors in public life if we each are not guaranteed decisional autonomy and relational equity in private life and if we do not all share the same freedoms to form and sustain families of our own choosing. Given the long history of government's gender and racial regulation of intimate life and the nexus among such regulation and political, economic, and cultural inequality, the struggle for intimate rights—to marry or not to, to bear children or not to, to parent our own children—has been a crucial dimension of race and gender democratization in the United States. Though stingy and disciplinary, welfare once contributed mightily to the struggle for intimate rights by enabling poor women to choose children, to parent them, and to do so while exiting or avoiding marriage. In contrast, welfare now expressly impedes nonmarital motherhood among poor women by withdrawing rights and enforcing poverty. Given the racially disparate distribution of poverty, welfare's marriage vise restores the color line to intimate freedom that *Loving*, in its day, took away.[25]

NOTES

This chapter originally appeared as an article in the *Journal of the Political Economy of the Good Society* 11, no. 3 (2002), and is reprinted here by permission.

1. According to a poll conducted by Andrew Kohut of the Pew Research Center in late March 2002, by a margin of 79 to 18 percent, Americans said they preferred government to stay out of the business of promoting marriage. Reported in David Broder, "An Unlikely Marriage Broker," *Washington Post,* March 31, 2002, p. B7.

2. *Loving v. Virginia,* 388 U.S. 1, 12 (1967).

3. *Boddie et al. v. Connecticut,* 401 U.S. 371 (1971). See also *United States v. Kras,* 409 U.S. 434, 444, distinguishing between unconstitutional state-imposed financial hurdles to divorce and constitutionally permissible bankruptcy filing fees.

4. *New Jersey Welfare Rights Organization v. Cahill,* per curiam (1973).

5. P.L. 104-193, Title I, Sec. 101, Sec. 401.

6. In 1999, in twenty-four states, women of color composed more than two-thirds of TANF enrollments. Relatedly, the decline in welfare caseloads has been more pronounced among whites than among women of color. Meanwhile, the percentage of single-parent families among blacks (62.3 percent) is more than twice that among whites (26.6 percent), and the nonmarital birthrate is substantially higher among non–Hispanic blacks (73.4) and Latinas (91.4) than among whites (27). U.S. House of Representatives, Committee on Ways and Means, *2000 Green Book: Overview of Entitlement Programs* (106th Cong., 2d sess., Washington, D.C., 2000), 1238, 1239 (table G-4), 1521.

7. U.S. House of Representatives, *2000 Green Book,* 1519.

8. U.S. Department of Health and Human Services, Administration for Children and Families, Office of Family Assistance, *Helping Families Achieve Self-Sufficiency: Guide for Funding Services for Children and Families through the TANF Program* (Washington, D.C.: U.S. Department of Health and Human Services, 2000), 3, 19.

9. U.S. Department of Health and Human Services, *Helping Families,* Sec. 403(a)(2).

10. P.L. 104-193, Title IX, Sec. 912.

11. Evan Bayh, "Demanding Responsibility from Men," *Blueprint Magazine* (Washington, D.C.: Democratic Leadership Council, January 22, 2002), at www.ndol.org/ndol_ci.cfm?contentid=250090&kaid=137&subid=258 (accessed January 22, 2002).

12. Will Marshall, "After Dependence," *Blueprint Magazine* (Washington, D.C.: Democratic Leadership Council, January 22, 2002), at www.ndol.org/ndol_ci.cfm?contentid=250080&kaid=114&subid=143 (accessed January 22, 2002).

13. Robert Rector, "Implementing Welfare Reform and Restoring Marriage," in *Priorities for the President,* ed. Stuart M. Butler and Kim Holmes (Washington, D.C.: Heritage Foundation, 2001), 71–97.

14. Wade Horn, "Wedding Bell Blues: Marriage and Welfare Reform," *Brookings Review* 19, no. 3 (2001): 39–42.

15. Bush Administration, *Working Toward Independence* (Washington, D.C.: Office of the President, February 26, 2002), 20, at www.whitehouse.gov/news/releases/2002/02/welfare-reform-announcement-book.html (accessed March 2002).

16. U.S. Department of Health and Human Services, *President's Budget for HHS, FY 2003: Ensuring a Safe and Healthy America* (Washington, D.C.: U.S. Department of Health and Human Services, 2002), 84.

17. U.S. Department of Health and Human Services, *President's Budget,* 22–23.

18. U.S. House of Representatives, H.R. 3073, *Fathers Count Act of 1999* (106th Cong., 1st Sess., Washington, D.C., 1999); H.R. 4678, *Child Support Distribution Act of 2000,* Title V (106th Cong., 2d Sess., Washington, D.C., 2000).

19. U.S. House of Representatives, H.R. 4671, *The Responsible Fatherhood Act of 2000* (106th Cong., 2d sess., Washington, D.C., 2000).

20. U.S. House of Representatives, H.R. 1300, *The Responsible Fatherhood Act of 2001* (107th Cong., 1st Sess., Washington, D.C., 2001), 469(D) (d) (2) (A).

21. U.S. Senate, S2524, *The Work and Family Act,* (107th Cong., 2d Sess., Washington, D.C., 2002); "The Bayh/Carper 'Work and Family Act': An Outline for TANF Reauthorization" (Washington, D.C.: United States Senate), at bayh.senate.gov/~bayh/workandfambillsum.htm (accessed March 2002). See also U.S. Senate, S. 653, *Responsible Fatherhood Act of 2001* (107th Cong., 1st sess., Washington, D.C., 2001).

22. U.S. Senate, S. 2052, Sec. 303, "Family Formation Fund," (107th Cong., 2nd Sess., Washington, D.C., 2002), (A)(i).

23. Daniel T. Lichter, "Promoting Marriage," *Blueprint Magazine* (Washington, D.C.: Democratic Leadership Council, January 22, 2002), at www.ndol.org/ndol_ci.cfm?contentid=250087&kaid=114&subid=144 (accessed January 22, 2002).

24. Data gathered from U.S. Census Bureau, *America's Families and Living Arrangements: Population Characteristics* (June 2001), especially table 2: "Family Groups by Type and Selected Characteristics of the Family."

25. In 1999, 25.4 percent of non-Hispanic white single-mother families lived below the poverty line as compared to 46.1 percent of African American and 46.6 percent of Latina single-mother families. U.S. Census Bureau, *Poverty in the United States, 1999* (Washington, D.C.: U.S. Census Bureau, 2000), table B-3.

Index

About the Contributors

Timothy J. Biblarz is associate professor of sociology at the University of Southern California. His research focuses on the demography of social inequalities, with an emphasis on family and intergenerational issues. Current projects include an investigation of historical change in the relationship between family structure and children's educational transitions, a test of an evolutionary theory of marital stability, and a study of social mobility patterns by sexual orientation.

Cynthia Burack is associate professor in the Department of Women's Studies at The Ohio State University. She is the author of *The Problem of the Passions: Feminism, Psychoanalysis, and Social Theory* (New York University Press, 1994) and articles on contemporary social thought, feminist theory, and political psychology. Her book on psychoanalysis and black feminist thought will be published by Cornell University Press.

Nancy D. Campbell is assistant professor of science and technology studies at Rensselaer Polytechnic Institute. Her research focuses on science in social movements and public policy involving women's health. She is the author of *Using Women: Gender, Drug Policy, and Social Justice* (Routledge, 2000). She is a 1995 graduate of the History of Consciousness Program at the University of California at Santa Cruz.

Victoria Davion is associate professor of philosophy at the University of Georgia. She is the founding editor of *Ethics and the Environment* and co-editor of *The Idea of a Political Liberalism: Essays on Rawls* with

230   *About the Contributors*

J. Clark Wolf (Rowman & Littlefield, 2000). Davion has published many articles on ecological feminism and the ethical dimensions of gender.

Jenrose Fitzgerald is a doctoral student in science and technology studies at Rensselaer Polytechnic Institute. She holds Master's degrees in women's studies (1998) and comparative studies (2000) from The Ohio State University. Her interests include U.S. welfare policy research, gender and economic development, and the discourse of globalization.

Suzanne E. Franks is director of the Women in Engineering and Science Program (Colleges of Engineering and Arts & Sciences) at Kansas State University. Franks earned her M.S. degree in nuclear engineering from the Massachusetts Institute of Technology in 1986 and a women's studies graduate certificate (1990) and her Ph.D. in biomedical engineering (1991) from Duke University. She has worked as a research associate at cancer research centers in Germany and the United States and in the pharmaceutical industry, and she has written and lectured on scientific topics as well as on gender and science. Franks now serves on Senator Pat Roberts's Advisory Committee on Science, Technology, and the Future and on that committee's Outreach Task Force.

Janice Haaken is professor of psychology at Portland State in Oregon and author most recently of *Pillar of Salt: Gender, Memory, and the Perils of Looking Back* (Rutgers University Press, 1998).

Valerie C. Johnson is assistant professor of political science at the University of Illinois, Chicago (UIC). She is the author of *Black Power in the Suburbs: The Myth or Reality of African American Suburban Political Incorporation* (State University of New York Press, 2002). Her research interests include urban politics, African American politics, and education policy with a particular emphasis on the politics of urban education. In line with her research interest, she has conducted research and education policy analysis for Rev. Jesse L. Jackson Sr. and the Rainbow/PUSH Coalition.

Jyl J. Josephson is associate professor and graduate director in the department of politics and government at Illinois State University. She is the author of *Gender, Families, and State: Child Support Policy in the United States* (Rowman & Littlefield, 1997) and co-editor with Sue Tolleson-Rinehart of *Gender and American Politics* (M. E. Sharpe, 2000), as well as articles on gender and public policy. Her two major current projects include a book project that examines privacy and intimate life from the perspective of groups whose privacy claims most frequently have been disparaged and foreclosed and an ongoing research project on the development of a faith-based community organization in west Texas. She is co-coordinator with Paula Ressler of the Safe Schools Project in Bloomington/Normal, Illinois, and president of the Bloomington/ Normal chapter of Parents, Families, and Friends of Lesbians and Gays (PFLAG).

Sharon Lamb, Ed.D., is a feminist author as well as a clinical and developmental psychologist who did her graduate work at Harvard University with Carol Gilligan and Jerome Kagan. She has published widely in the fields of moral development, girls' development, and abuse and victimization. She has taught at Bryn Mawr College and Dartmouth College and currently is professor of psychology at Saint Michael's College in Vermont. She edited or co-edited *The Emergence of Morality in Young Children* (University of Chicago Press, 1987), *New Versions of Victims: Feminists Struggle with the Concept* (New York University Press, 1999), and, most recently, *Before Forgiving* (Oxford University Press, 2002). And she is the author of *The Trouble with Blame: Victims, Perpetrators, and Responsibility* (Harvard University Press, 1996) as well as the recent book, *The Secret Lives of Girls: What Good Girls Really Do* (Free Press, 2001).

Valerie Lehr is associate professor of government and gender studies at Saint Lawrence University. She is the author of *Queer Family Values: Debunking the Myth of the Nuclear Family* (Temple University Press, 1999).

Gwendolyn Mink writes and teaches about law, social policy, and political movements affecting gender, race, and social justice. Her books include *Welfare's End* (Cornell University Press, rev. ed., 2002) and *The Wages of Motherhood: Inequality in the Welfare State, 1917–1942* (Cornell University Press, 1995), which won the Victoria Schuck Award of the American Political Science Association.

R. Claire Snyder is assistant professor of government and politics in the Department of Public and International Affairs at George Mason University. She is the author of *Citizen-Soldiers and Manly Warriors: Military Service and Gender in the Civic Republican Tradition* (Rowman & Littlefield, 1999), as well as numerous articles and essays on topics related to democratic theory and citizenship. Her current research interests include a number of projects on the New Right, including *Same-Sex Marriage and Democracy* (forthcoming from Rowman & Littlefield).

Judith Stacey is the Streisand Professor of Contemporary Gender Studies and professor of sociology at the University of Southern California. Her primary research interests focus on the relationship between social change and the politics of gender, family, and sexuality. Currently, she is conducting ethnographic research on gay male family and kinship relationships and values in Los Angeles. Her publications include *In the Name of the Family: Rethinking Family Values in the Postmodern Age* (Beacon Press, 1996) and *Brave New Families: Stories of Domestic Upheaval in Late-Twentieth-Century America* (University of California Press, 1998). She is a founding board member of the Council on Contemporary Families, a group committed to public education about research on family diversity.